Meredith Willson – America's Music Man

The Whole Broadway-Symphonic-Radio-Motion Picture Story

By

Bill Oates

1663 LIBERTY DRIVE, SUITE 200
BLOOMINGTON, INDIANA 47403
(800) 839-8640
WWW.AUTHORHOUSE.COM

This book is a work of non-fiction. Unless otherwise noted, the author and the publisher make no explicit guarantees as to the accuracy of the information contained in this book and in some cases, names of people and places have been altered to protect their privacy.

© 2005 Bill Oates. All Rights Reserved.

No part of this book may be reproduced, stored in a retrieval system, or transmitted by any means without the written permission of the author.

First published by AuthorHouse 08/09/05

ISBN: 1-4208-3525-4 (e)
ISBN: 1-4208-3524-6 (sc)
ISBN: 1-4208-3523-8 (dj)

Library of Congress Control Number: 2005901640

Printed in the United States of America
Bloomington, Indiana

This book is printed on acid-free paper.

Table of Contents

Acknowledgements vii

Introduction
"House of Melody" xi

Chapter One
"Iowa-It's a Beautiful Name" 1

Chapter Two
"May the Good Lord Bless and Keep You" 7

Chapter Three
"The Stars and Stripes Forever" 23

Chapter Four
"Local Boy Makes Good" 41

Chapter Five
"You and I" 55

Chapter Six
"Never Feel Too Weary to Pray" 67

Chapter Seven
"Radio Suite" 75

Chapter Eight
"A Handful of Stars" 91

Chapter Nine
"Seventy-Six Trombones" 109

Chapter Ten
"I Ain't Down Yet" 131

Chapter Eleven
"Thoughts While Strolling" 155

Chapter Twelve
"My White Knight" 167

Appendix A
Meredith Willson's Musical Compositions 181

Appendix B
List of Radio and Television Appearances 193

Appendix C
Selected Meredith Willson Recordings 199

Works Cited 201

Index 219

Acknowledgements

Attempting to show gratitude to all of those who assisted in getting this book published makes me think of Meredith Willson on the radio when he tried to be remembered to all of his "cousins" back home in Mason City, Iowa. He would start mentioning them but stopped short opting to quit before he forgot some. Writing a book holds a similar fate for those unintentionally forgotten, but to all of those "cousins" (the nicest Willsonesque that title I can give them) I hereby submit my thanks.

The book started ten years ago when I decided to expand my study of Meredith Willson for a wonderful Chicago magazine, The Nostalgia Digest and Radio Guide. This publication, old time radio guru Chuck Schaden's periodical preserving the good old days and especially the good old radio days, caused me to begin researching in Iowa after my 1993 teaching year was over. Thanks to Chuck for allowing me to use his bi-monthly platform as a writing outlet, for his undying devotion to old time radio, and most importantly for his friendship and support.

After calling a couple of 800 numbers that linked me with the Mason City Chamber of Commerce, I met my first Iowa cousin, a man who has opened numerous doors, shared his findings about Meredith Willson, and has become very good friend. Art Fischbeck loves to find new revelations about his beloved Mason City as much as Meredith Willson liked to share stories about the same hometown. Along with Terry Harrison at the Mason City library across from the Willson home, the three of us have bonded in the library's back room for hours and acted like children anticipating Christmas morning's presents when we find and share yet another Mason City fact. Art also introduced me to Fran Tagesen of the Kinney Pioneer Museum where more Willson mementos were available for scrutiny and inclusion in this book. To long-time Mason City broadcaster

Doug Sherwin, who had the foresight to save hours of his interviews with Meredith Willson, a tip of the plumed band hat. After meeting these Iowans, this author can see why Meredith Willson was eager to return home.

Because of Art's introduction, I met and fostered a friendship with another Willson lover, Jan Harshberger. What I have found and what she has discovered inevitably traversed the mail and the telephone lines from her home in Minnesota to mine in Indiana. We too have become Willson cousins, with her focus coming from a desire to perform songs written by Meredith Willson. Her contributions are priceless. In concert she shares her love for his music, and as friends we have swapped little known Meredith Willson numbers, a few of which need no further public display.

Among those who opened their memories of Meredith Willson and to whom I will be eternally grateful are Willson cousins Doris Blakesley, Ruth Scott, and the Reverend David Stone. Add to their lot so many other well-wishers from Mason City, and it is easy to see that "they'd give you their shirt and their back to go with it" in the time honored style that Meredith Willson so eloquently recalled as "Iowa Stubborn."

Throughout the years of research, many opened their archives and gave of their time to see this project through. My thanks go to the Library of Congress motion picture and recording divisions, the New York Philharmonic Society archivists, the New York Public Library system, the Museum of Broadcasting, the San Francisco Public Library system, the Pacific Arts and Library Museum in San Francisco, the Indianapolis Public Library, the Elkhart Public Library, and the Saint Joseph's College Library. Add to the list the support and devotion of hometown Marian the Librarians like those at the Kouts Public Library, whose workers Gladys Villars, Annette Hyndman, and Roxanne Shutske have always been eager to help in all of my projects.

Because of the emergence of the Internet and emailing another group of assistants emerged. Kudos for the information sent and invitations proffered to the following: Margaret Banks of The Shrine to Music Museum at the University of South Dakota; Joyce Slaubaugh of the United Musical Instruments Company of Elkhart, Indiana; Phyllis Danner of the University of Illinois John Philip Sousa Archives; Della McGrath of The Iowa Foundation; John Mead of the Oregon Historical Society; and the Walt Disney Archives.

Materials and encouragement came from all corners. Thanks to Rosemary Willson, Norma Zimmer, Rich Finegan, Annette D'Agostino, Dick Winland, Pat Koval, Bob Lewis, John Cyr, Norman Cox, Richard

Novak, Harry Brabec, Virginia Tulloch, Charles Kerlin, and Bob King. My gratitude likewise goes to Leonard Maltin for his encouraging words at Cinefest and tapes he shared with me. To my students and teaching colleagues like ex-band director Jim Earnest, who introduced me to Dr. Earle Melendy of Indiana State University, your help and support have moved me toward this completion. To Dr. Melendy who sent recordings and writings pertaining to Meredith Willson's 1970 visit, I truly appreciate both your contributions and the enthusiasm you exuded when talking about working with the music man. At this point a drum roll should be started for the all band directors who persevered with band members like me and tried to keep us marching and out of trouble. Likewise my thanks go to the members and contributors from SPERDVAC and the Radio Listeners Lyceum, who have the good sense to preserve radio shows like those on which Meredith Willson appeared. Thank you and keep up the good work.

Finally to my family, who supported me and goaded me into seeing this project finished, a big thank you. Your help means a great deal, from Bob Grahamslaw's book store trips with me to Ellen Jane Troyan's putting up with Bob and me, to my parents who patiently awaited this biography and to Aunt Jean Mitchell for housing me and spending time talking into the wee hours at her California home. Most importantly thanks and a big kiss for my wife who went along with this project, only complaining a little about the mountains of papers, books, and recordings that often cluttered the house and for reading along as the chapters neared completion. May you share with me the delight of those in Iowa who anticipate the publication of this labor.

May the good Lord bless and keep you all.

Introduction
"House of Melody"

On December 19, 1957, Meredith Willson, a rookie Broadway writer, composer, and lyricist, attended the premiere of his first musical. No stranger to the Manhattan theatre district, he had spent countless hours playing flute in the pit orchestras there and in the adjacent boroughs during the 1920's, when he was not touring with John Philip Sousa's band. However, never before had he poured so much time and energy into any one project, a full-blown Broadway musical comedy.

On opening night, along with the director and producer of the show, Willson and his wife Rini paced in the lobby of the Majestic Theatre on 44th Street. Prior to the overture, they moved inside and took their seats just before the curtain rose. Even though out of town audiences in Philadelphia and Washington, D.C. had given the show enthusiastic responses (famed playwright William Saroyan had even said that Willson had a "jackpot" on his hands) the composer and his wife waited in anxious silence, while the popular music literati prepared to review his production.

Just weeks before, the Willsons had paused to admire the marquee. The announcement acknowledged that Meredith Willson, the flute prodigy from Mason City, Iowa, had orchestrated this personal show. He was very proud of that moment of the project that he and his wife had nurtured for over a half decade. Staring at his name emblazoned in Broadway lights, he considered that the moment might be fleeting and not the more lasting stuff of which dreams are made.

As the orchestra warmed up, the couple took two seats near the exit, so they could beat a hasty retreat if the homespun wit which Meredith exhibited on radio, television, and at celebrity parties failed to please the first night crowd. Sitting hand in cold, sweaty hand, the Willsons waited as the house lights dimmed, the ellipsoidals and fresnels began to build on the act curtain, and the overture started with a whistle, a drum roll-off, and a march.

Should he have been more conventional with the opening number, "But He Doesn't Know the Territory"? Would the viewers be transported back to 1912 Iowa along with the train riders who debated the long-suffering business of salesmanship? Was the show too folksy for the sophisticated New York crowd? Was the show too long? Too short? The time for worrying was over, for the scene had already begun as a steam locomotive decelerated and approached the station, where it was time to meet the mythical inhabitants of River City through their song "Iowa Stubborn." The make or break opening for *The Music Man* was underway.

Pride in his Mason City birthplace swelled in Meredith Willson that opening night, and *The Music Man* quickly became a success. At some point during the premiere he discovered that the New York crowd enthusiastically embraced the story about his friends and family who lived over 1000 miles to the west. And as the caricatures of Mason Cityans came alive on stage, the real people, places and situations came back to Willson as he sat watching. A failure of this play might denigrate his friends and cousins left behind in north central Iowa almost forty years earlier. Yet as he eased into the opening night performance, he probably thought back to Mama, Papa, Dixie, and Cedric in the house on Superior Street and of those seemingly endless hours on the parlor piano under the tutelage of his mother Rosalie. Although her insistence that he practice detained him from playing circus or baseball, the hours manipulating the eighty-eight keys on the upright eventually led him to the Broadway premiere of *The Music Man*.

Chapter One
"Iowa-It's a Beautiful Name"

In order to understand how *The Music Man* evolved, one must know many of the elements that shaped the life of its creator. The musical is not an autobiography in its purest sense. It is, however, based on both the real experiences and dreams of a boy growing up in the early twentieth century Midwest. Like Samuel Langhorne Clemens, Meredith Willson created a world that combined actual people and events with creative fabrications. Clemens invented a persona named Mark Twain to recount adventures and characters from his childhood and created *The Adventures of Tom Sawyer* and *The Adventures of Huckleberry Finn*. In his own River City environment, Meredith Willson fabricated a caricature of himself, an average fellow from Iowa who simply enjoyed sharing stories about his "cousins." The complexities of both men ran far deeper than their surface storytelling personae.

As for Willson, before he could craft his masterpiece as an idyllic romantic comedy in song, he had to endure three decades of varied musical experiences. Some of these, like his time playing in John Philip Sousa's Band, became references, tributes, and music patterns in *The Music Man*. Others, like his membership with numerous symphonic organizations, taught him many different instrumental pieces from a wide range of composers, as well as rigid discipline for study and practice.

Finally, because Meredith Willson found within himself a comic character who appeared before millions of radio listeners he was able to mold him into a theatrical presence. The serious musician who came to direct music on many of NBC's most prestigious radio shows evolved into a naïve, dim-witted character whose presence in the script complemented stars of the show like Frank Morgan and Gracie Allen. Ultimately, these exercises with radio's top comedians helped him create the comic parts in his musical, just as his years with the New York Philharmonic and John Phillip Sousa's Band aided his knowledge of music.

The journey to the pinnacle of Broadway success included some hard knocks interspersed between the triumphs, but just like Willson's second great musical character, Molly Brown, he refused to give up. A failed expensive experiment in Seattle, critical disappointments, and working with studio personnel who sometimes edited out the composer's work might have discouraged a weaker person. Nonetheless, Meredith Willson regrouped each time and emerged stronger and wiser, fortifying himself with lessons well learned.

To fully appreciate Meredith Willson's journey to Broadway fame, one must start in Mason City, a town of some 30,000 people when *The Music Man* premiered in 1957. This town in north central Iowa emerged as adventurers set forth from the somewhat more tranquil settlements east of the Mississippi a decade and a half before the Civil War. Soon after Iowa officially joined the Union as the 29th state in 1846, hunters and land speculators began examining the area near Lime Creek in north central Iowa. When the early settlers arrived, the region did not even have its own name, until the state legislature created fifty new counties in 1851. However, timeliness identified the new county with a far different name than those surrounding it that were often derived from Native Americans, early founding fathers or war heroes. Because patriotic pride grew with the number of new Iowa residents, the north central region was given the name Cerro Gordo. The title derives from the most decisive Mexican War battle won by the young United States when General Winfield Scott defeated General Santa Anna in 1847. Mason City was established as the county seat and modest growth soon followed.

About half way between the Iowa capital of Des Moines and the settlement at the St. Paul cathedral that would become the namesake of Minnesota's capital, a small group led by Joseph Hewitt and James Dickirson began erecting cabins at what was originally called Shibboleth on Lime Creek in 1853. One early local historian said of the young town's name: it was "so rare and uncouth that its special significance has escaped the notice of inhabitants." No matter, for the town soon became Masonic Grove for the large number of Freemason inhabitants, and then it became Masonville and finally Mason City in 1855. Meredith Willson claimed that his grandfather Alonzo was responsible for suggesting the town's final name. However, arriving at a permanent name for the settlement posed a less urgent problem at that time than the Sioux who massacred thirty-three only 100 miles to the west at Spirit Lake in 1857, and the severe winters which provided these new residents with a challenge much different than those of the less hostile environments they left behind in cities like St. Louis, Chicago or Cleveland. As far as the problem with neighboring Native Americans was concerned, a "neutral ground" of non-aggression was created with them, and adaptations were made for the harsh prairie winters.

Among the thousands who sought their fortunes was Alonzo Willson. Born in Adams Center, New York in 1822, his trek west began when his family moved to Illinois in 1835. Before seeking his own fame and fortune, the thirty-year-old briefly courted a sixteen-year-old girl and married her in Paris, Illinois on February 2, 1845, much to her father's disapproval. Undaunted that Bernard Reynolds opposed daughter Catharine's elopement, Meredith Willson's grandfather took his new wife first to a rough-hewn cabin and later to a farm in LaSalle County, Illinois. However, before Alonzo finally traveled to Iowa, he saw a Blackhawk massacre that claimed three of his neighboring families, and made a round trip to the West that occupied two years of his life.

Ultimately heading for Iowa but detouring through California, Alonzo Willson was neither geographically disorganized, nor did he have a burning desire to avoid the straight route in favor of two trips over the Rocky Mountains. Braving hostile Native Americans and encountering weather unlike any he had experienced back East, he decided to head for the gold rush region of Northern California in 1853. His intention was not to pan for the precious metal, rather to escort forty intrepid pioneers and a herd of cattle, and to provide supplies for those who believed that their fortunes lay in the ground. After leaving his group in Marysville, where he acquired sizeable earnings from ranching and selling provisions, he returned to Illinois, gathered his family of four, and in 1855, transported them to Owens Township, Iowa. There he invested in land, the very commodity that was being sought by the steady stream of farmers who were pouring daily into the young Hawkeye State.

Initially, he purchased a sizeable area of timberland known as Owen's Grove just five miles southeast of present Mason City. After setting up a homestead in Cerro Gordo County, Meredith's grandfather sold 1,120 acres of land to new residents. Not only did he sell property, but he also loaned money to eager farmers, thus creating for himself a personal fortune. In addition, he built Owens Township's first stone schoolhouse, taught school and vocal music, and established the town's first library. He relocated a short distance away in Mason City in 1878, where four more children were born. As the town grew, Alonzo's status increased, and he eventually was named justice of the peace. Although his father-in-law had objected to the marriage, the first north central Iowa Willsons flourished as a family until Alonzo's death at age 90 in 1912.

Meredith Willson's practice of composing music to herald America's patriotic past was fueled by his knowledge of his paternal grandfather's pioneering contributions and his storied ancestry that included several who were participants in the country's early history. Benjamin Willson left England in 1694 for the American colonies, where he met and married his wife, Elizabeth Sprague. Their son Elebel became a ship's captain and distinguished himself during the American Revolution with Ethan Allen at the Battle of Bennington, Vermont and General Richard Montgomery at the battles of Montreal and Quebec. Richard Warran, Elizabeth's great grandfather, came to the New World on the Mayflower. (Coincidentally, a few years after the Warrans arrived, descendants of Meredith Willson's maternal grandmother, Lida Meacham, began their stay in Salem, Massachusetts before they eventually headed west through northern Ohio). Family archives and personal notes reflect Meredith Willson's interest in his family's genealogy that is clearly traceable back to England in the 1600's.

The first few decades of Mason City's existence witnessed moderate growth as early milling ventures utilized the natural resources of trees, water, limestone and clay. Throughout the middle of the nineteenth century, town plats were subdivided to offer homesteads to early Iowa residents. Although only a small village during the Civil War, Mason City sent its share of volunteers to join thousands of other Iowans in the Union Army. For those who died on battlefields far from their homes, a monument to Iowa Company B stands watch from the east end of the Cerro Gordo courthouse square, a tribute remaining in Central Park that would have been viewed by a young Meredith Willson.

Between 1869 and 1899, when rail lines traversing a growing nation increased markedly, the prosperity of Mason City burgeoned. Freight haulers like the McGregor and Missouri River Railway Company and the Chicago, Milwaukee and Saint Paul Railway Company (later the Chicago and Northwestern) transported Mason City commodities like lumber, sugar, and drain tile. Consequently, as the municipality prospered throughout the nineteenth century, so did Alonzo Willson's fortunes from selling property and brokering loans.

The financial successes of the Willson family provided the children with the opportunity to attend college. Born in 1866, youngest son John David had the rare chance to attend Notre Dame University. From that prestigious Indiana institution the young scholar became a graduate in the school's first class of law students. He had actually quit Mason City High School a year early rather than be delayed one year because only six students would have been seniors in 1883. As a result, when he took the bar exam in Indianapolis, he lied under oath that he was 21, when he was actually younger. After finishing his formal education, John began courting Rosalie Reiniger, an 1881 graduate of Chicago's Armour Institute and the daughter of a prominent Brighton, Illinois lawyer. He met her when he traveled to Chicago to play in an away Notre Dame baseball game.

After the couple married in 1889, they moved a hundred miles west of Mason City to Estherville, Iowa where John started a law practice and built a house for his wife, who was a primary school teacher and piano instructor. The local newspaper reported that the "upright grand, rosewood piano" was one wedding gift among those "many, costly gifts" given to the husband and his "highly cultured, winsome lady." Not only was Meredith Willson's mother an accomplished musician, but so too was his father. As a result of the growing popularity of band music in many nineteenth century American towns, John Willson joined the ranks of local musicians and played coronet and soloed on baritone with the Estherville band in 1892. With both parents active in musical endeavors, Meredith Willson and his siblings had a natural inclination to climb onto their mother's piano bench. However, before the young couple returned to Mason City in 1894, John D. Willson established himself as a prominent attorney, real estate agent, and loan manager, following his father's footsteps in the latter two ventures.

Rosalie Reiniger, the woman who inspired several Meredith Willson songs, came from a family who left north central Ohio and established itself first in northern Iowa and later in southern Illinois. Her attorney father, Gustavus, practiced law for a short time in Charles City, Iowa before he moved to Missouri where he ascended to the position of federal judge. He met and married Lida Meacham of Green Springs, Ohio in 1857. After establishing a residence, they produced four daughters and a son. Before the maternal grandmother of Meredith Willson joined her husband at his law practice in St. Louis, Lida Reiniger chronicled her journey from northern Ohio in a "Wapsie" coach to the Sherman House in Chicago and across the Mississippi to Dubuque via packet steamer in a journal that was serialized in newspapers. Along with his law books, Grandpa Reiniger brought his flute, an instrument that his daughter Rosalie later suggested that her son Meredith attempt and which eventually catapulted the boy to fame. After Grandpa Reiniger's death in 1869, his widow Rosalie moved the family back to Brighton, Illinois, where daughter Rosalie Reiniger and John Willson married. Among the six Reiniger girls and one boy was Lida, who frequently displayed her musical talents with sister Rosalie, and for whom *The Music Man* song "Lida Rose" was named. (Of course, grandmother Lida Reiniger's name might have played a part in the title of the song as well.)

Fondness for music came naturally from both sides of Meredith Willson's ancestors, but before he became a devoted music pupil, an older sister preceded him into the obligatory station of resident piano student. Born in Estherville in 1890, not only was she the first of three gifted Willson children to learn music from her mother, but Lucille, better known as Dixie, also became the first nationally famous family member when she became a prolific and successful writer during the 1920's.

The final years of the nineteenth century in Mason City witnessed John and Rosalie Willson raising a very creative daughter and attempting to expand their family. Sadly, a second child, a baby girl, died in infancy, but shortly after the turn into the twentieth century, Cedric and Meredith (born 1900 and 1902 respectively) joined the musical family on Superior Street. When they were able to seat themselves next to a lovingly strict yet doting mother, the children began the piano lessons that eventually became the springboard to a harp, a bassoon, a flute, and a very important piccolo.

Dixie holds Cedric (or possibly Meredith) circa 1901 in front of the Willson home on Superior Street, as father John looks on. (Mason City Library Collection)

Chapter Two
"May the Good Lord Bless and Keep You"

In May of 1958, soon after *The Music Man* became a hit on Broadway, Dixie Willson wrote remembrances of her younger brother Meredith's birth. At fourteen pounds and seven ounces, he was the largest baby recorded in Iowa at that time. She had the honor of pulling the name Meredith out of Papa's derby hat, which also contained Roderick, Rex, Alonzo and Buford. Sixteen-month old Cedric held the hat that contained his famous-to-be brother's name. Actually, the full name of the composer is Robert Meredith Willson, but while growing up in Mason City, the boy lost his first name. However, he frequently included the initial *R* when he played professionally in bands and orchestras as an adult. Perhaps the initial's revival was a tribute to his mother *Rosalie Reiniger* and her insistence on making him practice regularly, so that he might become a good musician.

Once all of the Willson family members arrived, and before the piano lessons began, church training began in earnest. Just a few blocks north and one to the west of the Willson home on Superior Street stands the First Congregational Church of Mason City. Mama Willson may have given up her teaching occupation at the private kindergarten that she held in her own home when her family began, but continuing her instructions in Sunday school was another story. When the youngsters departed her church school class, Rosalie Willson bade them all "May the good Lord bless and keep you." Perhaps the greatest dedication Meredith Willson created as a tribute to his mother's memory came when he took those words of her farewell and wrote them into the song he composed to end the National Broadcasting Company's *The Big Show* radio program in the early 1950's. He also shared memories of his mother when she became the inspiration for the character of Marian Paroo, the librarian in *The Music Man*. One particular representation of this embodiment stemmed from Mrs. Willson's insistence that her son practice the piano regularly, especially the dreaded five-finger exercises, a scene that Marian recreated with her young student Amaryllis. Recognizing the humor in the seemingly boring but necessary repetitive task, Rosalie Willson kept among her effects an old *Saturday Evening Post* cartoon showing a similar young piano student dutifully engaging in "That Last Survival of the Torture Chamber of the Middle Ages - Five-Finger Exercises."

When volunteers carefully restored the Willson home to visitors at the end of the twentieth century, the life of the family became vividly evident. Upon entering, the visitor can imagine where Rosalie's young students sometimes met. The parlor in the front of the house offered solace for the parents and the all-important musical instruments, including the piano, and sometimes John's guitar, Dixie's harp, Cedric's bassoon, and Meredith's flute. A living room, dining room, and kitchen also appear on the first floor. The front door opens to a staircase that leads to a nicely furnished home complete with nursery and three bedrooms (one for the parents, one for Dixie, and another for the boys.) The third floor became a playroom first for Dixie and her dramatic creations, and later the boys joined her.

Although Meredith Willson wrote fond tributes to his mother years later, getting out of Sunday school activities was the greater reality when he was young. He confessed that part of his reluctance to appear at church events emerged because Rosalie embarrassed the boy by making him wear black velvet pants in seasonal cantatas. Though uncomfortable in his outfit, the young performer also had a chance to observe Charlie Rau who operated the stereopticon at the Christmas pageants. Numerous times the composer recounted the impression that was left on the children of the twentieth century's first decade when that projector made the star appear over Bethlehem and later moved across the sky to the choir loft where the strains of "Joy to the World" emanated. Meredith proudly recalled that brother Cedric had the enviable job of assisting Rau in later years. The Willson boys' fascination with projected images continued during the first two decades of the twentieth century when they began frequenting local theaters with their mother.

Life in Mason City, Iowa during the first years of the twentieth century was not as idyllic as *The Music Man* suggests. The musical takes place during Fourth of July festivities, when River City was all gussied up for the holiday. Unlike its Technicolor counterpart, the real Mason City was typical of all Midwestern prairie towns, in that heat drenched the region in the summertime, and blizzards came whipping in from the north in the winter. The residents dressed for hard work at one of the many dirty factories, and passing trains added both soot and noise to the environs. True to the play, salesmen and nefarious characters passed through the town, and the town constable escorted some out just as quickly. Certainly, the Willsons enjoyed the fruits of John's success in local businesses, but even having a housekeeper did not keep Cedric and Meredith from enduring chores like emptying chamber pots, hauling ashes, pumping water, and pounding the beefsteak. The family grew during a time period in American history that was ripe for growth and commerce, and Mason City stood on the threshold of developing into an important contributor to the nation in the years prior to the First World War.

When the children were not carrying out household tasks or play-acting in one of the Willson home's upstairs rooms, church pageants often occupied their playtime. A natural attraction to the stage in Meredith Willson's adult life developed as he adapted to traumas as a child performer. At age four he presented himself before a local audience, bedecked with a Mother Goose Smock and a haystack hat. He was to recite the line, "Little Boy Blue, come blow your horn," but the future musical prodigy forgot his prop. He ran offstage, found the horn and holding it aloft, completed his part. In another episode, three years later, as a babe lost in the woods, he was to tell his counterpart on stage, "We will be safe, Francis, if we sit beneath this sheltering greenwood tree 'til dawn." After peering down at a rip in his velvet pants, he changed the line to "*stand* beneath the greenwood tree."

In another instance, the future host and actor in his own radio shows and others, he learned to cope with the realities of live productions during the Christmas pageant at the Congregational church in 1906. He and three others portraying shepherds approached the innkeeper to ask about the significance of the star they saw shining over Bethlehem. Hostess Sara responded that they should ask good father Joseph. Unfortunately, Joseph did not respond to his cue. She repeated her line, and then young Meredith ad libbed, "The good father Joseph will be here in a minute. He has gone to the toilet."

The first desires to appear on the secular stage really affected Meredith Willson at age six. Against his mother's knowledge, the boy sneaked off to the Princess Theatre, where he was told to get in a frog suit and hop around. Reluctant to play the fool, he was nonetheless forced to, for he had already accepted his wages, one penny. To make the experience worse, Willson had to place two flashlight batteries in his mouth, so that the amphibian's eyes would light up. The payoff was to have been a mass of chocolates purchased at the Candy Kitchen, but when proffered the penny, the storeowner only gave the boy one of his finest confections. Outside the store, a tearful youngster learned one of life's hard lessons: the exchange of frog suit humiliation for a measly penny was not worth its equivalent in one lone chocolate.

♪ ♪ ♪

During the Willson children's formative years, more renowned performers came to Mason City, not the least of which was the great boxer John L. Sullivan. Trips to the local theater were commonplace for the Willson boys. Meredith related how seeing his first moving picture, *The Highwayman*, left a lasting impression because of the forest fire scene that was printed on red tinted film. Another trip to the theater (the Willson children and their mother made frequent visits to the Princess, Airdrome, Bijou, Cecil, and Wilson) resulted in the boy seeing his first melodrama on stage, which he paid with "ashes money ... dropped regularly down the cold air register in the hall." (That is, the boys kept the money that they were supposed to pay to have the ashes hauled. Instead, they disposed of the load themselves and banked the profit.)

Within eyeshot of the Willson home in Mason City sat the town library, one of hundreds built with money from steel magnate Andrew Carnegie's philanthropy. Young Meredith availed himself to use the facility at an early age, preferring first the *White Fairy Book* and the *Green Fairy Book*. However, a seemingly unimportant part of the building caught his attention, the check out desk where a cadence of stamps and stamp pads met each other like a tap dancer's shoes on hardwood, and where muffled sounds and whispers represented the only other noises extant. He later reprised this haunting scene in *The Music Man* as the seductive "Marian the Librarian" song and dance number.

Winters in north central Iowa came with gusto in this prairie state. Willson fondly recalled the activities after fall popcorn balls as "snow, mackinaws, mittens, stocking caps and long underwear." A belly flop onto a sled before it headed downhill to the frozen creek was the order of the day. (Of course, dangers existed, for Cedric fell off a wall near the sledding grounds just the summer before, and, as Meredith later remembered, might have drowned if nearby neighbor Mrs. Burns had not exercised a folk remedy and "plied him with homemade wine.") However, the greatest winter pleasure came when the kids grabbed onto the runners of the Wells Fargo Wagon and hitched a ride "all day if you wanted to." No wonder the Wells Fargo wagon memory became immortalized in *The Music Man*, when these rides or the delivering of a new flute or piccolo by the same conveyance excited the young Iowan.

Also during this first decade of the twentieth century important architectural designer Frank Lloyd Wright came to Mason City. In the early years of his career, the draftsman completed a house for Doctor George C. Stockman, just a few blocks away from the Willsons, in 1908. Not yet designing his renowned completely original homes, for this one he used blueprints based on a prototype floor plan he published in a 1907 *Ladies Home Journal*, the "Fireproof House of $5000." This pattern for an affordable middle class home represented an early version of what would become his distinctive Prairie School style, and soon after he developed houses with singularly unique Wright designs.

After the town experienced four decades of growth thanks to the railroads transporting drain tile and meat to the east, The City National Bank executives determined that the lending institution needed a new building on the corner of State and Federal. After Frank Lloyd Wright's experience with the Stockman house, he was commissioned to design the new lending institution's home in 1910, at the urging of bank founder J.E.E. Markley. The banker's daughter became infatuated with the architect the year before when she was a student at Wright's aunt's Hillside School in Spring Green, Wisconsin. Another Mason City task required Wright to complete the Park Inn Hotel diagonally across from the bank and also to remodel a law office. After these next two businesses opened in 1910, Wright intended to continue his Prairie School style in Mason City, but personal matters sidetracked the famed architect, and he instead built many of his revolutionary homes in Oak Park, Illinois. A few years later, several of his pupils created a Prairie style "neighborhood" just a half-dozen blocks from the downtown center and only a few blocks to the east of the Willson home.

Meredith Willson fondly recalled growing up on Superior Street in his first autobiographical endeavor *And There I Stood with My Piccolo*. The memories included sounds that were peculiar to his family, such as "your front door opening in the winter and the screen door slamming in the summer, and Papa's derby hat hitting the newel post in the front hall, almost a dead heat with the six o'clock whistle you could hear all the way from the roundhouse, and 'The Toreador Song' on the music box while you had to take your afternoon nap." Sometimes Papa sang "Tipperary" at the breakfast table, Dixie helped with the alto, and, to his own amazement, Meredith discovered very early that he could harmonize. Sunday evolved from Mama starting the day playing hymns on the old upright in the parlor, while the two boys raced each other to get to the color newspaper comics first, to the trip to Sunday School, and finally to the lazy afternoons in Mason City that led to nap time on the day of rest. In all religion played a big part in the Willson household, because they usually made three trips to the Congregational Church on Sunday (Sunday school, a.m. service and p.m. vespers), Wednesday evening service and choir practice, and Thursday evening Christian Endeavor.

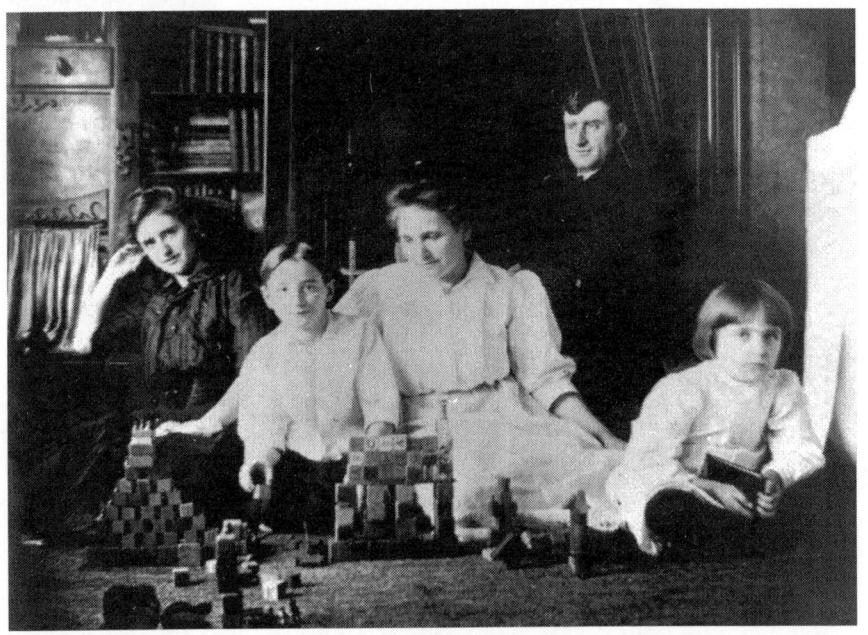

The Willson family circa 1908: (from left) Dixie, Cedric, Rosalie, John and Meredith. (Mason City Library Collection)

Other days of the week were equally predictable. Mama and Papa might play cribbage on Monday night, the boys frequently had band or orchestra practice on Tuesday, and a movie might be in store for Friday evening. Saturdays often meant traveling with Mama, perhaps to the library, and later the boys kept busy pumping water in the cellar (one hundred pumps per boy Meredith recalled) or pounding the beefsteak. Of course, Professor Harold Hill echoed these last activities from Willson's 1948 autobiography practically verbatim in his "Trouble" number in *The*

Music Man. By scrutinizing either the first installment of his autobiography or Willson's first musical, the examiner soon understands that the boys' preferences involved spending time with other boys, and ultimately, a good place for them to be was in a boys' band.

While the boys played or executed their chores, Mama Rosalie championed several causes from the trivial to encouraging a drastic innovation in public schooling. She failed in her attempt to get the post office to ease their burden by having addresses written in reverse order. "The last thing," she said, "that the Post Office people care about is the name of a person. The first thing they need to know is the country, then state, and so on." Her devout patriotism and a desire to make sense of the haphazard street naming system in her city caused her to join those who in 1916 renamed the thoroughfares in a more orderly manner, with the result that her own Superior Street became Pennsylvania Avenue. On the other hand, she believed that the restoration of Indian titles to places in the area was more in harmony with the spirituality ascribed by the original inhabitants. For example, because of her efforts, the European name for Lime Creek reverted back to the Winnebago River, a reference to the waterway where the Winnebago tribe established a village. At this point the river joins Willow Creek, and ancient beliefs espouse that the confluence of two such rivers creates a place ensuring peace and fertility, something like her own Mason City.

Rosalie Willson saw to it that animals received the same treatment that people did. She accomplished spearheading the construction of the first fountain and horse trough for weary beasts in Mason City and referred any driver passing her house who had not properly unhooked the checkrein to the Humane Society. She also started the Mason City Humane Society at the turn of the century, and often commandeered Aunt Minnie Brice's electric car to chase down violators. Eventually, in the spirit of Rosalie Willson's attempts to build character in children, she organized them to report offenders and rewarded them with special buttons. The society flourished until the gasoline motor displaced the horse as the prime mover of goods and people in Mason City.

Of greater importance in her crusades was her support of the new kindergarten movement being introduced in America. Rosalie Willson began this early education program in Mason City, after she helped organize the Chicago Free Kindergarten Association when she was a student at the Armour Institute. Among her papers are articles on the kindergarten movement, as well as an interest in a class at that grade level for African-American students. During the pursuit of these causes, she continued supporting the education department at the Congregational

Church, and, as a result, she was named superintendent of the primary department, an unusual position for a woman at the beginning of the twentieth century. Because of his mother's fervent devotion to the spiritual education of children, in 1960, Meredith helped finance and dedicate an educational addition to the church in her memory.

♪ ♪ ♪

While Mama rose in the ranks of responsibility and respectability at church, Papa kept busy in a variety of venues. Outside of playing in musical aggregations, he wrote poetry and fancied himself quite the local baseball player. His early accomplishments included striking out twelve men on the Austin, Minnesota team in 1888. One amusing remembrance of John came as a result of Meredith Willson witnessing his father entering the house with a bottle of beer given him by Ed White the butcher. Despite the ongoing movement to prohibit alcohol in America, John Willson endeavored to exhibit his manliness and down the whole container, even though it took a cheese sandwich to help choke down the brew. Fearing that drunkenness would soon be upon him, he quickly read the children a passage from *The Last of the Mohicans*, and then put them to bed. When the three young ones heard a clamoring downstairs, they feared that demon alcohol had taken hold of their Papa. The next morning their fears were allayed when the elder Willson prepared buckwheat cakes for their breakfast, where he announced that the ruckus the night before was his capture and execution of a rat.

Like his father before him, selling real estate and arranging loans occupied most of John Willson's business life, but because he was often away from home on business trips, he and Rosalie divorced in 1920. Even though he frequently traveled away from Mason City, his wife only took two trips her entire life: one to her sister's in Topeka, Kansas and another twenty-eight miles away to a funeral in Charles City. John Willson's final business endeavor in Mason City was a bakery he built and managed around the block from the family home.

Together, Rosalie and John gave their children encouragement and numerous opportunities to create. One poignant reminder of the importance of music in their lives, a piece of sheet music "My Rosalie" signed by John, resided among her effects after her death and was kept by Meredith until he returned it to a safe place in his hometown.

Meredith Willson – America's Music Man

Many pictures exist in Mason City of a doting Dixie Willson caring for her two younger brothers. She became the first creative Willson by winning recognition for her writing abilities, both musical and literary. Her earliest national accolade came when she received a twenty-five dollar check for a seven-stanza poem she penned praising Munsing underwear. "Be thankful, always, everywhere, that you have Munsing underwear" formed the basis of the lines that brought the prize money to the teenager. Unselfishly, she shared her first creative remuneration on sodas and candy for her high school classmates and music lessons for her two brothers. For a girl from Mason City, one of 2500 entrants nationwide, the thrill encouraged her enough to write dozens of poems, short stories, and novels. Some of her full-length stories were adapted as motion picture plays in the 1920's. In 1980, when *Family Weekly* magazine polled a dozen celebrities as to which books shaped their lives, famed writer Thomas Wolfe listed her "Honey Bear" narrative poem not only as inspirational, but also one which he quoted "in small slivers in everything" he wrote.

Dixie Willson's life included a variety of career opportunities. Like her brothers, she became an accomplished instrumentalist, mastering the harp and ultimately receiving an offer to play with the Minneapolis Symphony. However, true to her free-spirited nature, she declined the position so that she could ride a circus elephant, and years later her three ring experiences provided her with material for her writings. Her variegated five-decade career included teaching in Montana where she wrote and directed her own musical; writing short stories, novels, and poems in New York and California; creating children's toys and games; and contributing poems for Meredith's radio show in the late 1940's and early ideas for his musical *The Music Man*. Among her last writings are reminiscences of a loving upbringing in Mason City, and how proud she was of her younger brother's accomplishments, including his portrayal of their hometown values on the New York stage.

♪ ♪ ♪

Brother Cedric followed Dixie's lead as a performer and musician. Both he and Meredith assumed roles in church skits. They often played in musical organizations together, from their tenure in the local boys' band through their years together in the Mason City High School band and orchestra. By 1923, they both held chairs in John Philip Sousa's band. Cedric even sat in as a visiting musician with Meredith's orchestra on the *Good News* radio show in 1938. However, the elder Willson son departed his musical career and moved to Kansas where he received a degree in engineering at the

University of Kansas. Later he was awarded a master's degree in the same field from New York University. A Mason City newspaper article noted that Cedric, after overseeing the building of a $5,000,000 cement plant in Texas, established himself as a success equal to that of his famous musician brother Meredith. He lectured around the world on his innovations in the industry, and had many of those speeches published.

♪ ♪ ♪

By the time Meredith became a member of the Willson household in 1902, music was the watchword for the family's spare time. He was obligated to begin his lessons at age seven on the black upright piano in the parlor. A touching 1915 photo shows Cedric and Meredith hard at the piano, with Mama directing them. During that same year, the local school system listed Meredith on the "May Day Pageant and Festival," as presented by the pupils of the Mason City grade schools in East Park. Also on hand was the Jeffers Boys Band, a group that appears strikingly similar to the aggregation that is the center of attention in *The Music Man*. Just as relevant from this time period is a 1919 newspaper announcement that a group of local merchants bought the boys band dark blue uniforms: just as "sure as the Lord made little green apples, that band's gonna be in uniform ..."

Mama Rosalie directs piano practice for Cedric and Meredith in the front parlor on Superior Street. (Mason City Library Collection)

The Willson family's secondary public education took place only a few blocks to the northeast of their home on Superior Street. Old Mason City High School (the prototype for the River City High School of *The Music Man*) provided the learning ground for Dixie, Cedric, and Meredith. Not only was it a school for the best Hawkeye learning in the first half of the twentieth century, but it was also the place where the two Willson boys practiced with their first organized musical groups, the Mason City High School orchestra and the marching band.

After expending all of her piano teaching talents on her younger son, Rosalie Willson referred Meredith to Ed Patchen, the organist at the Congregational Church. Not learning from the disciplinarian that his mother was, the boy ending up skipping more and more lessons. When Meredith played truant, Patchen uttered his favorite non-vulgar expletive "my conscience" and headed for the pool hall to shoot billiards. The boy did tarry long enough to participate in a piano recital for "students of E. A. Patchen," when he played "Barcarolle" by Scharwenka and "Witch's Dance" by Schytte. Meredith Willson did not become a great pianist, but he represented his teacher in *The Music Man* as one who also spouted non-profane swear words like "Great Honk" and his diversion of the gentlemen's game of billiards, as opposed to its more despicable pocketed relative found in pool halls.

Meredith had a natural attraction to creating music from an early age. Sister Dixie recalled that he was often heard banging on Mama's sherbet glasses or on a piece of discarded pipe in the back yard. When the piano strings were exposed for repair or tuning, he amused himself by playing them as if they were members in a cloistered harp waiting to be exposed to his whims.

Diversions like playing circus and dreaming about Sousa's band frequently crept into the mind of young Meredith Willson. Both amusements enjoyed their heyday during the decades just before and after the turn into the twentieth century. By the time the Willson children were born, only remote outposts in America did not have ready access to rail lines. As a result, circus wagons and concert bands visited communities of all sizes, when their bookers simply followed the tracks to an open field, opera house, or any other available location. Of equal importance was the development of the cylinder phonograph and the disc victrola, both of which brought the marches of the greatest shows on earth like the Ringling Brothers' Circus and the music of "The March King" John Philip Sousa into the home. Needless to say, when the real performers came within reach of local audiences, the seats were packed.

After a few years of teaching her son the rudiments of playing the piano, Mama "scraped up some money" so young Meredith could take up the flute. She wanted him to play another instrument, because, in her words, he would "stand out better that way." Besides, a local musician indicated that the Mason City band needed such an instrument. The shiny, new woodwind instrument arrived, mail-ordered through a Chicago catalogue and sent from Boston. After hastily unwrapping the package, Willson stared in amazed disappointment, for it was not played with one end pressed to the musician's mouth like the brass and other woodwind instruments that he had seen, rather it was held sideways. However, he reasoned that learning the flute might be the key to one of his childhood dreams, to play in the famous Sousa band. This scheme to attain a station in the most famous American musical aggregation seemed to be only a remote possibility, for no one had ever learned to play the flute in Mason City before. First, the Willsons employed a piano instructor who used the leaflet "How to Play the Flute" to get the boy started. Eventually, a slightly more qualified teacher, a coronet player, kept one lesson ahead of the fledgling flautist. After working the instrument awhile, the young student became frustrated because the player could not see what was going on around him, because all attention focused between the lips and the left shoulder. Eventually, because the teacher instructed the boy to blow across the instrument as he had over a soda bottle's top, the child began his mastery of the instrument.

Meredith Willson's musical opportunities soon broadened. Ultimately, the boy learned from a real flute teacher, Squiz Hazelton, a local theatre pit orchestra member who suggested that the student add the banjo to his repertoire. In an anecdote cut from *And There I Stood with My Piccolo*, Willson recalled being a substitute flute player during a performance of the silent film *Ramona*. Unfortunately, the later prodigy on the instrument became completely lost and only "lasted out the matinee." After he improved his sight reading skills, he often found employment in pit orchestras for both silent films and vaudeville when he was a student in New York City. As he improved in Iowa, the flautist soon found his way into the Boy Scout band, an opportunity to provide Meredith and drummer friend Clare Williams with the chance to become professionals. The local GAR (Grand Army of the Republic veterans) received a request from nearby Belmond, Iowa for some musicians to perform at their Memorial Day celebration, with the result that both of the boys obtained free lodging and $1.50 to play martial music for the crowd.

Playing in bands was not the only source of income for the maturing music man. At age eight he sold lemonade from his front lawn, and soon he was delivering fresh radishes and lettuce to local restaurants. (Of course, it was Mama who planted, weeded, harvested and washed the crop before the sale.) By age twelve, he was delivering *The Saturday Evening Post* door-to-door. He recalled that it was much more fun in the spring when he could shed his mittens, where he kept his money, and stow the earnings in his pocket. Likewise, digging for the periodical without a mitten in his mouth was a far more savory exercise. His route cost him fifteen dollars from another boy, and he delivered about sixty copies on Thursdays. Sometimes an extra copy of *Country Gentleman* or *Ladies' Home Journal* might be thrown in to sweeten the subscriber. He delivered the periodicals before school and collected after, but he spent much of his profits enjoying performances at the Idle Hour Theatre where his early love interest Elsie Johnson sold tickets to the current melodrama.

Summer in Mason City represented some of the fondest childhood memories for Meredith Willson. The Fourth of July created one of the best-remembered evenings to the point that it became the time when romance was solidified between Harold Hill and Marian the librarian in *The Music Man*. Willson recalled when the town band played "Custer's Last Stand" complete with "red fire and everything," it set off the ultimate "whips and jingles" of excitement that a Mason City youth could enjoy.

Sporting knickers and an ivy league cap in the Mason City Boy Scout Band, Meredith is seated fourth from the right under a snare drum. (Mason City Library Collection)

By age ten Meredith Willson became an accomplished musician with an increasing adeptness on a variety of instruments. Consequently, this talent gave him the chance at age sixteen to travel with a local Erwin-Wells Society dance orchestra. After sufficient time on the flute, Meredith Willson found an opportunity to elevate his musical capabilities one notch higher when he augmented his talents by adding the piccolo to his repertoire. At age fifteen the young musician accepted a chance to play in a band at a summer resort in Lake Okoboji, about a hundred miles west of Mason City. When told he needed to double on the smaller version of the flute, Willson hastened down to Vance's and thumbed through catalogues until he stopped at a ninety-six dollar, silver-plated, gold key model. Arranging to make weekly payments of twelve dollars from his summer salary, he broke even on the instrument that arrived shortly thereafter from Boston on the Wells Fargo Wagon.

By the way, Vance's Music Store held a special place in Meredith Willson's heart. He and his musical friends often thumbed through the sheet music or listened to recordings to get free ideas for their instrumental trio. When Willson returned as a celebrity, he made sure that he would stop by and visit his benefactors. As a tribute, one of the buildings in *The Music Man* motion picture set bears the name Vance's.

The summer music engagement went well, with Meredith taking in just enough to pay for his piccolo. Fortunately, part of the financial arrangement included his room and board. At the end of the stay, two rather traumatic occurrences that directly affected Meredith Willson became the highlights of the job. Just prior to the last Saturday night dance of the season The United States Army called up orchestra leader Emery Moore as the country began its mobilization for the First World War. Willson was called upon to conduct the small combo for this last appearance. Nervously, the man who would become head of a number of world-renowned musical organizations started the band. When all of the instrumentalists finished at the same time, out of sheer relief, he collapsed onto his chair and, tragically, broke his new piccolo. The magnitude of second calamity was especially distressing, because just that day he had sent the last payment back to Mason City, where he would soon return with the bent instrument.

After Meredith Willson returned to his hometown, additional occasions presented themselves to increase his confidence and exposure as a musician. One early proud moment came when the young flautist played for the Rotary Club on a Wednesday at the Cerro Gordo Hotel. As a result, he eventually became a public relations representative for Mason City, and, as one of eight entertainers, he performed before The

Bureau of Manufacturers and Jobbers in 1918 on behalf of the Chamber of Commerce which was attempting to lure jobs to Mason City. His talents moved him to the Mason City Municipal Band, where he not only played, but also was proud to be allowed to sort the music, a task fondly recalled as a favored position with the director. The leader was so impressed with the boy's work that he shared with young Willson a first sip of alcohol, a glass of dandelion wine.

Being active in Mason City High School extra-curricular activities was paramount to the Willson children. Brother Cedric, senior class of 1918, played a year of football, worked on the school yearbook as business manager, and was active in Hi-Yi and German Club. However, he was not quite as musically active as was his brother. While at school that year Meredith also played the flute in the orchestra, the piccolo in the band, and became one member in a banjo threesome called the Jones Brothers (comprised of the brothers Willson and Harold Keidle.) In the first combined concert of the Mason City High School orchestra, girls' glee club, and band, the program opened appropriately and prophetically with John Philip Sousa's "Hands Across the Sea" and closed with the younger Willson brother playing the famed piccolo solo in The March King's "Stars and Stripes Forever."

Meredith Willson exercised other interests in high school that assisted his career path before the public. His performances in public speaking in 1918 included his interpretation of one of his favorite poems, "The Highwayman," prior to a supporting role as Tom the stable boy in the one-act comedy, "The Hollytree Inn." Meredith had his eyes on another member of the Public Speaking Department's performers, Elizabeth Wilson, a senior whose locker was close to his. For the "Line Most Proficient In" section in that year's *Masonian*, he announced that he would be "Consolidating Wilsons." However, he had to finish one more year of school before he would marry "Liza" as she was then nicknamed.

One further claim to fame during Meredith Willson's high school years resulted when the businessmen of Mason City raised important funds for the high school band to accompany the football team to play a formidable foe at the state capital in Des Moines. Little did the entrepreneurs realize that their generosity might have created in a win over Des Moines North. The game remained scoreless until the closing minutes, and when Mason City attempted a field goal, Meredith Willson let out such a shrill sound with his piccolo that the referee was shocked into distraction. As the small town fans jubilantly cheered that the drop kicked attempt sailed through the uprights unheeded, the official agreed and signaled the three-point attempt as good. The home team protested but to no avail, and the next day the Mason City newspaper announced that the 3-0 win resulted from an assist by the piccolo player.

Meredith Willson's senior year was abbreviated, for the horrific nationwide Spanish flu epidemic of 1918-19 closed down the school in the fall until it safely reopened later in the winter. These were the embryonic days of the Mason City High School Band, and because of the successes from the previous two years, the yearbook proudly reported that Mason City was "assured of a permanent High School Band," because it successfully rallied the football and basketball teams to victory. Another positive factor emerged when local merchants supported the band so that it could take two train trips, one to Spencer and Estherville and the other to Austin, Minnesota. Meredith's senior quote was "Great men are not always wise," and he continued on his musical ways, also singing in the chorus and performing in the annual minstrel show.

Many characters from Meredith Willson's childhood often flooded into his memory when he reminisced over the years with newspaper and radio interviewers. Even though his experiences placed him in the small and not always appropriately equipped high school band, the people and programs ultimately found immortality in *The Music Man*. And, in his words, after writing a "pretty horrible song" for the Mason City graduating class of 1919, he left to learn "serious" instrumental music in New York City. In his own words: "off I went to New York City with Papa's fried chicken, Mama's prayers, a mail order flute under my arm, and a bent piccolo in my pocket." Moreover, he departed with a cache of memories that would fill the radio airwaves with stories about his Mason City home, as well as ultimately becoming part of the inspiration for *The Music Man*.

Chapter Three
"The Stars and Stripes Forever"

The 1920's brought to the John Willson family of Mason City a period of disappointment, countered by the incredible successes of the children. The family's low point came when Rosalie asked John David for a divorce, because she was unable to cope with his constant traveling. On the other hand, Mama was buoyed by her children's accomplishments, starting with Dixie.

A product of her own progressive mother's insistence on modernizing American education by such revolutionary moves as establishing a kindergarten in Mason City, Lucille (Dixie) signed a three year contract in 1909 to teach in Japan. By 1913, she was in Missoula, Montana teaching primary students and composing programs for young children. *Primary Plans* magazine published her article "Programs for Special Days, Songs, Stories and Room Decorations" in 1913. Another of her activities that year involved her adapting "The Owl and the Pussycat" into a stage play and creating a "Friendship" peace plan, whereby all American towns would adopt a European counterpart to help each other in times of need. Hence, through international understanding a world war might be prevented. During the next decade she spent most of her energy writing poetry, short stories, novels, and screenplays.

In her teen years Dixie began exploring the creative avenues of writing and composing. In 1905, the Chicago *Herald Tribune* published "Fluff of Gold," a story written as a present to her grandmother. Her humorous poem praising Munsing Underwear appeared two years later. After marrying Benjamin Lampert in 1915 and divorcing him a year later, she sought her fame and fortune by joining the chorus of a musical comedy in Chicago. Eventually, she traveled with the troupe to New York and a landed a brief stint as a chorus girl in the prestigious Ziegfeld Follies.

Once established financially, Dixie persuaded her parents to allow Meredith to come to New York City for a visit. Even though he had only experienced a few trips outside of his north central Iowa home base, the fifteen-year-old seemed only moderately impressed with the metropolis. The night he arrived, his sister took him on an upper deck bus ride of 5th Avenue to view the big city. Assuming the visitor would be thrilled, she was surprised when he spied a large electric calendar with the July 12 date illuminated and reminded her, "Look at that, Sis. We're missing the county fair!" Although Meredith Willson acquired a fondness for New York a few years later, throughout his life Mason City and Cerro Gordo County remained his preferred leisure time destinies.

Like Meredith, when Dixie needed ideas for her stories, she tapped into family experiences. The plot for her first important publication, "Imogene Novre," resulted from a story she had heard in Mason City, about a bald-headed woman who rented an old log cabin from grandfather Willson. It took awhile for Dixie to establish herself professionally, and nearly destitute in New York City, her finances revived with a $55 payment for the story from *Munsey's* magazine. Instead of heading back to Iowa, she continued her writing in New York. Her next plan was to gain a variety of experiences on which to write. The scheme worked, because after she joined the Ringling Brothers Circus in 1920 for a year and a half, Dixie accumulated enough material for several stories, such as "Help Yourself to Hay," "Empty Elephant," and "Clown Town."

Paramount Pictures adapted her story "God Gave Me Twenty Cents" as a silent motion picture, and the company used this particular film to open its New York Paramount theater in 1926. The story was based on her naïve arrival in New York, where she boldly approached the biggest theatrical producer of the day, David Belasco, and tried to sell him on her playwriting abilities. She came to town with nine dollars, but it soon dwindled to twenty cents. (A little more than two decades later, brother Meredith reflected his sister's plight in the big city, when he wrote his first novel *Who Did What to Fedalia?*) The New York press enthusiastically reported on the feisty young female writer from Mason City and the opulent new motion picture palace where her film premiered, an occasion attended by Thomas Edison, Paramount head Adolph Zukor, and Mayor James Walker.

Dixie Willson rides a Ringling Brothers elephant during her circus years. (Mason City Library Collection)

The following year Dixie's refection of her chorus line years, "Here Y'Are Brother," was adapted into the Lewis Stone-Billie Dove vehicle *An Affair of the Follies*. The young Mason Cityan had come a long way from putting post cards in the soles of her worn shoes to keep the water out to become an important Broadway playwright. In a 1926 *New York Times* interview, Dixie said that she had realized the dream that she and her brother Meredith talked about on the steps of their Mason City home: "He promised that he would be a great musician and Dixie would say that she would be a great writer." Their prophetic discussion came true, for they were both in New York City at this time: he with the New York Philharmonic and she as a popular writer.

Dixie created a variety of writings, and nationally popular magazines like *Ladies' Home Journal, McClure's,* and *The Delineator* began running her work as early as 1920. During that year she was mentioned in the *Best Short Stories* series for the first time. Short stories like the "Penningwell Tuffingtons" appeared in the children's magazine *St. Nicholas* in 1923, and novels, like her 1928 *Little Texas* appeared in serial form. By the end of the decade, Dixie Willson adapted the Nunnally Johnson story "Rough House Rose" into a screenplay. Working with motion picture companies had been good to her in New York, because one of her first jobs there was as a scenario reader for Fox films, a job that also allowed her time to work on her short stories. Her $9 starting assets in 1918 grew to an income of $50,000 by 1927.

Her first love was creating for children. The long poem *Honey Bear* (1923) is her best-remembered contribution, but she is also credited with writing an instructional book for young airline stewardesses entitled *Hostess of the Skyways*. (1941) From the 1930's onward she developed a home make-up kit for children, published recipes for Betty Crocker foods, penned poems for greeting cards, and wrote for the "Goose Creek Parson" radio show.

♪ ♪ ♪

Brother Cedric Willson occupied most of his time in the 1920's following an interest in engineering that was sparked by trips with Mason City surveyor Chet Stevens when the boy was fourteen. Cedric also worked alongside county engineer R. E. Robinson. After his graduation from Mason City High School, the older Willson boy considered studying engineering at The University of Kansas. However, before he completed his degree work, Cedric made a brief attempt as a professional musician, when he studied bassoon at the Damrosch Institute in New York.

John Philip Sousa needed such an instrument in his renowned band, and a query to the school resulted in the older Willson boy's recommendation from Bassoon Master Maynard. When the bandleader contacted the instructor, Cedric was working with the Iowa Highway Commission. Soon thereafter Sousa offered him an invitation to join the organization simply on the instructor's word. The bandleader hired Cedric and told him to rendezvous with the band in Philadelphia, where the Willson brothers and sister Dixie reunited. A November 20, 1922 Mason City *Globe-Gazette* article proudly proclaimed that the two brothers would play together for the first time since they were in "The Jones Brothers Quartet" in high school, when they debuted with the Sousa Band in Philadelphia.

During the season that Cedric played without Meredith, the elder brother had the opportunity to be conducted by Charles Chaplin, when the famous film comedian exercised his love of music and seriously led the band for a Sousa birthday celebration. Cedric continued working on his engineering studies after the season's final concert in the fall. Eventually, he received his degree from Kansas and later a masters' degree in that field from New York University. After two seasons in the Sousa band, Cedric left the organization. He believed that because the "bandmaster's lameness [as a result of an earlier serious spill from a horse] prevented his appearance with the band ... its popularity declined." Other factors led to decreased interest in this style of band performances in the 1920's, but regardless of Cedric's reasons, the bassoonist returned to engineering. He became so accomplished that he shared his construction theories as a lecturer, some of which appeared in the book *Willson Symposium on Expansive Cement*.

♪ ♪ ♪

As for Meredith, the first of his long string of successes began after he graduated from Mason City High School in 1919. His local flute accomplishments landed him appointments, first with two very prominent musical establishments, the New York Institute of Music (later named the Juilliard School of Music) and the John Philip Sousa Band. During this period master musicians, such as celebrated French flautist Georges Barrere, Bernard Wagenaar, Mortimer Wilson, Julius Gold, and local symphonic virtuoso Henry Hadley applied the acid test of professional tutelage to this student from Mason City. To encapsulate Willson's success at the school, Hadley soon played next to Willson in the New York Philharmonic.

Meredith studied mornings at the Institute, and at night played at the Crescent Theatre on Boston Road or answered calls for flute players at the local union hall. Barrere made the suggestion of staying near the hall to the young musician, and one such call resulted in an invitation to play at the Winter Garden. Of course, the excited flautist sent a message to his mother that he would be at the famed Broadway theater. However, he did not have the nerve to correct the message when he found out that this Winter Garden was in the Bowery, a combination movie house and burlesque theater over a delicatessen and certainly not the more prestigious theater where the renowned Al Jolson often performed. Undaunted, the Iowan continued with Georges Barrere for the once weekly lessons, which allowed Willson to play in trios with professionals. Not only did this strengthen his playing abilities, but it also made his name known if an opportunity arose for a professional performance. By October of 1920, his musical talents had been appraised by Dr. Herman Goetchus, senior member of the faculty, and the young flautist won an artist's diploma at the conservatory.

While Meredith occupied the next phase in his life with music instruction and performing, he also took on the role of husband on August 29, 1920. After attending school in New York for one year, Meredith said that he would not return without Peggy. The two lived next to each other from their early childhood, and at least one neighborhood tree bore the initials "P.W. – M.W. 1910." Both their grandmothers and mothers had been friends, so Peggy and Meredith merely continued the family connections. In addition, Peggy taught Sunday school where her future mother-in-law held the position of superintendent. He borrowed $12 from his brother and looked for the "best looking parsonage" in nearby Albert Lea, Minnesota, where the couple eloped. (The reason for not celebrating their wedding at the Congregational Church in Mason City, might be because of Meredith's parents' marital problems at the time. The young couple began their married life nearly seven months after Meredith's parents divorced, an acrimonious separation that created an uncomfortable home life. The situation seemed to be tolerated as long as the children remained home, but once the youngest, Meredith, established himself in New York, the seemingly ill-suited couple began the dissolution of their marriage.)

Dressed in their finest, Peggy and Meredith pose for a picture in the late 1930's or early 1940's. (Mason City Library Collection)

After a Methodist ceremony the two headed to New York City to rent an apartment on 100 Northern Avenue from the Reverend Don Bean, a Congregational clergyman. Although Peggy waived her college plans in favor of accompanying her young husband East, she did eventually receive a teaching degree from the Ethical Culture School in New York. Years later, Meredith fondly recalled an O.O. McIntyre newspaper column that honored their relationship, when the writer referred to the musician as the "well known San Francisco orchestra leader." The Willsons remained married for twenty-six years, and ironically, Peggy's reasons for separating from Meredith echoed the very words Rosalie Willson blamed on her failed marriage to John: both men were away from home too much.

♪ ♪ ♪

As a youth in Mason City, Iowa, Meredith Willson experienced the excitement that accompanied a band in concert or one marching down his hometown's main streets. Musical organizations and Iowa had been linked in importance for many years before Meredith Willson appeared on the scene. Town bands and military muster increased with fervor in the Hawkeye State during the Civil War. This popularity intensified even more in the twentieth century, where ultimately a battle raged in the state's communities as to whether they wanted part of their tax millage to support a town baseball team or a band. In 1922, a Mason City baseball team seemed to be the sure bet for tax support until the final count, and the money instead funded a municipal band. In 1931, Iowa became the first state to allow municipalities to levy taxes to support a town band. Just like in *The Music Man*, Mason City did get its own band, and the town forever enriched Meredith's life by the organization's timely creation.

Two generations earlier another young boy began his long association with band music. In the nation's capital, where the threat of a Southern invading army ensured masses of military units constantly bivouacking, a young John Philip Sousa observed them and their pageantry in his hometown. From this location he created perhaps the greatest military band of all, and one which would eventually employ both Willson brothers

Sousa's own autobiography related how he had been an unruly child for his Portuguese immigrant father and Dutch immigrant mother. They finally decided to assign the musically talented thirteen-year-old to The United States Marine Band in 1868. The die that cast his devotion to music came early, because Sousa not only learned strict Marine Corps discipline, but he also matured with the organization, leading it from 1880 to 1892. After becoming the band's most distinctive leader, John Philip Sousa began composing some of the most famous marches the world has ever known. President Rutherford B. Hayes liked Sousa's band especially, because on cue the director would speed up the tempo of the performance, so that the President had to spend less time shaking hands after a particularly laborious procession of visitors.

The military did not want to lose Sousa in 1892, but the man who would be dubbed The March King at his height of popularity desired a decent royalty for some of the most popular music of the day. For five marches, including "Semper Fidelis," and "The Washington Post," he received only $35 apiece for their publication, as a result of being part of a military unit. On the other hand, after he left the Marine Corps, his popular 1893 march, "Liberty Bell," netted him $35,000 by his own reckoning. Encouraged by his business agent, David Blakely, Sousa defied then current wisdom against striking out on his own and began touring for the next four decades.

No greater debut for the new Sousa band could have been arranged than the 1893 Chicago Columbian Exposition. Although the official non-military Sousa band performed before the fair, the exposure gained by regular appearances when Sousa led the Marine band greatly fueled interest in the organization. Little Egypt's gyrations made curious Victorian Americans peer at her enticingly risqué belly dance, but even she could not compete with the audience pull of John Philip Sousa's Band. The conductor gave fairgoers the songs that they wanted to hear, and the crowds often sang along on hymns and popular favorites such as "Old Folks at Home."

The musical aggregation toured other fairs and expositions, such as Atlanta's Cotton States Exposition of 1895, the 1900 Paris Exposition, the Buffalo Pan American Exposition, and the St. Louis Exposition of 1904. In 1895, as the Sousa Band returned from a European tour, anxiously anticipating his arrival in New York City, The March King penned his most famous composition, "The Stars and Stripes Forever," in one draft. Of greater importance was that thousands of band lovers in the United States, as well as many other places around the world, had the chance to hear the most famous band in American history when a concert visited their local music hall or gazebo.

Sousa began traveling shortly after the American railroad system tied together all parts of the country, and "one night stands" by musical organizations, theatrical groups, vaudeville performers, speakers and a variety of other entertainment readily moved north, south, and west from New York or Chicago to opera halls and music academies. Not only was the timing perfect from a traveling standpoint, but it also came at a time when his marches experienced popularity through recorded music that was entering homes in the form of cylinder recordings and piano rolls. These two ways to enjoy Sousa's music often sufficed until the great man and his band visited the community; and in October of 1919, the people of Mason City, Iowa experienced the greatest band of its day in their armory.

The citizens were so inspired that in summer of 1920 they hired one of Sousa's own, coronet virtuoso Frank Simon, to be the star attraction of the new Mason City Municipal Band. He not only brought the Sousa style with him, but he also heard the talent of one particular local eighteen-year-old musician, Meredith Willson.

Harry Keeler, Vice President of the Mason City Brick and Tile Company and a driving force to get the band started, sought James M. Fulton of the Boston Theater orchestra to direct the new Iowa band. Keeler came to the town some years earlier to head Mason City's College of Music, and to organize a top notch musical group for summer productions, both of which were in keeping with his initial charge to give the city quality music in abundance. Keeler insisted that his current home rivaled larger East Coast cities for culture, and he helped earmark the Mason City Municipal Band as the town's primary musical organization, one that played "second fiddle" to no one. With Simon's influence, the musicians achieved Keeler's original intention to give the band a first class sound with a distinct Sousa flavor.

Frank Simon first heard Willson play when the teenager soloed before a combined Mason City Kiwanis-Rotary-Lions meeting. The famed cornetist recognized that the boy's talent must have come from his talented mother who accompanied him on the piano. Shortly thereafter Meredith Willson joined the town band composed of musicians from locations throughout the Midwest and who were on summer break from their regular organizations. During the summer of 1920, Willson played for ten weeks (every day except Monday) with the "$10, 000 band" and doubled as the organization's librarian. He gained for his flute and piccolo solos as much applause, the Mason City *Globe-Gazette* noted, as the whole band received. He repeated his solo performances a year later when he played with Simon in Sousa's band, with Willson handling the flute obbligato to famed vocalist Mary Baker's "The Wren," and the cornetist wowing the crowd with "Willow Echoes." Both musicians became highlights of the evening's varied offerings.

Simon wrote to Sousa, who was enjoying his summer hiatus before the next touring season, and recommended the boy for a tryout. Simon had already offered Meredith a flute seat in the famed Weber Band during the upcoming fall and winter engagements in Florida, but the teenager declined because in 1921 Willson was supposed to experience the dream of continuing his music education in New York. However, once Simon convinced Willson of the sincerity of an invitation to meet Sousa, the young flautist temporarily agreed to set aside his education and see if The March King really had an interest in him. Because Simon relayed to Sousa the young man's playing ability coupled with his fine family, good manners, and good looks, the famed conductor soon requested two pictures, one standing and another sitting, before Willson received a contract.

Not all of the chosen few in the Sousa band were legitimate performers. Cedric recalled that the first bass clarinet chair for years needed to leave the band quite suddenly in Wheeling, West Virginia. Usually, the band manager and trombonist Jay Sims easily remedied this situation. He merely moved the second chair up one seat. Unfortunately, the occupant, Ernie Johnson, had been pulling one over on the old bandmaster's eyes and actually had no idea what to play. Because the bass clarinet is not dominant in a marching band, no solos exposed the fraudulent player. The charade worked fine until the first chair got news that his father died, and the simple solution was to have Johnson move up temporarily. Sensing that his act of deception was to be exposed, "Ernie got his clothes and left. We never saw him again. For four years, he had been holding that clarinet and never playing a note." Meredith sort of remembered the same story in the first of his autobiographical works, *And There I Stood With My Piccolo*, but the person with the emergency was a similarly named Herman Johnson and the incompetent bass clarinetist was referred to only as "Mr. Softspoken."

Landing a spot in the Sousa band to a musician was akin to a baseball player sitting in the dugout with the famous and talented New York Yankees of the 1920's. Meredith Willson arrived to play in the famed band during the 1921 season, but the full realization of his dream came when the crowd-anticipated "The Stars and Stripes Forever" climaxed an evening's performance, and he literally had to come to the fore to "interrupt" the march with his piccolo solo. To recreate the scene: the consummate showman Sousa played his most famous composition to the hilt by having featured musicians in various sections of the march depart their seats and face the audience to symbolically assume control of the song. Of course, halfway through the song the woodwinds carry the melody in the piece until the trombones and basses take it from them before its memorable conclusion. As the audience anticipated the song's finale, Meredith Willson stood up with his fellow flute and piccolo players and lined up with their backs to the directing Sousa. As the young man offered his piccolo part, he received what he called the "electric thrills" that he felt during his performance.

Ironically, Meredith Willson's first opportunity to play "The Stars and Stripes Forever" for its creator met with near disaster. At age 17, the boy accompanied the Mason City Municipal Band to Des Moines, Iowa, where the Sousa band was appearing. When the time came for the lesser-known group to play the famous number, Meredith Willson, who had played the piccolo part dozens of times, butchered the solo before its maker.

When Meredith Willson played a Sousa Band concert in Washington, D.C., he used the opportunity to seek out Hanford MacNider, another important Mason Cityan in the nation's capital. Bedecked in his Sousa uniform, the young flautist located the office of the First World War hero. He announced his presence to the colonel's secretary, as if anyone cared, and was soon ushered in to see the man second only to Sergeant Alvin York in meritorious service during The Great War. Willson later recalled that the man who would eventually become the Assistant Secretary of War and a full general was just Iowa folk like himself. The two Hawkeye sons later developed a friendship which lasted through General Hanford MacNider's heroic service in World War II and Major Meredith Willson's leadership with Armed Forces Radio during the same conflict to the days when the music man visited their hometown years later and stayed at MacNider's Indianhead homestead.

R. Meredith Willson was no slouch on his instrument, as noted by the *Philadelphia Record* of September 3, 1922, when the music critic remarked that the last concert of the Willow Grove season was noteworthy because of a twenty-year-old flautist from Iowa. Sousa frequently included Charminade's "Concert in D" as part of the program, and the reporter continued that the solo in the "difficult and delectable offering" belonged to the flute soloist: "The composition presents many difficulties - all disappearing before the musicianship of Willson." Unfortunately for music lovers, the 1922-23 season with John Philip Sousa was the young Iowan's last before moving up to an even greater rung in performing.

Of course, touring with Sousa meant long hours on trains, often a time to review new music. Meredith Willson recalled one such opportunity to pour over a pocket score of the "Nutcracker Suite," but the young musician was baffled by the intricate moves. While Willson scrutinized the material, John Philip Sousa came down the aisle, and the young Iowan determined that it would duly impress The March King if the young flautist examined the music as the bandmaster passed. Detecting a pretender in his midst, Sousa took Willson aside and began tutoring the young musician. The military muster of the seemingly rigid conductor metamorphosed into a paternal leader intent on securing the well being of one far from home and with whom he would soon perform.

Projecting forward three decades to *The Music Man*, the incredible feelings Willson had touring with Sousa "from coast to coast and from Ottawa to Cuba" were captured in the exuberance the fictitious River City residents felt imagining Sousa playing in their town. Their enthusiasm fueled a desire to involve idle children in a wholesome program such as a town band. Willson's musical is at first a tribute to the gentle days and people of Mason City and second to John Philip Sousa's tremendous influence on the composer. From Harold Hill's chanted words about trouble in River City to just before the rousing "Seventy-Six Trombones" to the fireworks named after a Sousa performance favorite "The Last Days of Pompeii," the story oozes with obvious and sometimes less direct references to Willson's days with The March King. The inspiration for "Seventy-Six Trombones" may have come from one of the Sousa reunion concerts Willson played, such as the November 5, 1922, Hippodrome performance. Dozens of former members of the famed band wore a variety of uniforms from different time periods to play "The Stars and Stripes Forever" *en masse*. If seventy-six trombones did not perform in that aggregation, it must have seemed like it.

Sousa directs an oversized band in "The Stars and Stripes Forever" on its 25th anniversary in 1921. (The University of Illinois Sousa Collection)

A tip of the hat for recommending Willson to Sousa came to Frank Simon in the form of a letter years later, when Willson said, "I once wrote a song about 76 trombones and 110 cornets. This is a good time to reveal that there was only one cornet all the time ... they just sounded like 110 cornets because you [Simon] were the cornetist."

Years after Meredith and Cedric Willson made great names for themselves in their respective occupations, they continued their ties with John Philip Sousa. By 1943, ex-members of the famous band began meeting for reunions and to swap stories about themselves and "The Old Man." By the next year, the Sousa Band Fraternal Society organized and soon thereafter the Willson brothers joined. Fortunately for the siblings, both the New York and Los Angeles meetings accommodated members closer to one site or the other. The Los Angeles chapter paid Meredith Willson an early honor for his radio work at a meeting in 1946. Coincidentally, one West Coast member, former Sousa flautist Jack Bell, played in the orchestra of *The Music Man* on Broadway. The group effort to preserve memories with Sousa initially succeeded with its objectives, but the organization faded away as its members died.

♪ ♪ ♪

After Meredith Willson returned from touring with John Philip Sousa, he resumed his studies and weekend engagements as a musician. The routine for a student at the New York Institute of Music included classes during the day and performances in the evening. While working in the Times Square Rialto Theatre orchestra conducted by Hugo Riesenfeld in the winter of 1923-24, Meredith Willson became part of an experiment that would revolutionize motion pictures. At a time when all films were silent except for pit orchestras, piano players, and organists, Dr. Lee DeForest experimented with his Phonofilm process, one that recorded sound on film in light waves alongside of the picture. In order to get inexpensive talent to play before his microphone, DeForest engaged the young flautist from Mason City, and as a reward, gave Willson a share of stock in the company. By the end of the decade, talking pictures had revolutionized the motion picture world, and this brief encounter with the medium was just the first of many for which Meredith Willson contributed to the music.

During his time in the Rialto Theatre pit orchestra in 1924, Meredith Willson also made his first important composition, *Parade Fantastique*, a song which, to put it mildly, was not enthusiastically embraced by critics. When he appeared at the publisher to collect his royalties on the song, he was given pocket change and ushered unceremoniously to the door. Intended to be the combination of a traditional march with macabre musical images reminiscent of the Halloween season, the number enjoyed a prestigious premiere performance by the New York Philharmonic-Symphony Orchestra. Willson joined this august organization later that year when he made an impressive career change and became their first chair flautist, a seat he also held in the New York Chamber Music Society. Throughout the decade, Meredith Willson continued learning from both resident and guest conductors. He never received a formal music degree from the New York Institute of Music, rather he learned from those who were in the American musical Mecca of the 1920's, New York City.

♪ ♪ ♪

When R. Meredith Willson took his place in the flute section of the Philharmonic Society of New York in the fall of 1924, he found himself in the midst of an exciting time period in the symphony's growth. The competition and power struggle during his stay would forever change the orchestra from a predominantly Germanic led group to the world-renowned orchestra under the baton of the fiery Arturo Toscanini. Willson also found himself in the transition between primarily Old World musicians and those American born. He had faced a similar problem in the Sousa organization. Sousa noted that when the Willson brothers joined the band in 1921 and 1922 they were two of only four non-foreign born members, but by the time the young Iowans finished their two-year tenures with The March King, all except four of the musicians were American born.

Meredith Willson's first conductor when he joined the New York Philharmonic Society was Willem Mengelberg, a Dutchman, whom Winthrop Sargeant described in his *Genius, Goddesses and People* as one with a "Teutonic military mind. He demanded respect not for his personality, but for his rank as conductor." His leadership resulted in one of the best-trained orchestras in America. During the 1924-25 season, he and Willem Van Hoogstraten directed the orchestra primarily at Carnegie Hall, the Metropolitan Opera House, and the Brooklyn Academy of Music. On several occasions the orchestra traveled to nearby halls in Stamford, Connecticut or to Massachusetts colleges and public auditoriums. Before the season ended, internationally famous instrumental soloists Efrem Zimbalist, Pablo Casals, Ossip Gabrilowitsch and, making his first American visit, Igor Stravinsky appeared with the orchestra.

Listed with three other flautists, "R. M. Willson" played in his first symphony performance on October 16, 1924. Under the direction of Van Hoogstraten, the evening offered Weber, Respighi, Mozart and Wagner. Exposure to these and other composers of the season, like Strauss, Dvorak, Brahms, Bach, Reger, Beethoven, and Tchaikovsky caused Willson to lovingly include their work on his radio shows years later. He also joked on one such program that when Van Hoogstraten assumed that the young Iowan was familiar with certain famous symphonies, Willson replied that he had never heard of them but that he was happy to learn the pieces. The dumbfounded conductor retreated to his daunting duties with the depressing prospect of such an unversed musician but was immediately revived by the young man's ability to learn so quickly.

During the next two seasons, the New York Philharmonic Society proffered its customary bill of fare, its annual trip to Pittsburgh, and guests like Pablo Casals and Lauritz Melchior. However, during the 1925-26 season, Arturo Toscanini, Milan's La Scala conductor, led the group for the first time as a guest and set his sights on a more permanent position with the organization. By February of 1928, the iconoclastic director began conducting in New York regularly and almost one year later he officially lorded over the musicians.

Even though the orchestra was one of the best trained, Toscanini, in Sargeant's words, shook "the New York Philharmonic to its foundations." A young Meredith Willson observed how a group led by Toscanini's "towering rages in which he broke his baton in half and kicked over his stand" supplanted Mengelberg's "carefully contrived systems." As a result, the young flautist always took rehearsals seriously, and later, when he conducted his own practices or performances, his normally easy-going Hawkeye demeanor turned resolute.

In keeping with the rigid discipline of the orchestra, the Philharmonic's manager kept careful notes on attendance and imbursement. For example, R. Meredith Willson received $90 in 1928 for seven performances in Pittsburgh. When fellow flautist John Amans became sick during that same season, Willson received $25 extra during the week he covered the additional duties "Sickness" seemed to be a common reason to note members' absences, and one special mention proudly reported that the Iowa piccolo player had an illness but still appeared in concert. In another place, the monosyllabic "sick" and "late" for rehearsal recorded the comings and goings of the tightly controlled organization.

Although Toscanini demanded a rigid decorum, orchestral etiquette frequently took a back seat during practices. One time when Walter Damrosch returned to guest conduct the orchestra, unlike his usually placid demeanor, Damrosch began to imitate Toscanini's tirades. When fledgling American composer George Gershwin came for a special visit, an air of European snobbery and artistic egotism pervaded the direction. On this occasion the Philharmonic was to play Gershwin's *Concerto in F* for piano and orchestra, a composition by the upstart jazz prodigy. Under the leadership of the primarily European/classical musicians, the orchestra members rebuffed the young artist's work and misplayed it at rehearsal, feigning not to understand the new jazz patterns. Returning to get their haughty goats, Gershwin attended a later rehearsal not wearing traditional formal wear. Instead he played the piano sporting a derby hat, while smoking a big, fat cigar, much to the chagrin of the stuffy assemblage.

Not only did symphonic music in New York enjoy prosperity during the 1920's, but also other American orchestras experienced sustained audience growth in many cities remote to the older, established Eastern locations. For example, the Minneapolis Symphony began in 1903, the San Francisco Symphony in 1911, the Detroit Symphony in 1914, and the Cleveland Orchestra in 1918. However, just as they began to attract subscribers to their seasons, they needed to clear hurdles, not the least of which was the First World War, before these organizations became financially stable. One early success, The Los Angeles Philharmonic Orchestra, began in 1919 and premiered its long-running "Hollywood Bowl Under the Stars" just three years later. Coming through the instrumental music ranks at a very opportune time, Meredith Willson later guest conducted with all of these newer organizations from the late 1930's through the 1960's.

The prosperity that followed the end of the First World War, coupled with, ironically, The Jazz Age and the desire for its devotees to be entertained and be seen at gala social events, helped increase interest in all arts during the 1920's. Likewise, the purchase of recorded symphonic music grew with the nation's post-War prosperity, and better quality disks became available when electronic transcriptions replaced inferior acoustic recordings. If listeners could not get to a live concert, either a recording or a concert via radio, the newest entertainment medium of the decade, might placate the music lover until he or she could be found seated in one of the many new performance halls. Unfortunately, a number of the gains that symphonies made during these years were reversed when the New York Stock Market suffered its worst crash in 1929 and audiences reconsidered spending money on live entertainment.

♪ ♪ ♪

In 1926, three young radio stations banded together to create the first media network, the National Broadcasting Company. Later that year, to establish an air of legitimacy, the expanded twenty-five-station chain broadcast the New York Philharmonic on the network's premiere offering from the Waldorf-Astoria Hotel on November 15, 1926. With Walter Damrosch conducting and Meredith Willson playing the flute and piccolo, the orchestra headlined a four-hour long bill that included humorist Will Rogers, the famed comedy team of Weber and Fields, and additional musical groups ranging from the Metropolitan Opera to local dance bands. The symphonic organization later found a home at the rival Columbia Broadcasting Company from 1927-1950, when Damrosch moved to the National Symphony Orchestra and created his own show for NBC. Appropriately, twenty-five years after the network's origin, Meredith Willson penned the official anniversary song, "Three Chimes of Silver," honoring the company's quarter of a century on the air as well as offering his own thanks for what would become two decades of affiliation with the National Broadcasting Company. (Incidentally, these three notes that usually signified the end of a radio program on NBC originated as a tribute to the network's parent company and were based in the three initial letters of the General Electric Corporation.)

Incidentally, John Philip Sousa initially dismissed radio as not being capable as a conveyor of "serious music." However, once Sousa realized the potential of sharing all forms of music with audiences who might be too busy to hear a performance live, he changed his earlier opinion of the medium and likewise presented his music on radio. Not coincidentally, the amount of money that could be generated for a network appearance also convinced him to rethink his position.

Although Meredith Willson gained a tremendous education about notes and their arrangements with The Philharmonic Society of New York through the 1928-29 season with guests like Bela Bartok, Paderewski, Vladimir Horowitz, Alan Jones and Yehudi Menuhin (at age twelve), the young Iowan once again considered altering his music career. For his next major change he set his sights on conducting, as positions opened on the West Coast.

Chapter Four
"Local Boy Makes Good"

During the 1920's, Meredith Willson's stature as a musician propelled him from youth prodigy in the Mason City Municipal Band to an accomplished flute and piccolo player with renowned organizations such as John Philip Sousa's Band and the New York Philharmonic. Willson adapted to a musical lifestyle that took him on the road and eventually found him located in New York City. By the end of the decade, he would meet a variety musical opportunities that would bring him to additional locations. He found both on the West Coast in 1928, when he ascended the podium and raised the baton during the facet of his life that would occupy the next two decades.

The National Broadcasting Company began in 1926 as the first American radio network, and the Columbia Broadcasting System debuted two years later. Within a few years NBC acquired enough stations to spilt into two networks, the Blue and the Red. The network maintained a primarily East Coast broadcasting chain, as well as one that better addressed the needs of listeners in the Western time zones. Also at this time in the late 1920's several smaller groups of stations, like the Don Lee Network in the West, formed as small regional chains that worked to provide outlets for the larger national networks. Although he would find fame on all of the major American broadcasting companies, as well as spend time with the smaller groups, the first network that invited Meredith Willson to be its musical director was an upstart named the American Broadcast System in the Northwest. (This early radio network should not to be confused with the American Broadcasting Company, which emerged when NBC's Blue division was forced to become independent in 1946.)

Meredith Willson went to Seattle in 1928 at the request of Adolph Linden, owner of radio station KJR. Willson became the musical director there and helped his innovative new boss with a grandiose project. Transcontinental radio networks were not complete in the late 1920's, and Linden devised an ingenious figure eight pattern from the West to East Coasts to facilitate program flow. Simultaneously, the farsighted Linden created another novel plan for his city that had a long-term affect on the Iowa musician, when Willson received his first opportunity to direct an orchestra.

At Linden's urging in 1929, Meredith Willson proffered his plan to conduct a West Coast orchestra, while providing fine artists for the new network. In order to organize Seattle's symphony orchestra for a summer series at the University of Washington stadium, the young conductor convinced some of his New York musician friends to join the organization. Although it was a long train trip to a summer gig, the summer was often a lean time for such players and they trusted Willson's home grown sense to steer them right. When the young music leader arrived in New York to round up his fellow musicians, and before he headed west, he stopped on Park Avenue to have a formal picture taken. This would be the first photo that Willson had taken in a number of years. He identified himself to the photographer as being unused to such a shoot, because he had not been before a camera since his Uncle Ed's funeral in Charles City, Iowa several years earlier. The photographer fell into a nearby chair and said that he had a shop on Main Street in that same Iowa town. Willson later recalled that this chance meeting seemed to be a favorable omen and another pleasant reminder of his hometown connections.

When the thirteen anxious musicians and Mrs. Peggy Willson arrived in Seattle in early June, Mayor Frank Edwards greeted them formally at the train station. The *Mason City Globe-Gazette* referred to R. Meredith Willson (a common moniker when he performed in New York as well) as a young sensation, a local prodigy who had achieved a level of greatness. The article continued by outlining the twenty-week performance schedule, which was to end on August 18. It also indicated how these broadcast concerts were just the beginning of the new network and that this orchestra, now named the American Philharmonic, would soon be ready to originate programming from studios in New York. However, at age twenty-six, the "youngest philharmonic concert master in America," as he was called in the *Seattle Times*, quipped in his first autobiographical work, "we laid a very large egg in the shadow of Mount Rainier."

The city was eager, the New York musicians were ready to enjoy a full summer of employment to help make up the seventy-piece American

Philharmonic Orchestra, and the preparations were elaborate. However, the weather did not co-operate. Willson reported that, after "one cold and gloomy audience after another," coupled with Linden's mounting financial problems of hiring a dozen notable instrumentalists and trying to start a radio network, the funds to fulfill the contracts soon evaporated. Two noble ideas folded, and regrettably, Meredith Willson had to return to the East Coast and face his fellow musicians and the $100,000 owed them.

Back in New York, the young Iowan felt that he had no place to hide from those whose contracts were worthless, yet he had to perform in public to pay his own bills. Demoted from symphony conductor to on-call piccolo player, he grabbed his old Sousa uniform and joined a band playing in Central Park. After determining which park held the man whose name sealed their bogus contracts, the musicians located Willson, playing his familiar solo in "The Stars and Stripes Forever." Although he was worried if he would ever have a woodwind lip again after the group got through with him, he was relieved when they eventually tore up the contracts and wished him good luck.

♪ ♪ ♪

After a brief stay in New York City to pick up a few dollars performing, Willson decided to take a musical chance on the burgeoning California Coast. During one early stop, he visited his old friend Abe Meyer, the man responsible for getting the young composer's first song published and who moved West to become the musical head of Tiffany-Stahl. This small Hollywood production company's greatest claim to fame was perhaps the silent film *Peacock Alley* (1926) with Mae Murray. The studio later earmarked the film to be remade as an early talkie starring its foremost box office attraction. However, the 1929 version did not receive the same accolades, as did the first. Mae Murray was so disappointed with the finished product that she sued the studio for ruining her career. Fledgling conductor Meredith Willson arranged the music for the talking version. He admitted to not knowing anything about his new job, but then few did in the early years of talking pictures. To at least create an aura of an artist in residence, he took to smoking a cigar while walking around the studio early in the morning to meditate on his work.

The problem with the musical "score" on this and many early sound films resulted from incorrectly using the music to enhance the scene. For example, Willson's work on *The Lost Zeppelin* (1929) had no mood music to bridge scene changes: an actor entered a room, turned on the radio, and the music started. After a few lines of dialogue, like "Shall I turn the radio off?" the music went silent until the next literal need arises. Meredith Willson might have been captured on film directing the band in such a scene, for at the very end of the zeppelin saga, a dance number in a nightclub takes place in front of a "live" orchestra. Willson is probably conducting, but he is difficult to recognize because the leader's back is to the audience the whole time.

Thrilling poster art for The Lost Zeppelin entices viewers to see this early Tiffany-Stahl talkie. (author's collection)

Many melodies that Willson created during the late 1920's and early 1930's found their way into a number of early talking picture scores, not necessarily originating from Tiffany-Stahl. When motion picture companies simultaneously released both silent and sound films, publishers provided a reservoir of useful tunes to augment the story's mood. The Edward Everett Horton comedy *Wide Open* (Vitaphone 1929) used Willson's "Skyline," while the Douglas Fairbanks, Sr. and Mary Pickford adaptation of *The Taming of the Shrew* (United Artists 1930) incorporated his "Tornado" in the sound version. Other Meredith Willson songs used in early sound films include "The Siege" (*Second Floor Mystery* Vitaphone 1930), "Defiance" (*Czar of Broadway* Universal 1930), as well as "Phenomena" and "Parade Fantastique" (*The Last Performance* Universal 1929). The haunting "Parade Fantastique," often found usage in films, including eleven times in *Love In the Desert* (FBO 1928). Even the foreign version of *Dance of Life* (Paramount 1930) employed excerpts from "Skyline." Most of these songs listed by ASCAP on the film cue sheets are identified as "partial," but complete versions of many of them became available to the public through Kalmus or Witmark publishers. Although these early writings do not necessarily represent memorable tunes, they did give the young composer a variety of opportunities to develop his film scoring skills, which would mature by the end of the 1930's.

♪ ♪ ♪

After a few exercises in scoring motion pictures at Tiffany-Stahl and contributing numbers like the title song for *My Cavalier*, the radio medium again beckoned for Meredith Willson, this time with longer lasting and more positive experiences. In 1929, he traveled to San Francisco, which was host to a number of important radio shows in the early 1930's, as well as the location where up and coming performers teethed in the medium before the Western network focus shifted to Los Angeles. The radio connection for Willson came from a writer friend named Merle Matthews. A Willson acquaintance from the Seattle days, she moved to Don Lee's San Francisco station KFRC, and soon after, Willson became the station's music director in 1929.

The relocation proved to be one that Meredith and Peggy treasured. After the motion picture *The Music Man* became a hit in 1962, Meredith Willson recalled his "second home," San Francisco, for a *San Francisco Examiner* reporter. He remembered that he "went down from Seattle to see a football game in 1929 and stayed." The recollection conflicts with his story in *And There I Stood With My Piccolo* wherein he stated that he returned to New York after the symphonic radio debacle in Seattle. Regardless, Peggy and Meredith Willson developed a fondness for the city by the Bay, as well as a closeness to radio that would continue for the next twenty-five years.

Settling in at KFRC meant that Meredith Willson would arrange and create music for a premiere American station, as well as an early West Coast hub from which many popular programs and personalities came to Bay area and later network radio. The station became the flagship of the Don Lee network in 1926, when Lee used the profits that he made as a Cadillac automobile dealer to buy the station. After the NBC network began to grow in the East, Lee envisioned his own group of stations in the West. Consequently, in 1927, he purchased KHJ in Los Angeles and revamped his Cadillac dealership there into a radio studio. With two of the most prestigious broadcasting outlets in California's biggest markets, Lee set about to rival the National Broadcasting Company for audience share. In 1929, he convinced CBS president William S. Paley to allow KFRC and KHJ to represent the network on the West Coast. In order to develop as a talent laden force in radio, Lee started by hiring artists like Meredith Willson, who joined the San Francisco station to guide the music for a variety of network shows.

During the early 1930's, before regular broadcasting flowed endlessly from coast to coast from the network hubs in New York, Chicago, and Los Angeles, and because of the time differences, West coast stations presented a great deal of network quality original programming for the Western divisions of NBC and CBS. Willson recalled one such show that he worked on in San Francisco named *Captain Dobbsie's Ship of Joy*, a variety show that showcased a wide range of talent, some very unusual. Possibly the first ship-to-shore radio broadcast occurred in 1933, when star Hugh Dobbs and the entire "crew" transmitted a show from mid-Pacific aboard the cruise ship *Malolo* en route to Honolulu. The character of Dobbs was likeable on or off microphone, and his forgetfulness was legendary. During one show he invited a South Seas ethnologist onto the program to play an instrument called a *lala*. When this long tree trunk instrument was struck, it called natives for miles. To prove the point Dobbs sent his listeners away from their radios to hear the sound live. Willson and the orchestra began playing music so the recipients of the sound would be in place. In the meantime the good but forgetful Captain Dobbsie began a conversation about ancient Peruvian stone carvers and forgot about those he had sent off. Fifteen years later in his first autobiographical work *And There I Stood with My Piccolo*, Willson wondered if the faithful were still waiting for the noise.

Among others who frequented KFRC were Carlton E. Morse, a top-notch writer whose famed *One Man's Family* started its twenty-seven year run with the Barbour family of the Seacliff district of the San Francisco in 1932. In Willson's words, Morse wrote "practically everybody at the station" into the serial, which later became a mainstay on the NBC network. Others who went on to fame at NBC in San Francisco included KFRC staff announcer Bill Goodwin, who would spend half of his eight years on the *George Burns and Gracie Allen* show with Meredith Willson; future band leader Phil Harris, who was getting his start as a drummer in the Loughner-Harris orchestra at the St. Francis Hotel; and from the Peacock Court of the Mark Hotel, Xavier Cougat commingled with Anson Weeks' orchestra. Also beginning their radio careers in San Francisco in the early 1930's were singer Nelson Eddy, Chicago breakfast club host

Don McNeill, comedienne Vera Vague, orchestra leader Kay Kyser, the "Great Gildersleeve" Harold Peary, as well as game show emcees Ralph Edwards and Art Linkletter.

♪ ♪ ♪

Meredith Willson found himself writing a variety of pieces in these early days of San Francisco radio. Some shows required opening and closing theme music, and the young musical director even found time to write original songs and have them published. His "Show Us the Way, Blue Eagle" (1933) was an inspirational and patriotic song that heralded the eagle as both the symbol of America and the image chosen to lift the hopes of those looking for relief from the Great Depression. Centered on the cover of the sheet music, with the NRA eagle behind him, Meredith Willson strikes a somber and formal pose. Two years later he again adorned the cover of another popular song sheet, but not as its composer, rather as its promoter on his many radio shows. For the sheet music "Red Sails in the Sunset" (Jimmy Kennedy and Hugh Williams 1935), Meredith Willson posed clutching an NBC microphone.

The sheet music cover for "The House of Melody" includes photos of West Coast radio personalities John Nesbitt and Meredith Willson. (Arthur Fischbeck collection)

Perhaps one of the longest acquaintances Meredith Willson made during his stay in San Francisco was with famed storyteller John Nesbitt. Nesbitt originated his romantic and moving stories in *The Passing Parade* and split the half-hour of *House of Melody* with Willson from KFRC's Van Ness Avenue studios. In 1937, their collaborative work, the theme song from "House of Melody" appeared in print. The light and airy waltz tempo piece expounded on the ideal dream house filled with the perfect blend of love and melodies. When Meredith Willson had his own radio program, a summer replacement for *Fibber McGee and Molly* in 1942, Nesbitt rejoined his friend and offered his inspirational stories, often undergirded with Willson melodies.

This particular Bay area station had a wide variety of shows, many of them parodies or counterparts to successful East coast network shows, but one of the greatest features of KFRC, as well as one of the most popular West Coast originated radio shows in the early 1930's was *The Blue Monday Jamboree.* Kissing cousin to the seemingly eternal *Grand Old Opry* from Nashville and the popular *WLS Barn Dance* from Chicago, this two hour, down-home variety show ran from eight until ten o'clock PM with its own stock company of performers provided the listener with just about anything in radio entertainment. Program pianist Edna Fischer later recalled that the show had "naturalness and the freedom to be yourself ... [and] you didn't get a second chance." Remembering years later that there were probably very few recordings of the show, she continued, "If it was a great performance, it was gone. If it was bad, then everybody heard it." She was probably correct about the likelihood of many recordings surviving, for their fate might have been like so many of the pre-War glass or aluminum transcription disks: they ended up broken or collected in a scrap drive during the Second World War.

Thanks to Fischer, at least one related KFRC program survives. Because of her popularity on *Blue Monday Jamboree*, she made a rare guest appearance on *Carefree Carnival* in 1937. She was given a nearly 12 minute recording of the program because it featured her music. After two songs by Fischer, she and Willson "convince" host Ned Tolliver to give "Our Destination Is Heaven" a hearing. She had written the words to the Willson music. Immediately after the romantic ballad finished, Willson's "Smile with Me" theme for the Signal Oil show abruptly closed the program. Fischer presented this rare recording to the Museum of the City of San Francisco very late in her life.

As for her memories of *Blue Monday Jamboree*, Fischer recalled the time when station manager and master of ceremonies Harrison Holliway played a trick on his father, who was waiting in the wings until the show was over. During the performance, the elderly gentleman fell asleep on a couch and began snoring. As a gag, and to reinforce the impromptu nature of the show, Holliway placed a microphone under the sleeping man's nose and then invited listeners to write in their guesses as to what the sound was for a prize.

Meredith Willson recalled when he orchestrated the Ferde Grofé piano piece "Metropolis" for the show, the arranger decided that a rivet gun would be the only instrument that could sound like the pneumatic tool written into the piece. The sound effects man, also station janitor Mr. Bunce, hooked up the apparatus to a compressed air tank. No time had been allotted to rehearse the sound, because the cast and crew had only one hour to get everything ready for the two-hour show. Willson raised his hand for this first number of the evening, but when he dropped his hand as a cue for Bunce, the effect did not work. The janitor tried the tool again and again during the number; however, it did not start until after the last note of the piece, and then would not shut off until after the broadcast ended.

The Blue Monday Jamboree attempted to showcase different occupations, and when the chance came to honor railroad workers, Bunce attempted another unusual sound effect. When radio broadcast all shows live and recording equipment could not easily reproduce believable sound effects, the crews used the actual item as much as possible. What better way could there be to salute the railroad industry than to blow a Southern Pacific engine whistle in the studio? Again without the luxury of a rehearsal, when the four hundred and seventy-five-pound whistle arrived, the janitor put it in its place untried. After emcee Holliway asked the engineer guest which whistle was his favorite, the answer came back "Three longs and a short - that lets my wife know she can start fixing breakfast – I'm only fifty miles up the line." At that point, Mr. Bunch, who had attached the whistle to his compressor and set the sound effect near the microphone, pulled the trigger line. No one had calculated what a steam whistle, intended to send a call miles away, would do in a broadcasting studio. After the mechanism rang out, the studio windows fell in, the roof collapsed, and some audience members sued because they thought that they had broken eardrums. Worse, the station had to go off the air for two weeks to repair the damage.

Blue Monday vocalists warbled a variety of music from highbrow to hillbilly, while Al Pearce provided comedy with his moronic Elmer Blurt character. The husband and wife team of Harry and Betty Gibson performed domestic skits as Doakes and Doakes. The entire range of talent on the program, as well as the overall variety of programming on KFRC, appealed to Meredith Willson's love of all forms of entertainment. As a result of the show's popularity, Meredith Willson became such a star at the station that sponsor Golden State Eggs felt he would be a good representative in a lengthy advertisement that heralded its products as prepared by wife Peggy. After revealing her husband's personal preferences for salt on his grapefruit and not on his eggs in a 1929 newspaper testimonial, Peggy continued her recipe tips by describing how to make homemade noodles like the ones she had been preparing during their ten years of marriage.

♪ ♪ ♪

From his first published composition, *Parade Fantastique*, Meredith Willson wrote, by his reckoning, over 400 pieces of music. The number probably is not exaggerated but cannot be verified, because the composer often penned songs for radio show use, such as "The Jamboree March" for *The Blue Monday Jamboree*, and ones for which he was sometimes credited but frequently not given recognition. One of his finest creations in the 1930's was the *O.O. McIntyre Suite* (1934), a three-part composition in tribute to the great New York columnist, who died in 1938 at age 54.

Meredith Willson made the acquaintance of Oscar Odd McIntyre when the two were trying to gain their fame and fortune in New York after they left their respective Midwestern homes in Iowa and Ohio. McIntyre attracted his audience with writings that addressed the needs experienced by displaced non-native Gothamites. Consequently, his following as a Hearst syndicated columnist in 380 newspapers grew to an astounding 7,000,000 readers by the 1930's. His "New York Day by Day" exhibited a cockeyed optimism about a city so often painted as a hostile and unfriendly environment and, as a result, endeared him to readers from New York and across the country. He delighted in simple things, especially dogs, and this fondness for the mundane inspired Willson to compose the following three parts that made up the suite: "Thingamabobs," "Thoughts While Strolling," and "Local Boy Makes Good." Paul Whiteman's orchestra first played the piece, and the middle section was later adapted as the 1945 Bing Crosby hit, "Whose Dream Are You?"

O.O. McIntyre's writings touched so many readers that thirteen years after his death, NBC radio's *The Big Show* offered a tribute in his behalf. In a quiet moment on radio's major last variety program, Meredith Willson directed the orchestra in "Thoughts While Strolling," while host Tallulah Bankhead read a poignant column by McIntyre about the loss of the columnist's dog. Willson recalled the writer: "Perhaps a good one word simile of Americana is MCINTYRE." Continuing with his reflections that justified the subject of his music, Meredith Willson related, early in his own career, all of the qualities for which he wished to be remembered, a

> hero, having made good in the big city, returning for a brief visit to his hometown. As the train slows down at the station you hear the enthusiastic reception of the native son by the local band ... a few well-chosen remarks ... and the Local Boy is speedily returned to his New York Day-by-Day.

Willson might have been prophesying the achievements that he would realize when *The Music Man* debuted six years later.

♪ ♪ ♪

Although San Francisco radio mogul Don Lee imagined that network radio broadcasting would soon shift to Los Angeles, Meredith Willson did not move to Lee's new headquarters at KHJ, rather he stayed in the city that captured his heart, San Francisco. In addition to KFRC, the musical director shared new offices at both KGO and KPO, two NBC Bay area affiliates. After being encouraged by Abe Meyer to include more current popular hits on his programs, Meredith Willson sought out *Variety*'s top ten list and played them on his new program, *The Big Ten*. Soon after NBC borrowed the idea and transformed it into the network's long-running success, the *Lucky Strike Hit Parade*, which debuted with the same format. NBC sold the rights to the new show to the Brown and Williamson Tobacco Company, but because Meredith Willson was already on the network payroll, he did not receive any compensation for the idea, even though the program ran successfully on radio and television from 1935 to 1974.

Other shows on which Meredith Willson worked in San Francisco included *The Heckler Surprise Party*, *The Carefree Carnival*, *America Sings*, *Chiffon Jazz*, and *Waltz Time*. Of equal importance to his ascendance in the world of radio was the musician's opportunity to compose his first symphony. The inspiration came from glancing out of his twenty-second floor office in the Hunter Dublin Building on Sutter Street to the San Francisco Bay and the circle that would be closed when The Golden Gate Bridge was completed. He later recalled that the final notes of his *Symphony Number One in F Minor* or *A Symphony of San Francisco* emerged at about the same time as the great cables and rivets completed a masterpiece of American engineering. He also related that, even though the symphony and the bridge were finished at virtually the same time, the bridge "made more money."

Attempted as a musical composition reflecting the varied moods of the City by the Bay, the symphony, in the words of the *San Francisco Chronicle*, painted its history in "haunting nuances ... its tears, its tragedies, its laughter, its streamlined future." To say that Meredith Willson found a very favorable home away from his Iowa home would be an understatement. Like his later musical masterpiece, *The Music Man*, the composer endeavored to pay homage to the admirable personality of the city and its inhabitants.

The day after the symphony's premiere and seated at the piano in his NBC office, Meredith Willson played the first movement for an interviewer. The performance began with the rugged pioneer motif intended "to catch the virility of San Francisco's past" and then segued into, in Willson's words, a "feminine theme. It's a little hymn. It's simple and foursquare." The melody builds and then subsides, but the movement always ascends to the next plane as it progresses majestically higher and higher. The second movement reflects the desolation in the city as a result of the great earthquake of 1906, with very quiet, melancholic tones moving slowly toward a hopeful civic renaissance. In true Willson style, the piccolo attempts to buoy the rest of the more somber instruments, but devastating horror pervades the section. Lilting piccolos rapidly begin the third movement, a tribute to the city's diverse population. Finally, the concluding music emanates as the result of the composer watching over one of the greatest engineering feats in American history, a hopeful artifact constructed during The Great Depression, *The Golden Gate Bridge*. Like the structure, the composition rises musically in an impressionistic mood and inches powerfully to the conclusion that reflects the confidence and love of its composer. Deep brass and percussion lead the accelerating allegro movement to its triumphal conclusion.

The debut of his new piece occurred on April 19, 1936, at the War Memorial Opera House, where Willson conducted the San Francisco Symphony Orchestra as its youngest leader at age thirty-three. The *San Francisco Chronicle* of April 20, 1936 praised Willson's work as favorable for "a young composer." It also stated that it was less an exploration of "new paths, but it is more imitation of familiar models." Reporting on its definite American flavor, the reporter noted that Willson's symphony filled out the "patterns of sonata-allegro, passacaglia and scherzo without academic fuss and feathers." Reservedly impressed, fine arts critic Alfred Frankenstein liked the instrumentation and saxophone quartet, but felt that "the attempt at a sonorously built-up, climactic conclusion does not quite come off." The critic continued to suggest that the first effort was reason enough for Willson to "dispense with the subtle 'Symphony of San Francisco' and the rather obvious program associated with it" and to keep composing. The fact that the journalist praised the composer's directorial talents seemed overshadowed by the disappointing critical reaction to the symphony itself. The mayor of the city expressed a more favorable analysis and honored the proud writer with "Meredith Willson Day" after the premiere. Daunted but not depressed, Meredith Willson offered another such piece when he debuted his *Missions of California Symphony* two years later.

However, before he began this second symphony, Meredith and Peggy took a six-week cruise through the Panama Canal, and eventually to familiar people and places in New York City. On the return trip to California, the composer reassured friends and family in Mason City that his current home had not displaced his Iowa birthplace in his heart. After visiting Peggy's mother, the composer announced that he intended on writing a Mason City symphony. Instead, twenty years later he completed his own hit musical that honored his beloved hometown.

San Francisco became a much loved second home for the Willsons. As national radio networks continued to move their programming to Los Angeles, the Iowa musician assumed directorial positions in both major California cities. And even after he relocated to southern California, numerous occasions presented themselves, so that Willson could return again to the north where he could conduct musical organizations, and especially the San Francisco Symphony. However, by the Second World War, the opportunities became less frequent, as new professional demands kept him busy in the Los Angeles area.

♪ ♪ ♪

Although the 1930's evolved as a period of great professional advancement for Meredith Willson, he also suffered tremendous personal losses. In 1931, both of his parents died: John Willson on January 10, and Rosalie Reiniger Willson on September 15. During the couple's separation, Rosalie continued fighting for important social causes, while devotedly serving at the Congregational Church. John Willson remarried and operated a bakery in a Mason City building one street to the west of the house where he raised his children. (Interestingly, his second wife, Minnie Hartzfeldt, spent a great deal of time raising Dixie's daughter Dana after John died and until her own passing in 1940.) In later years, Meredith fondly recalled "Mama and Papa," but the positive memories of his mother eclipsed those of his father. John Willson found difficulty accepting and acknowledging the magnificent strides that his youngest son had made in the world of music.

One year after the deaths of Willson's parents, father figure and mentor John Philip Sousa died the day after conducting the Ringgold Band in Reading, Pennsylvania. Late in his life interviewers asked The March King what song he would last like to hear, and strangely enough it was the final number that he directed, "The Stars and Stripes Forever." From the time of his mentor's death through the end of his directing days, Meredith Willson often included Sousa's marches in his own programs, and more often than not, his tribute included "The Stars and Stripes Forever."

Chapter Five
"You and I"

In order to continue his success in network radio, Meredith Willson moved to Los Angeles. He mused about leaving San Francisco: "There must have been gloomy days when I lived there, but I don't remember them." Likewise, he pondered the aura of working in the city where by four o'clock the fog rolled in, "which didn't make things gloomy, only cozy, or strong, or moving, or wild, or beautiful, or friendly." Regardless of his increasing fondness for living in San Francisco, important network radio programming migrated from the Bay area. In order to advance in the medium, Meredith Willson decided to move to southern California.

Regretting the inevitable, Meredith Willson permanently departed to Los Angeles. The natural reservoir of talent primarily from the motion picture industry, the larger metropolitan region, and the fact that NBC built a new studio in the city created the key reasons why the area began attracting personalities, first from its sister city to the north, then from Chicago, and finally from New York. Before moving south Meredith Willson signed with George Gruskin of the William Morris Agency, and, already an active player with the network, arrived in the City of Angels to become the head of music at the NBC's Western division and to work on the popular *The Maxwell House Show Boat* program.

In order to mirror the quality radio production house at Rockefeller Center's Radio City Music Hall in New York, NBC needed to build similar broadcasting studios in Los Angeles. The network opened the swank new Hollywood facility on December 7, 1935, with a two-and-a-half hour broadcast extravaganza. After a medley of both old and current tunes, ending with "You Are My Lucky Star," Ken Carpenter, the first of several announcers, started the festivities by presenting Meredith Willson to direct the first number, "Dardanella," in "Willson style." (Willson's "Chiffon" style of arranging popular numbers included more flutes, piccolos, and strings than did more brass dominated arrangements.) Those who followed in the gala evening included host Al Jolson, who introduced the leading network talent of the day, like singer Bing Crosby, Victor Young's Orchestra (from the Jolson radio show), announcer Don Wilson, dancer Bill "Bojangles" Robinson, announcer Jimmy Wallington, Johnny Green's Orchestra, motion picture censor Will Hayes, singer Rudy Vallee, comedians Jack Benny and Mary Livingstone, actress May Robson with a tribute to the late comedian Will Rogers, sportswriter Grantland Rice, Hollywood columnist Jimmy Fiddler, tenor James Melton in Baltimore, Ben Bernie's orchestra from New York, singer Ruth Ettington from Hawaii, and actor Buddy Rogers and others at a party in London. These celebrities echoed the theme that NBC dedicated itself to present the best radio programming from around the globe, while giving a special nod to including many from the moving picture industry.

This particular program heralded network broadcasting from a state-of-the-art facility, especially designed for the big broadcasts that would occupy the airwaves for the next decade and a half. NBC opened another studio in 1938, while CBS also constructed a similar building in Los Angeles that year. The exodus of most network radio programs to southern California began in earnest during these last years of The Great Depression. After Meredith Willson returned from the aforementioned dedicatory broadcast to shows like *Carefree Carnival,* which still emanated from San Francisco, he made his final move to Los Angeles.

One very popular, long running NBC program during the network's formative years in the early 1930's was the *Maxwell House Show Boat.* Emcee Charlie Winninger, who introduced acts like the show's lead singer Lanny Ross and the blackface team of Pick and Pat from its radio port in New York, captained this latter day minstrel show. Patterned after the popular Jerome Kern musical *Show Boat*, the radio version offered numerous acts reminiscent of those who performed aboard paddle wheelers on the Mississippi. Winninger was an appropriate radio captain for two reasons: he really did entertain on showboats, and he also starred in the musical both on Broadway and in an early film version. However, after Winninger temporarily resigned and the show moved from New York, Maxwell House reconsidered its property. Three *Show Boat* specials from Los Angeles replaced the weekly series that appeared through October 28, 1937, and for these final specials, Meredith Willson came aboard to direct the music.

Willson fondly recalled the days of conducting at Warner Brothers Stage Three where NBC broadcast the show. At the end of its run, the renamed *Hollywood Showboat* offered regular cast members performing adaptations of musical theatre. Willson recalled one anecdote about radio censorship from his first excursion on May 14, 1937, when he noted that the studio clock ran a little bit late. Words of congratulations, such as "good luck, Charlie" to stars Charles Winninger who returned to the cast temporarily, and "Give 'em hell, Hattie," to Hattie McDaniel, escaped over the airwaves. The last salutation is remarkable, because radio actors did not say the word "hell" over an open microphone in those days, unless uttered as a reference to the Devil's abode in a religious broadcast. Unfortunately, for this mainstay of early network radio, the program had been losing listeners as a result of new radio programming and cast changes, not the least of which was the temporary loss of favorite Captain Winninger. The show's final broadcast included Thomas L. Thomas, Nadine Conner, Virginia Verrill, Hattie McDaniel, Alma Krueger, Warren Hull, and Eddie Green. No more would the famed show come "Puff, puff, puffing along" into living rooms from coast to coast as it had for five seasons. Instead the *Good News Show* replaced it as Maxwell House's premiere Thursday night show.

While Meredith Willson ascended to the position of musical director at the network, his job took him to a variety of programs. As early as April 22, 1935, he hosted his own musical program, *The Meredith Willson Orchestra*, which first appeared on NBC's blue network at 8:30 p.m. Eastern Time and continued until he moved to the *Good News* show in the fall of 1937. His other directorial chores included guest conducting with the San Francisco Symphony and on the RCA *Magic Key* program in 1936 (two chances to return to his beloved San Francisco), a visit to the *Ford Sunday Evening Hour* and an appearance on the *National Rededication Movement* special in 1938. He continued similar guest appearances across the country for the next twenty years.

The new program that would occupy Meredith Willson's time through the end of the decade was the result of a merger between a Hollywood film studio and coffee money. Metro Golden Mayer pictures wanted to showcase its talent on the radio and Maxwell House wanted the best representatives to sell its "Good to the last drop" beverage. The result was *Good News of 1938* (and subsequent years), one hour of MGM stars backed by Meredith Willson's orchestra. Beginning on November 4, 1937, shortly after the *Show Boat*'s demise, the program became a veritable who's who of singers, actors, directors, producers, and behind-the-scenes artists and technicians from one of the most prestigious Hollywood film factories.

The opening show premiered at Hollywood's Paramount Theater with a newly reconditioned stage decorated to resemble Nashville's Old Maxwell House restaurant, complete with a crystal chandelier and butlers serving coffee. The orchestra and chorus of seventy people rehearsed several days before the initial broadcast, and, as a result, the then astronomical $25,000 premiere outdistanced the budget for anything ever broadcast on network radio from Hollywood. For the expense NBC treated its listeners to a stellar cast including both veterans and newcomers to the performing arts: actress-singer Jeanette MacDonald, singer Sophie Tucker, producer Gus Edwards, and actress-singer Eva Tanguay. Proud Mason Cityans read in their *Globe-Gazette* that they were not listening to *Good News*, rather to *The Meredith Willson Show*.

The results of the *Good News* program's first season demonstrated ratings success, with an impressive finish against its popular rival at CBS, *Major Bowes' Original Amateur Hour*. Because of shooting and location schedules, the program did not have a regular master of ceremonies from MGM, although Robert Montgomery, Robert Taylor, and Robert Young frequently played the role of leader. However, the strength of the NBC program lay with the diversity of very popular cinema personalities. During the first season, which offered stars like Judy Garland, Eleanor Powell, Allan Jones, Mickey Rooney, and Louis B. Mayer himself, motion picture fans savored additional time with their film favorites via a different medium. No matter that the hour-long show essentially represented a double sales pitch, one for the studio and another for the coffee company, charming moments with singers, comedians, stage actors, and even dancers more than compensated for the frequent commercial reminders.

♪ ♪ ♪

With time off during the summer of 1938, Meredith and Peggy Willson took a long desired trip to Europe. Staying for six weeks the couple cavorted with luminaries such as *Variety* magazine editor Abel Green, film star/director Erich Von Stroheim, and Twentieth Century Fox head Darryl F. Zanuck. At the British Broadcasting Company in London, Willson viewed an early television program and was invited to conduct the orchestra on the air. He declined after catching a cold and was embarrassed when the program went on as planned, dedicated to "conductor, Mr. Willson of the NBC ... on his couch of pain." The ambulatory Iowan beat a hasty retreat to his room when he heard the broadcast, for he was having a cocktail in the hotel when Fred Bates, the BBC official who invited Willson to conduct, walked in.

By the second season opening in September, *Good News* began with Meredith Willson establishing a persona on radio. Prior to the late 1930's, musical directors rarely moved from the podium to the microphone. However, when comedians like Jack Benny bantered more and more with his conductor, the bandleader soon became a regular member of the cast, as well as the frequent subject of a script. In one early broadcast during the *Good News* season, George S. Kaufman wrote a skit for four men entitled "If Men Played Bridge," a roll reversal satire with the guys bringing their masculinity to a then common women's diversion. The initial three actors in the cast included host Robert Taylor, guest Spencer Tracy and regular cast member Hanley Stafford, while the lesser-known actor Meredith Willson joined the trio to round out the players in the card game. According to the musical director, the skit was so successful, especially the smaller part designed for Willson, that during the season the show presented special reprises of the gag like "If Men Do as Women Do," an opportunity he said to play "a perfectly practical radio stooge."

One anecdote that Meredith Willson related about getting all of the talent to fit into the sixty-minute framework of the show involved the dismissal of a future star. Metro-Goldwyn-Mayer scheduled leading lady Norma Shearer to appear in a sketch from her 1938 film *Marie Antoinette*. However, unaccustomed to the time constrictions of a weekly radio show, the movie star exercised her artistic license to the extent that the program's young producer had no idea when the piece would end. Midway through the performance time ran out for the live radio show, and the next day saw the firing of the well-meaning producer, Ed Gardner, who later starred as Archie on the popular *Duffy's Tavern* radio and television shows.

Because of their film shooting schedules, the hosts of the show changed in its early days, but the program succeeded nonetheless, and competing movie companies planned copycat shows. Surprised by the early strength of *Good News'* revolving masters of ceremony and their stellar guests that Warner Brothers and Paramount attempted to race their own programs onto the air. Unfortunately for them, the MGM offering became the most successful studio show in terms of ratings and duration on the air, even though it did not receive the critical accolades that might have accompanied such an expensive and talent heavy show. *Newsweek* magazine reported that listeners "couldn't decide whether Metro-Golden-Mayer was trying to sell Maxwell House, or if the coffee makers were putting Metro-Goldwyn-Mayer in airtight containers."

One attribute of the show is certain: the thirty-five year old musical director not only showcased his directing and arranging abilities, but he also improved his radio acting ability on air when he bantered with program regulars like Frank Morgan, Fanny Brice, or Robert Young. After Meredith Willson moved back to the podium from being the character of a naïve Iowa boy in the big city, he included in his repertoire of music numbers songs that would be a part of his broadcast favorites for the next twenty years: Sousa marches, classical numbers, and time worn favorites (those he later called America's most beloved), like "Liza," "The Lambeth Walk," or "Tea for Two."

As Willson's homegrown Iowa character gained prominence on the show, back in Mason City the residents experienced having a part in celebrity with their now nationally famous musical director. On May 19, 1939, the *Globe-Gazette* reported that Meredith Willson's hometown named him Honorary Chief of Police as a result of a special Mason City connection to *Good News*. Three prominent residents wrote a script for guest star Wallace Beery to read on the program, and after making the presentation, the actor asked Willson if such participation from the Mason Cityans warranted the waiving of any speeding ticket through the Iowa town. To appreciate the status that Meredith Willson achieved on the show, he conducted a special number, "The Stars and Stripes Forever," in honor of the late John Philip Sousa and in celebration of his own thirty-seventh birthday. While the real Mason City Chief of Police presented the musician with a scroll and badge, the band and chorus sang "Happy Birthday," and the cast members offered their congratulations to Willson.

The format of the show usually included banter from the host, a musical number, guests in skits, nonsense from the Baron Munchausenesque Frank Morgan, a Baby Snooks routine with Fanny Brice and Hanley Stafford, and the promotion of the guest stars' current cinema venture. On rare occasions the writers created a theme for an entire show, as was the case for the June 29, 1939 program. This final *Good News* show for the 1938-39 season presented "for the first time on the air" a medley of songs from *The Wizard of Oz*. To herald the motion picture's August 25, 1939 release, most of the original actors presented songs from the film. The program's guest list included Judy Garland, Ray Bolger, and Bert Lahr. Already part of the *Good News* cast, Frank Morgan moved from his normal radio role to the Wizard and the others that he played in the film. One key cast member, Jack Haley did not appear as the Tin Man, because, as host Robert Young explained, the actor was appearing in New York. However, it might be less than coincidental that his absence was also connected to his status as a Twentieth Century Fox property and appearing on the MGM show aided the competition too much. Young assumed the part of the Tin Man on the air.

Numerous thematic segments filled this particular show. Endearing actress Fanny Brice played her usually obnoxious and precocious Baby Snooks character on this special show, but was rewarded for her good behavior by "Daddy" Hanley Stafford telling her the story of *The Wizard of Oz* (the two exited the microphone singing "We're Off To See The Wizard.") Judy Garland then recalled receiving the film role of Dorothy, and Frank Morgan did the same for his part of the Wizard. The next related segment took the listener to a mock rehearsal with the Cowardly Lion working on his part and Harold Arlen and Yip Harburg explaining the songs, including Judy Garland's first public singing of "Over The Rainbow." Not having sung it very many times, she had a little trouble with one of the familiar lines of what would become her signature song. During his lengthy career on radio Meredith Willson often included "Over the Rainbow" in his list of all time great songs. One of the evening's unusual guests was original *Oz* stage cast member (1904 vintage) Fred Stone, who discussed his scarecrow part with Ray Bolger. Essentially, the one-hour presentation represented the epitome of MGM self horn tooting, but with a polish that made the program very entertaining.

Good News offered MGM's finest, and those appearing through the show's final season (1939-1940) included Walter Huston, Lucille Ball, Marlene Dietrich, Fay Wray and Hattie McDaniel. During its three-year run, one obvious non-catch from the studio, Greta Garbo, did not join the coffee hour. Apparently she wanted to be left alone. Many others who seldom visited radio programs found their way to this self-promoting studio vehicle. By the time the show finished its run, it did not exhibit the enthusiasm that the program promised in the first season, partly because Maxwell House and MGM severed their partnership, leaving the coffee without the large and relatively automatic talent pool.

By the end of the show's final season, the ratings declined and Maxwell House opted to change the format. Fanny Brice, Hanley Stafford, Frank Morgan, Robert Young (regular emcee as his schedule permitted), and Meredith Willson continued in a half-hour show. The sponsor added Mary Martin as the featured singer and Don Wilson, Jack Benny's renowned announcer for JELLO, another General Foods product. The retitled *Maxwell House Coffee Time* included about a quarter of an hour of Morgan and the same for Baby Snooks and Daddy. Shortly thereafter Meredith Willson departed for his most ambitious radio stint when he decided that American Armed Forces needed his help during World War II.

The Maxwell House program continued with Frank Morgan through the War years and with Fannie Brice until she left to do her own show in 1944. When Meredith Willson returned from his tour of duty with Armed

Forces Radio in 1945, the sponsor bolstered its ratings by luring George Burns and Gracie Allen to NBC and returned Willson to the coffee maker as its orchestra conductor.

♪ ♪ ♪

During the years Meredith Willson directed the music on *Good News*, he developed an enthusiasm about the possibilities of radio programming for young musicians and endeavored to encourage them to follow their dreams. Published in 1938, his *What Every Young Musician Should Know* was a presentation of practical answers to important musical questions in a "casual every day discussion that should be easily read and understood." He avoided previously difficult textbook terminology, which he felt confused the readers and instead encouraged them by offering his familiar, folksy radio style to keep readers interested. He walked the curious young musicians from learning how to use the baton to the particulars about the orchestra, before venturing to the modern radio studio and its peculiar problems for the musical director. The same radio voice that had been bantering with Frank Morgan on *Good News* used his plain talk Hawkeye delivery to successfully manage musical problems like key changes, to "get blood out of a turnip" (arranging to suit a band's peculiar needs, rather than paying an "arranger ... $75.00 a piece"), and to help the reader understand musical jargon like rip, button, spat, and kronk. Holding with his plan to simplify lessons for the young musician, just as abruptly as he started the guide, he ended it with "Good-Day."

♪ ♪ ♪

In 1940, Meredith Willson endeavored to write his second symphony. Years later he joked that at a luncheon with fellow musicians, Los Angeles Symphony conductor Albert Coates prompted Willson to write another long musical piece. At an earlier gathering of musicians, Coates told an anecdote about a Boston Symphony conductor who insisted that all of his musicians must know Tchaikovsky's *Sixth Symphony*, and to prove that the challenge was real, the orchestra leader randomly chose a surprised trombonist and ordered him to play his part. The embarrassed man admitted that not only did he not know it, but also that he had never heard of it. The shocked conductor could only respond, "I hope you enjoy it."

After a modicum of laughter followed, Willson then corrected the English storyteller and related that the conductor was the New York Philharmonic's Van Hoogstraten, the piece was Beethoven's "Lenore

Overture," and the instrumentalist was a flautist, one R. Meredith Willson. After Coates took the correction in good stride, the eager Willson mentioned that the Los Angeles Orchestra might like to play Willson's *San Francisco Symphony* some time. "I'd rather play your second symphony," Coates' replied.

"I haven't written any second symphony," Willson responded.

"Exactly."

Meredith Willson was less insulted than challenged and began his second major work. He completed his *Missions of California, Symphony Number Two in E Minor* in 1940, and Coates conducted it in April of that year.

The first movement of *Missions*, "Juniperro Serra," combines powerful deep tones with brisk higher pitched ones in an Iberian flavor that heralds the majesty of Old California. The next section, "San Juan Bautista," moves slowly like an ancient hymn and reflects Willson's first encounter with the old mission. Just like the swallows that return to Capistrano, the notes of the third movement, "San Juan Capistrano," float high above the score. Anticipating Meredith Willson's successes with composing marches in the upcoming next three decades, "El Camino Real" moves the listener down the old Spanish road in a triumphant sojourn to the beauty of these religious buildings. Together the four sections reflect the many moods experienced by the modern visitor, from centuries old traditions to the placid sanctuaries that still provide a safe harbor for the weary.

When Meredith Willson visited San Juan Capistrano for inspiration to compose the second movement of the symphony, he was met with a rather amazing revelation. After requesting samples of eighteenth century music common during the mission's founding, resident Sister Agnes shared a song that was popular two hundred years previous. To Willson's surprise the piece fit perfectly as a counterpoint to the section that he had written several months before, and, consequently, he adapted the old creation to compliment and complete the most reverent part of the symphony.

Nearly sixty years later in 1999, the symphony became available to the public once again, when the Moscow Symphony Orchestra recorded it and Willson's *The San Francisco Symphony* on a compact disk as part of its American Classics series.

♪ ♪ ♪

After having nearly a dozen songs published during the 1930's, Meredith Willson achieved important accomplishments in the popular music vein when he composed two love songs the year before America's entry into World War II. He first enjoyed success when his spiritual "Never Feel Too Weary To Pray" for the film *The Little Foxes* was published in 1941. However, shortly thereafter Music Dealers Service, Inc published his first popular romantic number, "You and I."

On a return trip to Mason City, Meredith Willson shares his new hit song "You and I" with KGLO listeners. (Mason City Library Collection)

The melody of "You and I" surfaced as a replacement for "Always and Always," the theme for *Maxwell House Coffee Time*. The necessity to write a new piece came when an ASCAP (American Society of Composers, Authors and Publishers) strike forced the radio networks to drop the organization's protected songs and find new music. Founded in 1914 to direct payment for the use of music in live performances and on recordings, what had been modest usage fees for radio stations and networks to use ASCAP music initially ballooned to millions of dollars. In late 1939, when the contract between the broadcasters and ASCAP expired, the group representing the writers attempted to increase the fee even more. The stations objected and formed their own organization, BMI (Broadcast Music, Inc.) The United States Department of Justice settled the disagreement a year later. However, in the meantime, many stations modernized public domain folk songs, resurrected spirituals and pre-ASCAP numbers like those by Stephen Foster, while others commissioned their resident musicians to write new songs.

To comply with his employer's request, Willson wrote the new opening song, first known only as the theme for *Maxwell House CoffeeTime*, as he had done for radio programs several times before. However, after the melody received lyrics and the title "You and I," numerous important artists like Bing Crosby, Benny Goodman, and Tommy Dorsey recorded the love song, which quickly rose in popularity as a listener favorite. Eventually, it became the most popular in America and remained at number one for nineteen consecutive weeks, ironically, on *Your Hit Parade*, the radio program that Willson originated a few years earlier. As a result of the song's radio tie in, Woody Allen revived the Dorsey rendition in the 1987 film *Radio Days*.

Willson wrote his next hit song, "Two in Love," virtually simultaneously with "You and I." When the composer received a first edition sheet music printing of "You and I," he noticed that the back page of the music contained no teaser. Frequently, the last page contained the first part of another song or songs to generate future sales. Disappointed at seeing the area blank, Meredith Willson penned the second song to complete the sheet music and scored another minor triumph when *Your Hit Parade* featured both of his love songs in its weekly countdown of the country's most popular. Willson claimed that he meant this second song as a tribute to his marriage to Peggy. Perhaps out of sentiment, after "Two In Love" appeared, she admitted that she preferred this number to the better remembered "You and I."

At the time Willson's popular songs ascended high on the *Hit Parade* list, an informal debate over big band music emerged. Although many voiced their preferences toward either the "swing" or "sweet" dance band style, when Meredith Willson directed orchestras on the radio, he played both. His own "chiffon swing" walked the line between the two schools. Willson's musical groups evolved from what had been traditional bands to ones with more strings and woodwinds. As some directors followed his lead and increased their groups to include more normally orchestral instruments, they also experimented with Benny Goodman's style of louder and more percussion driven swing numbers like his "Sing, Sing, Sing." By the Second World War, most big band broadcasts offered both types of music during a typical set.

The most poignant composition Meredith Willson made just before America's entry into the World War II was "The Jervis Bay," a tribute to the fortitude of combatants facing overwhelming odds. Touched by the actions of a British freighter crew, the songwriter heralded the heroism of the sailors as this particular ship sank at the mercy of a more powerful German battleship. Soon after Willson completed his song, the *Greek War Relief Program* needed a new and inspirational piece to encourage listeners to support those fighting the Axis. He brought along "The Jervis Bay" to this special radio program, one for which the show's organizers also asked writer Gene Fowler to create a poem. When the verse arrived, "The Jervis Bay Goes Down" fit perfectly when read during Willson's song. During a deeply poignant moment, as Willson conducted the number at the broadcast from Grauman's Chinese Theater in Hollywood, English actor Ronald Colman presented a moving rendition in tribute to his fellow countrymen.

As has already been stated, Meredith Willson conducted on a number of special radio shows, and the early 1940's necessitated his increased activity on such broadcasts. In January of 1940, Willson contributed to the Franklin D. Roosevelt birthday tribute, a March of Dimes special broadcast in sixteen parts to increase public awareness of polio, the crippling illness that plagued many Americans including the President. In the fall of that year the gala *Tenth Anniversary Salute to Movie-Radio Guide* aired in recognition of the weekly periodical that listed what the reader could find over the airwaves and on the screen. The cast of this festivity included radio luminaries such as the comedy couple Jim and Marian Jordan (Fibber McGee and Molly), comedian Hal Peary (The Great Gildersleeve), singer Connie Boswell, Meredith Willson, Frank Morgan, announcers John Conte, Harlow Wilcox and Harry Von Zell, as well as Gordon Jenkins and his orchestra. In addition, Meredith Willson hosted *The Johnson's Wax Program* or *Meredith Willson's Musical Revue*, a musical variety replacement for the very popular Fibber McGee and Molly show, during the summer of 1940.

During the following year, even more opportunities resulted as Meredith Willson guest conducted both regularly scheduled and special programs. As the Second World War gained momentum in Europe, he directed the music for shows like 1941's *America Calling* for the Greek War relief and an early USO Program. Willson also guest conducted on *The Ford Summer Hour*, the *CBS Symphony Orchestra*, and the four-part *Rexall Parade of Stars*. He even imparted his knowledge of radio production necessities when his treatise *How To Write A Script* appeared in print. At the end of this very busy year, the infamous event of December 7th and America's subsequent entry into World War II changed his career once again.

Chapter Six
"Never Feel Too Weary to Pray"

Motion pictures grew in popularity during the 1930's. Even though The Great Depression adversely affected live entertainment, some film companies flourished. Studios like Warner Brothers, Universal, RKO, 20th Century Fox, and MGM kept active as Depression-weary filmgoers scraped up the dime or quarter admission price to escape hard times in a movie theater. By the end of the financial crisis, the aforementioned studios emerged stronger, providing audiences with a new cadre of screen stars to augment those few who remained popular from the silent era. When Meredith Willson returned to score motion pictures, the medium was experiencing its most active period.

In 1938, silent film comedian Charles Chaplin faced the reality and permanence of talking pictures, a dilemma that he had been avoiding since the advent of sound movies in 1927, and decided that his on-screen character would finally be heard. The long-running king of cinematic comedy made millions of early motion picture patrons laugh from the first time he wobbled in front of a hand-cranked camera in 1914. Honing his acting skills in British music halls gave the young comedian an opportunity to explore communicating without words. After starting at Mack Sennett's Keystone Studio, the famous tramp character soon ascended to the position of most popular funnyman in film. Believing the Warner Brothers' ventures into talking pictures in the late 1920's to be a mere fad, Chaplin continued making essentially silent films. To appease distributors who had wired their theaters for sound, he displayed another of his talents and scored the background music for his films *City Lights* (1931) and *Modern Times* (1936). He even allowed his normally silent

"Tramp" character to sing a nonsensical song in the second of these films, but just as this was the Tramp's first time to be heard in a film, it was the last time that he appeared on screen. Not even the film's hopeful end song "Smile" prevented the comedian from getting by with the only sounds being music, sound effects, and evil Big Brother's voice. The next Chaplin film had to be a proper "talkie."

Meanwhile, the attempts of Adolph Hitler and his allies to achieve world domination gained momentum in late 1930's as Axis troops began their land-grabbing move across Europe. While the megalomaniacal plans of *Der Fuehrer* squeezed the freedoms of many Europeans, Charlie Chaplin chose the opportunity to allow his comic persona to satirize the German leader and his Italian counterpart Benito Mussolini. In *The Great Dictator* Chaplin ironically created the role of The Jewish Barber who bore a haunting resemblance to another character in the film, Adenoid Hynkel of Tomania (a not so subtle parody of Hitler and Nazi Germany's Third Reich.) In a chilling comedy of errors, the barber is mistaken for the demented dictator. With Jack Oakie playing the jovial Benzino Napoloni (a caricature of Mussolini), he and Hynkel dance playfully and symbolically with the fortunes of the world, while they float an inflated globe between them. When Chaplin devised the screenplay, the horrors of the Second World War were not yet fully evident, and so, the light-hearted parody of Hitler and Mussolini seemed relatively harmless. The comic surmised that if one could portray the folly of the leaders' aspirations, then perhaps through humor another major global conflict might not develop within a generation of the First World War.

After hearing Meredith Willson's second symphonic piece, *Missions of California Symphony*, Chaplin contacted the composer to score *The Great Dictator*. Having spent hours in youthful sojourns to Mason City theaters to watch the Little Tramp's escapades, Willson's first face-to-face meeting with Charlie Chaplin was one of awe and admiration. Called to the filmmaker's office, the musician approached Chaplin with questions as to how this very different project without the famous tramp character would develop. Willson soon discovered that his ongoing task was to underscore the film's action and to mirror the moods the filmmaker desired. In some cases he wrote new music, and in others he adapted music by several composers, including Chaplin. For this particular film, the director and star relinquished some of his usually tightly held creative reins to allow Willson to collaborate on the vehicle. The result contributed to Chaplin's biggest box office success.

Charlie Chaplin and Paulette Goddard plan their escape, as storm troopers from Tomania interrogate a Jewish family in The Great Dictator. (author's collection, United Artists, 1941)

Meredith Willson primarily worked with Chaplin to create mood music for *The Great Dictator*. The film's opening number is militaristic and upbeat with heraldic overtones, and it sets the first scene, a World War I battlefield. Typical martial music with underlying musical commentary pervades. For example, at the war's end "When Johnny Comes Marching Home Again" is ironically interwoven into the melody as the hero languishes in a hospital bed. Two outstanding scenes punctuate the great comedian's art and use of music. The first occurs when in pantomime Chaplin as the Jewish barber cares for a customer with actions choreographed to Johannes Brahms' "Hungarian Dance Number Five." The second transpires when Chaplin as Hynkel dances with an inflated globe to light and airy ballet music from Richard Wagner's "Prelude" to *Lohengrin*. Adapting folksongs and classical pieces fit well with what Willson had been including on his radio programs.

Willson appreciated Chaplin's film genius as a comedian, director, and composer before he joined the project and accepted the challenge to develop crucial musical choices. One early trial of the musician's talent came during the scene with the Jewish barber shaving a customer while dancing to Brahms. In order for Willson to synchronize his orchestra to what already had been filmed to an offstage record player, his orchestra required a couple of weeks to reconstruct the music for the soundtrack at no more than eight measures at a time. The composer overwhelmed Chaplin with the time expended, as well as the satisfactory results. Following his intuition, Chaplin had secretly ordered a recording of the music (film was a relatively inexpensive commodity) when Willson was ready to share his adaptation with the comedian. To the composer's credit everything fit perfectly, and this clandestine recording is the one heard in the film.

One peccadillo that bothered Willson was Chaplin's uneven work regimen. To his credit the director usually arrived at the sound stage at about ten o'clock in the morning to fine tune the music. Relying on his instinct, Willson often had to convince his aides that the music was just right, for example, not too loud or brassy as they had believed it should have been. In a couple of hours he would win them over, but then Chaplin listened and saw room for additional improvement. "There wasn't enough wail in the brasses when those newspaper headlines come up," he instructed at one session. However, by the end of the day, he joined Willson and shared the baton to create the best effect for that particular scene.

On the other hand, the composer, who had learned strict rehearsal discipline under Sousa and in the New York Philharmonic, became frustrated when the star/director entered his brooding times. Sometimes Chaplin would work extra long days, and on others he would stop midday. He also took off unannounced long periods of time, sometimes days, to mull over his next creation. The final results showed true genius, but the nerves of the cast and crew suffered as they had little clue as to what and when the next move might be.

Willson and Chaplin generally worked well together, as is evidenced by the final product and by the selfless way they shared the credit for the musical score. As is often the case when two geniuses come together on one project and desire to protect their creations, conflict over control and credit emerged. However, they eventually found agreement and continued the filmmaking.

The Great Dictator got into trouble after the project began in January of 1939, but by the time the studio released the motion picture, the public rallied behind it. What had started out as German border expansions soon threatened the peace of the entire world. When filming first began, the studio warned Chaplin that this particular satirical subject was too volatile, and after Britain declared war on Germany in the fall of 1939, production on the film was halted. According to Chaplin, United Artists gave him "alarming messages ... by the Hays Office" that there might be censorship problems. After weighing his options, Chaplin decided to continue, even sinking two million dollars of his own money into the project.

After six months of filming, final editing and scoring, *The Great Dictator* opened in New York simultaneously at the Astor and Capitol theaters on October 15, 1940. Because the Axis plan for world domination became glaringly evident by the film's release, not all of the Hitler jokes were funny in the way they were originally conceived, and the initial audience response was lukewarm. Nonetheless, the project became one around which many who detested the maniacal ruler's plan rallied, and, as a result, the film gained momentum. German and Italian officials had the film banned in the countries they controlled, and attempted to prohibit its exhibition in Latin America. Ironically, Chaplin withdrew the film after the Academy Awards of 1941, when it became evident that America was moving closer to participation in the Second World War, but re-released the film after the deaths of Hitler and Mussolini. Ultimately, the public supported *The Great Dictator* with an impressive five million dollar gross, and a one and a half million-dollar profit for its creator.

When Willson asked Charlie Chaplin how he should react to the newly completed film, the great comedian responded that the two should attend an obligatory neighborhood showing before the world premiere. (At the time, major production companies surprised a small neighborhood theater with a pre-release screening to get the audience's reaction. If the director or his staff found problems with the film, then last minute editing could be made.) After Chaplin had the cans of film delivered to the projectionist, he told the thirty-eight year old composer, who was finally realizing what scoring a real motion picture was like, that the two should vent their anxieties by both going out in the alley behind the theater and throwing up.

In his *New York Times* review of *The Great Dictator*, Bosley Crowther heralded Chaplin's return to the screen after a four-year absence. Essentially, the critic pointed out the power of the diminutive character, reminiscent of Chaplin's "tramp," standing against tyranny and "directing his superlative talent against the most dangerously evil man alive." The review continued by adding that, in addition to Chaplin's trademark slapstick, the comedian undertook social satire of monumental proportions. Except for the facts that Crowther believed the film to be somewhat repetitious and "overlong," he praised the film from Chaplin's mockery of Hitler and Mussolini to the aforementioned Hungarian Dance scene. During a revival of the film in 1958, German critics even hailed the film as a "macabre masterpiece." Three years later, when the film first appeared in Italy, Roman audiences made it the hit of the year and loved Jack Oakie's parody of their former dictator.

In his 1949 autobiography *And There I Stood With My Piccolo*, Meredith Willson distanced himself from the controversial genius, calling

Chaplin "selfish and in many ways inconsiderate." One transgression that bothered Willson was the fact that Chaplin never became an American citizen, which was to the composer "a real lesson in patriotism." Willson did add, "it was a real pleasure to watch [Chaplin] day after day and see him tick." From eating lunch with the comedian daily for ten weeks to watching him labor intensely on the set, Meredith received valuable lessons in comedic timing that he later adapted for radio use. Perhaps it is because of Willson's 1949 assessment of Chaplin's lack of patriotism that The Little Tramp's 1964 autobiography made scant reference to Willson's contributions to the film. However, in interviews years later Willson more fondly recalled their acquaintance.

Since its initial release, critics and film students have hailed *The Great Dictator* as one of Chaplin's masterpieces. Even though it did not win any Oscars, Chaplin as actor and Meredith Willson as musical director did receive nominations. Sadly, the film represented the last great Chaplin creation and another by the comedian did not appear for seven years. Appropriately, The Academy of Motion Picture Arts and Sciences finally honored him with a special Oscar in 1972. As for the 1941 Academy Awards, Willson's score was one of seventeen nominated, but it lost to Walt Disney's animated feature film *Pinocchio*. However, as a result of his effort on *The Great Dictator*, other Hollywood directors recognized his talent, and soon thereafter a different offering elevated Willson's prestige in film scoring.

Moving from Chaplin's studio at United Artists to the RKO lot, Meredith Willson endeavored to score *The Little Foxes*. The studio, whose fortunes during the 1930's vacillated from extreme success with films like the Fred Astaire and Ginger Rogers musical series to near bankruptcy, experienced a period of creative and financial success just prior to the Second World War by producing quality films like *Abe Lincoln in Illinois*, *Irene*, *Kitty Foyle*, and *Citizen Kane*. With the acquisition of Lillian Hellman's successful play and having Bette Davis in the lead role of Regina Giddens, following Tallulah Bankhead's triumph in the stage version only two years earlier, this William Wyler production had the preliminary earmarks for success. The company also had an advantage to be aligned with Samuel Goldwyn who produced this as the first in a series of quality productions for his own studio. The film would be this studio's tale of the South as a response to MGM's immensely popular *Gone With the Wind* (1939). Coincidentally, both Bankhead and Davis had been candidates for the lead in that film.

Much of Willson's music in *The Little Foxes* fits into three categories: mood setting melodies, literal tunes coming from within the scene, and spirituals, such as the one he wrote for the opening and closing credits. The musical themes, sometimes reminiscent of Max Steiner's creations for *Gone With the Wind*, range from ethereal passages punctuated with a few notes by Stephen Foster to brooding minor-keyed melodies that represent the characters who are hell bent on self-destruction. A long period of no music occurs in the film when infirm husband Horace Giddens (Herbert Marshall) returns to his conniving wife Regina. The only musical interruption in the scene comes from the freed slaves who are singing a beautiful hymn, and about which Horace philosophizes: "The white folks have the pianos, but the colored folks have the songs." This statement underlies the film's truth that the "haves" are a greedy, cutthroat lot, but those in servitude appear to exude basic human sympathy and kindliness.

Musical director Willson experienced disappointment when some of his contributions fell to the cutting room floor. He felt especially proud of his "Never Feel Too Weary to Pray," an original spiritual that was cut drastically in the finished print and appeared only in a shortened version during the closing, abbreviated credits. The song did appear on sheet music in 1940, ironically labeled as music from *The Little Foxes*. Perhaps the greatest lesson Willson learned about Hollywood music editing during this project was that a great many notes fell to the editor's whims. Later, when Willson hosted the Johnson's Wax summer radio show in 1942, he included a segment entitled "Lost Songs," a time to resurrect musical numbers cut from films and a chance to give them a second hearing.

Not only did Willson object to the butchery of his songs in the movie, but he also argued with the director about the ending. The story concludes with conniving Regina Giddens traveling to Chicago in triumph as a wealthy woman. The very idea did not sit well with the composer, who even suggested that the ending be re-shot. After director Wyler laughed at the thought, Willson decided to make his own statement over the closing credits. Bette Davis' face is the last shot of the film, and as the credits roll, the chorus sings the lyrics "Oh Lord, sound the trump of the Judgment." Willson believed that at least his lyrics could indict her wickedness and satisfy his "Iowa conscience" by reinforcing the idea of goodness eventually winning in the end.

The final results for the production included Oscar nominations for best picture, actress, supporting actress, director, screenplay, art direction, film editing, and score. Unfortunately, *The Little Foxes* won not one award (a year with numerous films later deemed classics.) For the second time the music director's efforts came up short to Bernard Hermann's music for *All That Money Can Buy*; however, two decades later Willson music did win an Oscar when Ray Heindorf adapted the score of *The Music Man* into a feature film.

If Meredith Willson's musical path seemed to be moving toward scoring motion pictures in 1940, the events of the following year sidetracked such plans. As the war in Europe continued to accelerate and America seemed inevitably headed for a part in what became World War II, Willson contributed to the effort on the home front by writing special music for radio programs. He never did return to film studio composing, except when his Broadway musicals came to the big screen in the early 1960's.

Chapter Seven
"Radio Suite"

When World War II involved America after the Japanese attack on Pearl Harbor on December 7, 1941, the country's entertainment community raced to do its part to help the War effort. Meredith Willson joined the initiative and made his own contributions. When he decided that he might best serve his country in a military uniform, he approached the local recruiting office to offer his services and was subsequently ushered to a special location. Upon arrival he observed a number of familiar faces. Willson and his cronies from the instrumental music field seemed to be on the "oldish" side for boot camp; nonetheless, they received military assignments in a new weapon against the enemy, Armed Forces Radio.

After the 1940-41 Frank Morgan-Fanny Brice season on radio, Meredith Willson busied himself on programs that helped keep America informed of the needs in the European war with shows like the Red Cross shows *Bundles for Britain* and *Russian Relief.* After the Japanese attacked Pearl Harbor, he did not go to his local recruiting office at first, because he believed his role on morale boosting radio shows and composing specially written songs might be more valuable to the War effort. Among the songs he penned during the early days of the Second World War included: "My Ten Ton Baby and Me" (the Office of Defense Transportation asked Willson to write a tribute to the truck drivers who spent long hours to supply service personnel), "Gangway, You Rats, Gangway" (a 1941 song written for the USO after Willson and a friend heard the line shouted by a g-stringed performer in a burlesque house), "Yankee Doodle Girl" (for the Women's Army Corps), "Fire Up - Carry On To Victory" (the requested but not official song of the Chemical Warfare Service), and "Hit the

Leather" (for the U.S. Cavalry just before it changed from a horseback unit to the tank corps.) Meredith Willson even acquired production support for a naval counterpart to Irving Berlin's *This Is the Army*. However, because this musical, originally written for the First World War, was so successful in its revival during the Second World War, the navy did not wish to take a chance on a less impressive show. Nonetheless, because of his patriotic devotion, Meredith Willson's civilian projects ceased on November 26, 1942, when he became serial number 0920625 in the United States Army.

Soon after the Japanese attacked Pearl Harbor, the War Department determined that keeping overseas forces in touch with their homes via radio was essential to morale. The Armed Forces Radio Service began on May 26, 1942, when the army and navy named radio ad executive Tom Lewis to head the new broadcasting organization. From the start, the new radio network operated without any studios of its own and developed programming as an effort to remind allied personnel what they were defending. Later that year, Meredith Willson became the first AFRS musical director. (Prior to his arrival, visiting artists like Bing Crosby brought their own cast and orchestra to create a special version of their shows for military programming.)

Armed Forces Radio slated as many as eight musical programs for recording per day, and their production values equaled, and in some cases exceeded, network standards. All radio unions, facilities, and personalities saw to it that the soldiers, sailors, and marines would hear the most supportive of shows; hence, performers relinquished tremendous salaries in favor of getting incredible entertainment recorded and shipped free to Allied fighting forces around the globe. Military personnel sometimes lined up outside of the Columbia Broadcasting System's Los Angeles Sunset and Gower studio for hours to be audience members for programs like *Command Performance* and *Mail Call*. Meredith Willson's task was to have the music in place, sometimes with last minute changes or no rehearsals, so that the transcription disks could be pressed and mailed on schedule. For the most part, AFRS broadcast virtually none of these programs live.

The shows ranged from a disk jockey style program of popular hits to classical music. GI Jill spun the current top songs with a beautiful female delivery that reminded those far from home the reason they were fighting. A very entertaining program designed for the segregated forces, *Jubilee*, heralded the finest black entertainers, like Eddie "Rochester" Anderson and Lena Horne, who were just beginning to make in-roads into mainstream radio. *Mail Call* presented a pseudo on-air magazine that proffered a variety of entertainers. Other shows included *At Ease, Concert Hall,* and *Front Line Theater*; however, the most prestigious show of the military network was *Command Performance*.

Time magazine described *Command Performance* as "the best program in wartime radio." Estimates indicate that the show's ledger could have exceeded $75,000 per installment, yet no budget existed and the talent was gratis. The program's director gave up a $1,000 a week job on *The Fred Allen Show* to volunteer his services, while many other talented artists received only their military pay. When the average half-hour commercial network radio program had usually one or two guest stars, *Command Performance* had as many as six or seven.

AFRS engineers usually recorded the program late in the evening at donated NBC and CBS studios, after the prime time shows had been aired. The advantages of doing most of the shows from Los Angeles at this time were two-fold: the Hollywood area already held most of the requested talent, and the time difference meant that the studios were basically free of nationwide network programming, given that late evening on the West Coast was very early morning in the East. Broadcasting from the West Coast also created a good time for celebrities to appear, because they were usually free from their radio or motion picture jobs.

Essentially, the program followed a regular format for the duration of the War. Meredith Willson's bugle call fanfare started the show, just before the spirited "Over There" theme song. Its significance was doubly important, because it was revived as a rallying song to announce that "the Yanks were coming" once again to preserve democracy as they had in the First World War. Also, the song's composer, George M. Cohan, died near the end of the first full year of the Second World War, three weeks after Meredith Willson was called to head Armed Forces Radio's musical division. The opening words uttered on *Command Performance* first from Jack Benny's long-time announcer Don Wilson and later from Ken Carpenter of the Bing Crosby show issued the edict that this program would continue "Till it's over, over there." From this point, an honorary emcee, such as James Cagney, George Raft, or Humphrey Bogart, presented the evening's fare.

Service personnel, like "Sad Sack" Smith, "Two Drink Tommy," or the 405th Engineers, sent in requests from the mundane to the bizarre. Some desired sounds from female movie actresses included sighs from starlets like Carole Landis, Lana Turner sizzling a steak in a pan, or Bette Davis sewing a doily. Other audiences enjoyed actors Alan Hale guzzling a beer or Errol Flynn taking a shower before an audience of WAVES (Women Accepted for Voluntary Emergency Service.) Sometimes, just simple sounds, like slot machines turning or the hustle of streets like Fifth Avenue in New York, augmented the free talent with the show's main intention being to temporarily soothe the homesick for a half-hour. Eventually, a letter from an under-appreciated four-legged member of the military led to a special theme show. The response came on program number 173, an all-animal show with representations by cartoon character voices from the Disney and Warner Brothers studios.

Generally, the AFRS shows lasted thirty minutes, thus allowing one transcription disk to hold the complete program on its two sides. After the disk was pressed, copies were shipped to 300 stations around to world to be broadcast locally to service personnel. Forty weeks after it began as a military tool to counter the enemy propagandists like Tokyo Rose and Axis Sally, *Command Performance* broadcast a special Christmas Eve program on December 24, 1942, and included its first non-military audience. Sent out over the four American radio networks (NBC Red and Blue, CBS, and Mutual), as well as being recorded for shipment overseas, the plan was to bring together the military around the world with those who were waiting for their return into one large audience. Because it was impossible to conduct all of the AFRS radio shows, Meredith Willson did not direct the orchestra for this particular show, but he did conduct on subsequent holiday installments. Instead he yielded the baton to motion picture composer Alfred Neuman. This holiday show opened with a statement by Chief of the War Information Office Elmer Davis and continued with the usual guests from host Bob Hope to Kay Kyser's orchestra. Although numerous non-serious moments occurred during this stretched version of the show, the cast and audience rose to their feet at end of the program to sing "The Star Spangled Banner." Three years later, also on Christmas Eve, Meredith Willson and a similar cast gathered to celebrate victory over the Axis forces, and they also vowed that *Command Performance* would continue "Until they're back from over there."

Bob Hope and Bing Crosby, two top-notch performers who could have done just a slight amount to help the War effort, instead availed themselves to appear on the show so frequently that they were among the favorite guests on *Command Performance*. Through their endeavors they led War Bond drives, entertained troops overseas, and offered emotional pleas for a variety of causes on their own programs. As a result, they were without peer in leading the Hollywood propaganda machine against the enemy. Not only were they on the radio in weekly programs of their own, but they were also two of the most popular motion picture box office champions of the day. Hence, when they took time from their busy schedules to appear on an Armed Forces Radio show, Meredith Willson had to have all of the music in place and ready to go.

Young upstart singer of the day, Frank Sinatra, threatened "The Crooner" Crosby for the adoration of females in the popular music listening audience, and the friendly feud played itself out on what was to have been simply *Command Performance* number 122. The transcribing schedule had come up short one show, so AFRS planned two half-hour, back-to-back programs for the largely military audience. In the first episode, Crosby was to "meet" his new singing rival, Frank Sinatra. The two were to spar melodically as Bob Hope refereed. However, when the three got together they often abandoned scripts to the delight of the audience and the consternation of the director who monitored the studio clock. The first program came off without any major hitches, but the show to follow caused Major Meredith Willson to maintain decorum for a sensitive segment in the show.

Major Meredith Willson autographs an AFRS publicity still to brother Cedric. . (Mason City Library Collection)

The engineers recorded number 123 very late, as the audience continued on a mirthful high thanks to the antics of Hope, Crosby, and Sinatra during the first show. After hearing who would be the guests for the second program, the primarily young male audience eagerly awaited an "all female" show. Having singers Connie Haines, Lena Horne, Shirley Ross, and Francis Langford was more than enough to keep the attention of the uniformed personnel. However, when the aforementioned male trio, perched on seats just off microphone, ad libbed as the show progressed, one final guest's song might have been destroyed during the highly festive atmosphere. Opera star Lotte Lehmann was ill scheduled near the end of the show to sing the very placid Brahm's "Lullaby." Prior to her very serious number and knowing the more raucous mood of the crowd, Meredith Willson gestured to the audience to be quiet. With little hope he started the orchestra, but to his surprise the Lehmann number went unspoiled, and for a few minutes attention remained rapt.

Perhaps the greatest *Command Performance* broadcast occurred near the end of the War, when "Dick Tracy in B Flat" was the subject of a February 15, 1945 recording session. Based on the popular comic strip detective, this installment featured an expanded cast that included: Hope, Crosby, and Sinatra, as well as comedians Jimmy Durante, Frank Morgan, and Cass Daley; singers Dinah Shore, Judy Garland, and the Andrews Sisters; and announcer Harry Von Zell. Even though *Command Performance* usually ran thirty minutes, this program ran nearly an hour. Imbedded in the evening's chicanery were original songs by Meredith Willson, including his silly "Happy, Happy, Happy, Happy, Happy, Happy, Happy, Happy, Happy, Happy, Happy Wedding Day," a song written for Dick Tracy and Tess Trueheart's impending nuptials. Rarely did so many stars gather together and share so freely for a program that is now among the best that Armed Forces Radio produced and one of the most entertaining of what was has become a classic old time radio show.

Although the War restricted travel, and the rigors of keeping the music together for Armed Forces Radio became a virtual around-the-clock effort, Meredith and Peggy Willson found time to return home to Mason City. Because of a rare hiatus in the otherwise hectic transcription disk pressing schedule, Major Willson and his wife enjoyed two days during the 1944 Christmas season in their hometown on the way back from a trip to Washington, D.C. After the music director finished recording special Christmas programming in the nation's capital, the couple left for the brief stay in Iowa, and then quickly returned to California.

One of Meredith Willson's saddest tasks was to conduct the Armed Forces Radio Service Orchestra for the NBC tribute to Franklin Delano Roosevelt on April 15, 1945, three days after the President's death. The entertainers who buoyed the spirits of radio listeners during The Great Depression and the Second World War combined their talents to honor the man who was the symbol of the nation and who led the country against the Axis forces for three and a half years. Meredith Willson's musical talents appeared alongside those of actor Ronald Colman, comedians Eddie Cantor and Jack Benny, husband and wife radio comedians Jim and Marian Jordan, actor James Cagney, singer Ginny Simms, and many others in a two-hour, somber tribute to FDR. For his contribution Willson conducted one movement from his *Missions of California Symphony*, the hymnlike "San Juan Bautista Suite."

The four radio networks joined together again in 1945, when they beamed a very special Pentagon AFRS broadcast, a lengthy *Command Performance* to quietly celebrate the end of the Second World War. On August 14, 1945, after decisive and controversial atomic bombs fell on Hiroshima and Nagasaki, the Japanese offered a final surrender. *Command Performance* responded with its longest show, and this time the program was not fraught with the silliness that so often sustained those who were waiting until "it was over, over there." For more than two hours the "Victory Extra" edition of the program offered a variety of stars who thanked their God that the fighting was finished. From Lionel Barrymore, Ronald Colman, and Bing Crosby to the normally zany comedians Bert "Mad Russian" Gordon, Ed "Archie" Gardner, and Bob Hope, the tributes poured in. Hope was especially serious as he recalled the words of the late, popular Scripps-Howard columnist Ernie Pyle to set the tone that even though the comedians were jubilant, they were not inclined to be funny on that night. No sense of triumph was evident; instead, feelings came from the satisfaction that right surfaced over the forces of hatred. The tone was solemn out of consideration for those who made the ultimate sacrifice for their country and were not alive to enjoy the hour. Having risen to the rank of major, an honor for which he was forever proud, Meredith Willson again conducted the orchestra that set the mood.

AFRS programming continued after the war and eventually became the Armed Forces Radio and Television Service, especially for the thousands of service personnel stationed around the world. Months passed before those billeted at remote outposts after the Second World War ended would again taste the lifestyle they left at home. Many of them listened to one more important post-War *Command Performance*, the first peacetime Christmas show, broadcast on December 24, 1945. For two hours singers, comedians, and bandleaders celebrated the season with a special "Peace on Earth" message. As a special addition to the program, President Harry S. Truman included his wishes to those who would be delayed slightly in coming home because their job was part of the tying up and mopping up after the War.

Command Performance continued on AFRS until December of 1949, but just as Major Meredith Willson's services were no longer needed to oversee the productions, the gala cast pool eased back to their pre-War jobs and the program quality diminished. In some instances, the military network pieced together parts of old shows to create "new" programs. In 1947, NBC studio director Meredith Willson did have an opportunity guest star on *Command Performance.*

To follow on the heels of the success of *Command Performance* during the War, the Campbell's Soup Company attempted to popularize the show on commercial radio and debuted *Request Performance* on CBS on October 7, 1945. It ran until April 1946, but the program that utilized so much valuable talent for free in the AFRS version appeared as a shadow of the original when the sponsor had to budget $15,000 per week for its guests. Following his newfound popularity on the *Burns and Allen Show,* Meredith Willson did make a visit to the January 27, 1946 installment.

Willson's energies were not totally devoted to Armed Forces Radio during the Second World War. Because he was an accomplished musician and had causes to promote, the composer responded to a number of musical opportunities. Special appearances at War Bond drives, short term radio series such as two installments entitled "Three Thirds of a Nation" (the first a 1942 summer program celebrating the unified American War effort and the other a 1944 series celebrating steel production), as well as summer replacement programs to allow the radio stars some rest and relaxation before their fall season opener, added to the musician's musical chores during the early 1940's.

One chance for Meredith Willson to take over a program for the summer came before the War, when the extremely popular *Fibber McGee and Molly Show* left the air during the summer of 1940. Sponsor Johnson's Wax still had to fill its Tuesday time slot, so Meredith Willson accepted the responsibility as he hosted *Meredith Willson's Musical Revue.* Harlow Wilcox, the long time *Fibber McGee and Molly* announcer, appeared on the replacement show, as did the show's quartet, the King's Men. The series bore the early trademarks of Meredith Willson's own musical preferences with his tributes to songs from earlier eras, and especially Sousa marches.

This series included singers Ray Hendricks and Kay St. Germaine coupled with the comedy of Cliff Nazarro. Because the program was packed with music, titles were not announced prior to the song medleys to save time and to provide the audience with a guessing game. Lyrics in the melody that indicated the title were replaced with "la, la, la" to not give away the answer. Sometimes referred to as the "folk songs of tomorrow," Willson mixed a variety of numbers like "A Pretty Girl is Like a Melody" with Sousa's march "Manhattan Beach." When the segment finished, Willson queried Wilcox as to what he thought the titles might be. Another Willson gimmick during the show was to engage two seemingly incongruous numbers simultaneously, as was the case on the July 30, 1940 program when the early twentieth century popular hit "Somebody Stole My Gal" played in counterpoint to segments from a dozen pieces starting with Beethoven's *Fifth Symphony*. These early experiments with merging two pieces concurrently later evolved into a Willson trademark in his musicals. In *The Music Man*, for example, the barbershop quartet of school board members harmonizing "Goodnight, My Someone" counterbalanced women from the town warbling "Pick-A-Little." Other musical segments in the radio show included Connie Haines and Bob Carroll singing twenty songs in a one minute and forty-five second segment. The program ended with a Johnson's Wax Car-Nu commercial and Willson's song "What Dream is This?"

The 1942 summer show for Johnson's Wax showed more polish than did its predecessor. Long-time Willson friend and renowned storyteller John Nesbitt became an important addition when he related *The Passing Parade* stories that he had established on radio and in movie shorts in the 1930's. The friendship of the two men complemented each other to the point that Willson's patriotic music during this War era program and Nesbitt's tales of courage and human perseverance created an inspiring half-hour. One outstanding collaboration occurred when the two reprised Willson's "The Jervis Bay" and Gene Fowler's poem on the same subject.

Because RKO editors had substantially pared down Willson's "Never Feel Too Weary to Pray" for *The Little Foxes*, the composer decided that a place for a second hearing should be created on his second summer show for musical numbers that were in some cases totally deleted from a finished film. In the first "Lost Songs" segment, he offered "A Handful of Stars" for reappraisal. Studio editors deleted this Ted Shapiro number from a 1939 film, and the radio host insisted that if given a hearing, the song might become a hit. Willson assisted in its promotion in other venues, for after his own theme song "Mail Call March" opened *Mail Call* on AFRS, the bridge music from the announcer to the guest host included a few bars from "A Handful of Stars." This particular "lost song" resurfaced again when Willson renamed it as "A Pocketful of Stars" or a "Parlor Full of Stars" and made it the opening music for radio's *The Big Show* in 1950. Shapiro was so touched at the initial resurrection that he contacted Willson to offer thanks and to write a special number for Willson's *Musical Review*.

Bill Oates

Even during the War, Meredith (top row next to Gracie Allen on the far right) was able to appear at events like the annual Hollywood Bowl celebrity concert. (author's collection)

♪ ♪ ♪

After the Second World War ended, Meredith Willson experienced mixed feelings about V-J Day, the surrender of Japan to end the Second World War: he was happy about the victory but unsure of a job. Jubilant but temporarily lost, Meredith Willson headed for a good meal at the Los Angeles Brown Derby restaurant, where he talked to Chester Lauck, Lum of the *Lum and Abner* radio show, and Ray Noble, musical conductor on the Edgar Bergen-Charlie McCarthy *Chase and Sanborn Show*. The small party bolstered the Iowan's spirits, and soon after two impressive offers to become musical director emerged. The first came from motion picture studio Metro Goldwyn Mayer, then known for producing many of the finest motion picture musicals, and the other was at the Hollywood branch of NBC, where Willson first gained national recognition and a job for which he was also qualified. He refused both offers. The musician felt that after his experiences in radio during the War, many untapped creative possibilities loomed for musical programs and directors. Among the potential innovations, he believed that the bandleader could be more active as a character on the program, rather than merely directing the song that had just been announced. He also wanted to see musical variety on radio compete in the medium's Hooper ratings, so he decided to try his own show. Unfortunately, nobody bought the idea because of its cost, but he had another chance to try these ideas a year later.

As a stroke of good luck for Meredith Willson, Maxwell House assumed sponsorship of the *Burns and Allen Show* right after the War, returning it to NBC and an envious Thursday nighttime slot. During the 1944-1945 radio, season Frank Morgan continued as the star of the *Maxwell House Show*, after Fanny Brice left to do her own General Foods show for Post Toasties. Reconsidering its property, the coffee company approached George Burns about leaving CBS and sponsor Swan Soap. After hearing the Iowan on *Good News* and working with him from time to time on Armed Forces Radio, George Burns asked him to be the musical director to replace Felix Mills. Willson agreed because he would be joining one of the premiere radio comedy shows, and he was happy to be back with the sponsor that had launched his talents on a nationally popular program almost a decade earlier. Additionally, he would be able to undertake the conductor-character he had been imagining. He quickly fit into the cast and routine, so much so that after the first year on the program, George and wife Gracie Allen asked Meredith Willson to host their summer replacement.

As was often the case, networks considered summer shows for full time status on the fall radio schedule. Although the ratings did not have the strength to merit a Willson program on NBC, Canada Dry ginger ale bought his first regular, primetime network program, *Sparkle Time*, which debuted during the fall of 1946 on CBS. Meredith Willson's show remained on the air for two years with Canada Dry and continued as the *Ford Music Room* through 1953. Even sister Dixie Willson contributed some limericks to the show, such as

> Said a brainless young lady of Wales,
> "A smell of escaped gas prevails!"
> So she searched with a light....
> And later that night
> Was collected in seventeen pails.

However, a most creative innovation to radio came when his "Talking People" began delivering novel commercials. .

Introduced on a 1946 *Music Room* program, the Talking People consisted of five singers coordinated to speak advertising jingles in unison, like a Greek chorus. The program's music arranger wrote the chorus parts on music paper, with "notes" represented as a percussionist might see a drum part, with quarter or eighth note tails attached to X's, instead of rounded and blackened musical notes.

Generally, they queried the star in unison: "Mr. Willson? Oh, Meredith Willson?" To which he responded, "Oh, it's the Talking People." One early routine was for the group to follow with "Tell us a story, Meredith. Will you, huh?" He usually answered with a story that heralded the sponsor's product. On some occasions the chorus was allowed to exhibit their singing abilities, as they did on *The 1947 Christmas Seals Show*.

In the fall of 1947, the Talking People presented some of *The Aldrich Family* commercials on radio. General Foods owned Maxwell House Coffee and JELL-O, so when Meredith Willson found success on the *Burns and Allen Show* with his symphonic coffee ads, the sponsor loaned him and The People to the *Aldrich* program. The group jiggled vocally in six delicious JELL-O flavors so well that they won the New York City College award for the best gimmick in radio advertising that year.

Norma Zimmer, one of the five "People" and Lawrence Welk's Champagne Lady on his television show in the 1950's, recalled how the group performed one of the most novel ideas on radio. Reading the aforementioned "notes," they practiced to speak in the same pitch. Whether they were laughing, stressing certain words, or emitting onomatopoetic sounds, their goal was to talk as one person. Rehearsals were frequently held in Willson's home, and if she or the other female member of the group, Betty Allan, broke up with laughter, serious Meredith would give them the same disciplinary scowl that he often used on wayward instrumentalists. Although known for comedy, rehearsing music was serious business to Willson. John Rarig, Bob Stevens, and Bob Hamlin completed the quintet that worked so closely together that they became an audience favorite and just what the originator wanted for radio advertising: clever, musical entertainment with an embedded message.

During the summer of 1947, Willson replaced good friend Dinah Shore on Wednesday nights. The singer, later closely associated with her television sponsor Chevrolet, then represented the Ford Motor Company. Willson had frequently worked for the auto manufacturer on radio when he guest conducted the *Ford Symphony Hour* from Detroit. The composer once again created the show's theme song, "Ford's Out Front," based the auto company's contemporaneous advertising campaign. He merely set the slogan to music for the Talking People. This program included the usual Willson mix of familiar popular and classical songs, examining similarities between melodies, funny stories from the newspaper, and interaction with the Talking People. Other regulars on the show included

South African singers Joseph Moray and Miranda, singer Ben Gage, and child prodigy pianist Paulina Carter.

While Meredith Willson's *Music Room* continued on radio, yet another Willson program with the Talking People debuted on April 4, 1950. *The Falstaff Show* from Hollywood, which aired in Tuesdays, Wednesdays, and Thursdays at 10:30 p.m. Eastern Time, appeared as a short-lived, fifteen-minute program that was broadcast to regions where Falstaff was distributed. Introduced as "light but lively" (like the frothy brew), the show opened with Meredith Willson and perhaps one of the newly renamed "Singing People" Norma Zimmer commenting on the news of the day. After some trivial patter, she and the four other members of the group sang old favorites like "Put on That Old Gray Bonnet" and "Sweet and Low." By half time, the program's host reminded listeners of his Iowa stubbornness that drove his preference for Falstaff beer. Before the show ended, young Paulina Carter played a piano number with the band.

Not only did his musical show (under several names, times, and networks) continue through the 1940's, but also did Meredith Willson's association with George Burns and Gracie Allen as a cast member. The custom of including the orchestra leaders in the story dialogue was relatively new in the late 1930's and not embraced on many shows. Several of radio's music directors, like Ray Noble of the *Charlie McCarthy Show* and Phil Harris of *The Jack Benny Show*, exhibited enough acting talent to assume recurring roles in the scripts. The character built around Meredith Willson's hometown naïveté made him a good one to listen to Gracie's illogic or to represent an innocent male character different to that of the eternally woman chasing announcer Bill Goodwin. And frequently, when Goodwin and Willson got together for an integrated commercial, the advertisement percolated as some of the best presented over the airwaves.

According to Goodwin, the "good to the last drop" flavor of Maxwell House resulted from the perfect combination of a variety of beans (monezales, metalins, and bucaromangas). To emulate this harmony of flavors with music, Goodwin often worked with the conductor to parallel popular songs, such as "Oh, What a Beautiful Morning" or Willson's own "Iowa," and dissect the tunes part by part. When the song was reconstructed with all of its melodies and harmonies intact, it became a blend as masterful as General Foods' best coffee. The final product was a commercial that rivaled the show for entertainment value.

Typical of many radio programs of the late 1940's, considered to be the heyday of classic old time radio, the success of the *Burns and Allen Show* lay in its carefully choreographed rehearsal schedule. At 10:30

a.m. on Thursday, dress rehearsal began with two run-throughs, so that last minute adjustments to the script might be made. At 1:30 p.m. the orchestra practiced its songs and transition pieces. The cast gathered one more time for a light reading at 4:30, and shortly thereafter, the audience began filtering in. At 5:15, Pacific Time, announcer and cast member Bill Goodwin (Toby Reid was also around for special announcing tasks in the show) warmed up the audience. Willson later reasoned in his autobiography that because comedies were usually a half-hour long, someone needed to set the audience in a humorous frame of mind before the program's first funny line was issued. Also, at this time Goodwin introduced the cast members, except George and Gracie. Three minutes before airtime, and with the momentum before the show building, one of the most popular and long-lasting comedy couples entertained the studio audience with one of their tried and true vaudeville routines. Two hours later the ordeal repeated itself for the broadcast to the West Coast (this was in the days before pre-recorded programming, when virtually every program was broadcast live.)

Meredith Willson felt that he had fallen into another "lucky Thursday" stint when he joined the cast. He surmised that because he delivered the *Saturday Evening Post* in Mason City on Thursday (a fairly lucrative job for a boy of his age), played numerous New York Philharmonic concerts on that day, conducted his earlier Maxwell House shows at the same time (sponsors bought time slots on certain days, so that even if the genre changed, the sponsor still owned the time), and recorded *Command Performance* on Thursdays, that the experience with George and Gracie was destined for success. Maybe his logic was askew, but his success on this well-received program was legitimate. As a tribute to the program, Meredith Willson wrote *Radio Suite* in 1946, a five part tribute to the characters and named in their honor: "George," "Gracie," "Postman," (Mel Blanc), "Postman Visits the Burns House," and "Bill."

Unfortunately, just as Meredith's fortunes in radio skyrocketed during the last half of the decade, his relationship with wife Peggy became strained. Life with a musician takes a special kind of spousal tolerance, what with late night performances, constant travel, and Hollywood socializing. As his professional demands increased, she endured them less and less. In July of 1947, *The American Home* magazine article "The House That Music Built" featured the seemingly blissful home of Meredith and Peggy Willson. By early 1948, she divorced him on the grounds of "mental cruelty." In the settlement she received twenty-five percent of his earnings, which would have escalated dramatically in the next ten years, their Beverly Hills home, a gas station, and over fifty thousand dollars in bonds, insurance and securities. Peggy returned to Iowa, and then later married wealthy businessman Leroy Van Bomel in 1950 and relocated to the East coast. After her death in 1986, her ashes came to Mason City from New York and were quietly interred in Elmwood Cemetery.

Meredith Willson had rekindled a friendship with Russian singer Ralina Zarova, someone he helped to promote on radio and to receive her citizenship in the late 1930's. Ironically, after *The Music Man* was a success and while Willson was finishing *The Unsinkable Molly Brown,* the new home that Meredith and Rini occupied in March 1948 was featured in a September 1960 issue of the aforementioned home magazine. She would inspire him and help promote his career until her death in 1966.

In 1948, Meredith Willson published the first of his autobiographical writings, *And There I Stood with My Piccolo.* With the voice of the composer who had become familiar to radio listeners for almost twenty years, Iowa's most recognizable media luminary retold the Willson family story through the events that seemed to be the pinnacle of his radio career: musical director on the *Burns and Allen Show.* The folksy recollections include Meredith's youth in Mason City, his early days in New York City, the two-year sabbatical with John Philip Sousa, and trips to the West Coast that brought him into the early days of radio. As the book traces his career from coast to coast, it continually returns to Mason City, where his stream of consciousness recalled something in his hometown as sparked by a stimulus in New York, San Francisco, or Los Angeles. He remarked, "The farther I get from Mason City by the calendar, the faster I seem to be coming back to the old values and things we used to take for granted back home." As he waxed nostalgic about such seemingly mundane tasks as filling the cheesecloth bag with crab apples in his home on Pennsylvania Avenue, he likewise fondly related contemporary experiences that he was adding to his trunk of memories. Unfortunately, just as the autobiography starts with the dedication "To My Rini," it likewise omits any reference to first wife Peggy.

Although Meredith Willson finished his autobiography when he was forty-six years old, his greatest fame-producing years lay ahead. Writers sometimes told their life stories early in their careers, as was the case when the great humorist James Thurber did so at age thirty-nine. The Ohio humorist quipped in his autobiography, *My Life and Hard Times,* that writing one's memoirs early in life had the advantages of being closer to the actual time of the events and having facts that were not as misremembered as they might be when the author was older and possibly more forgetful. Willson had become so popular as a radio character that he read from his own pages when the *Hallmark Playhouse* dramatized his book on March 10, 1949. Extremely happy in his new marriage and very satisfied with what he had accomplished in music and radio, Meredith Willson little conceived that the "biggest" radio show that he would ever direct and the creation of a Broadway hit loomed ahead in the next decade.

Chapter Eight
"A Handful of Stars"

During the 1947-48 radio season, Meredith Willson's radio career experienced major changes. Because of increasing activities in his own programs and as General Foods gave him more chances to create JELL-O spots on *The Henry Aldridge* program, the musician left the Burns and Allen show. He did return to their program as a featured guest star on December 30, 1948, and conducted the orchestra on the program several times the following spring. Though he kept busy writing music and working on his own radio shows, Willson briefly entered the newest medium that would showcase his talents in 1949, when he hosted the four-week summer television series, *The Meredith Willson Show*.

Television had been developing during the 1930's, but the lack of programming at first and the expense of a set kept many people tuned to their radios for entertainment. The Second World War temporarily halted the medium's growth, because the military needed the material for equipment and electronics engineers directed the technology toward the production of sonar and radar detection systems. However, shortly after the War ended, television manufacturing resumed with a fury, creating the fastest growing entertainment medium ever.

With the help of one of the Talking People and future Lawrence Welk Champagne Lady Norma Zimmer, the Iowa musician appeared on television for the first time. In his premiere show on the NBC network, Willson tried a stunt on his own Talking People, who were still popular after their radio debut two years earlier. He used two dogs as silent Talking People to show how difficult it would be to train this particular ensemble as compared to educating real "people." With comedy guests like Imogene Coca and Edward Everett Horton, *New York Telegram* critic Harriet Van Horne gave the program a good review. (Only three years earlier she had panned his summer replacement radio show for George and Gracie.) Her only major complaint in this otherwise complimentary assessment of his first television venture was that he "still refers to Mason City, Iowa at every possible opportunity." Although the television ratings were positive, Meredith Willson remarked that he preferred "a real dependable medium with a future – radio."

Willson's only long-term venture into television came when Bill Goodman and Mark Todman created a game show entitled *The Name's the Same* on ABC, a counterpart to their successful *What's My Line?* The musician related in his second autobiographical work that he got the part on the show because he pulled a piccolo out of his pocket to illustrate a musical point to those auditioning him. Robert Q. Lewis hosted the program, which was sponsored by Johnson's Wax one week and Swanson's chicken products or Bendix Washers and Dryers on the others.

The premise of the show involved a group of celebrities who guessed what famous people or everyday objects or actions might be the names of the contestants. For example, a child had the name Ingrid Bergman, a gentleman contestant sported the moniker Rip Van Winkle, one man was called Will Tickle, and another had the misfortune to be called A. Pig. Willson, actress Joan Alexander, comedian Jerry Lester, game show host Bill Cullen and humorist Abe Burrows were among those who regularly filled the three slots on the panel. One highlight of the show occurred midway during the thirty minutes when a guest star appeared and the panel had to determine who the celebrity would like to be. In an even more complicated twist on the game's premise, a young boy named Monty Wooley appeared just before the real Monty Wooley came on the set. The elder Wooley continued the game by allowing the panel to guest that he would like to be pop singer Johnny Ray. The program ran for four years starting late in 1951, and Meredith Willson regularly guessed names from the show's inception until 1953.

The Name's the Same sends Christmas Greetings in 1951. (Mason City Library Collection)

♪ ♪ ♪

Although television was the entertainment buzzword for the 1950's, NBC made one last gallant attempt to keep a respectable radio audience. On November 5, 1950, *The Big Show* (not to be confused with *The Big Show*, a 1935 CBS review hosted by the vaudeville team of Jesse Block and Eva Sully) premiered as radio's greatest variety show offering to date. On the much-heralded debut, famed stage and film star Tallulah Bankhead introduced her first guests (Fred Allen, Jimmy Durante, Jose Ferrer, Ethel Merman, Paul Lukas, Danny Thomas, Russell Nype, and Frankie Laine) with the proven assistance of musical director Meredith Willson. Not only did Willson lend his down home presence and musical skills to the proceedings, but he also wrote a number of songs to enhance the hour-and-a-half production.

The emcee of the program, "the glamorous and unpredictable Tallulah Bankhead," set the pace for this ninety-minute extravaganza, which ran the gamut from broad farce to Shakespearean tragedy. Her own path to this last great radio show followed a lengthy and distinguished acting career. Born in Huntsville, Alabama in 1901, the daughter of the Speaker of the United States House of Representatives William Brockman Bankhead and granddaughter of United States Senator John Hollis Bankhead, came to New York City in 1917 after winning a *Motion Picture Photoplay* magazine beauty competition and subsequently began her stage career. From the start, her husky voice, which soon lost its Alabama accent, enabled her to climb to the pinnacle of New York theatrical success. Her greatest achievements on Broadway included starring roles in *Rain*, *The Little Foxes*, *The Skin of Our Teeth*, and *Lifeboat*.

As Tallulah Bankhead's stage career rode a crest of productivity in the late 1940's, NBC summoned her to head up their new radio show, which was supposed to capture some of the fluid ad money that had begun shifting toward television. In 1948, she starred in the theatrical revival of Noel Coward's 1931 hit *Private Lives*, and by the time *The Big Show* debuted on November 5, 1950, the play was successfully entering its third season at the Plymouth Theatre. Enticed by a good salary and easy work, Bankhead struck a deal that if the radio program failed, she would be able to leave after the first four weeks. This was not the case, because the seasoned actress who was nervous about performing in uncharted waters (her previous radio visits were limited) showed that she became a most capable host. Her presence established a reliable program format (referred to by entertainment luminaries like Groucho Marx and Fred Allen as "The Tallulah Show") as she guided it through two critically successful seasons. Unfortunately, *The Big Show* represented the climax to her long and productive career, for she would not star on radio again and she enjoyed only a few more Broadway productions until her last in 1964, four years before her death.

Tallulah Bankhead's outrageously flamboyant radio character aptly reflected her personal life. For example, she had a penchant for sneaking uniformed service personnel in ahead of long lines of anxious audience hopefuls that alone would have more than filled the huge theater. Meredith Willson might have agreed with her on this patriotic infraction, especially since the Korean War raged during the radio program's brief life. After giving one g.i. a lift on the way to the theatre, he exited the car bidding her a "good luck." When he left, she broke into tears saying, "Imagine, he's going off to Korea, and he wishes me good luck."

Essentially, *The Big Show* followed a revue format with Tallulah opening the program. Capable writers like Goodman Ace, Selma Diamond, George Foster, Mort Green, and Frank Wilson created barbs pointed at the hostess, ones that usually satirized her age, loss of sex appeal, proclivity to an overindulgence in alcohol, and androgynous musical renditions. Television became another target, especially when frequent guest and anti-TV crusader Fred Allen appeared. Their slurs against the upstart medium held a special significance, given that one of the few regular sponsors of the show was the "new" RCA Victor television.

The list of Broadway, Hollywood and sports luminaries who visited the show reads like a who's who of mid-century talent. Into New York's remodeled Center Theater trouped Ethel Merman (several times during the show's run), Danny Thomas, Groucho Marx, Fanny Brice, Jose Ferrer, Mindy Carson, Bob Hope, Leo Durocher, Ed Wynn, Ed "Archie from Duffy's Tavern" Gardner, Jack Carson, Eddie Cantor, Louis Armstrong, Dean Martin and Jerry Lewis, Margaret O'Brien, Edith Piaf, Vivian Blaine, Ken Murray, and Gloria Swanson to name but a very few. Even though the show garnered generally favorable reviews, because it had an immense budget for radio (as well as television in those early days), NBC lost over one million dollars during its two year run. Trips to Los Angeles to infuse Hollywood talent did not help the show's ratings. Even the first program of the second season emanating from England failed to stem the tide of departing audience members who preferred watching their new, expensive television sets.

Coupled with Tallulah Bankhead's potential for hosting the radio show efficiently, Meredith Willson was brought on board to give the program an eminent radio name and to offer expertise that had been his trademark for over fifteen years. He fulfilled his duties as musical director, utilizing one of the finest instrumental groups ever gathered for network radio, a forty-four piece ensemble with some members doubling in the renowned NBC orchestra. Likewise, the network employed the talents of a young choral director, Ray Charles (not to be confused with the later blind singer and composer), and sixteen singers to present vocal numbers ranging from musical comedy to religious and patriotic. As adept as Willson was at arranging and directing songs from raucous vaudeville tunes made popular by Jimmy Durante, the director was also able to display the more highbrow fare presented by, for example, Ezio Pinza or the President's daughter, Margaret Truman.

Willson's key task as musical director was to incorporate a variety of musical numbers to fill the ninety-minute segment. Many of the tunes were very Willsonesque and reminiscent of melodies that he used on his own programs. As has been mentioned in an earlier chapter, the opening theme came right from the "Lost Songs" segment of Willson's 1942 Johnson's Wax program. The Iowan wrote new lyrics for the Ted Shapiro song "A Handful of Stars" and adapted it for *The Big Show* to read "we're going to fill your 'Parlor Full of Stars'" and sometimes "Pockets Full of Stars." Of course, old Willson songs heralding life in Iowa and Sousa marches appeared quite frequently. However, one of Meredith Willson's finest contributions to the program and American popular music resulted when he composed the closing number.

Meredith Willson reads from The Big Show script.
(Mason City Library Collection)

Intended to be used only once, "May the Good Lord Bless and Keep You" became the permanent concluding number because Tallulah Bankhead insisted that it remain in that place on the show. Though a staunch supporter of the song, Tallulah had to learn it by having Willson sing it for her one note at a time until her unpolished near bass voice captured the tune. After the third program in the series, all cast members joined in. A strange yet delightful moment occurred when many non-musical performers "sang" a line from the hymn. Even though Tallulah's voice presented a rather interesting rendition of the song, at the program's end every guest, ranging from often-sinister film actor Peter Lorre to comedians Dean Martin and Jerry Lewis, added a line. Not only did the regular NBC listeners warm to the modern hymn, but also many military personnel during the Korean War took the song to their hearts. "Durable Iowa Boy," a May 14, 1951 *Time* magazine article, reported on the popularity of "May the Good Lord Bless and Keep You" and stated that after the song debuted on the show, Willson received up to 2,000 fan letters a week. It continued by calling him "probably the most durable composer-conductor in radio."

As *The Big Show* continued during the 1950-51 radio season, songs like "This Is It," "It's Easter Time," "Here Comes The Springtime," "Hullabaloo," "How I Love the Music of a Band," "You Can't Have a Show Without Durante," and *The Big Show* incidental music occupied the bulk of Meredith Willson's composing time. If he did write a popular non-radio initiated song, the music often appeared later as a special number on the show. When one is the musical director he is able to include his own tunes like "I See the Moon," "Let Freedom Ring," and even the "Iowa Fight Song" as part of the program's bill of fare.

Because The University of Iowa needed a newer inspirational melody, Willson's "Iowa Fight Song" replaced "The Corn Song" and "On Iowa" as the Hawkeye's rallying tune. Les Zacheis, former band member and music writer for *The Cedar Rapids Gazette*, expressed concern over the "rickey-tickey tune that fate wished on them [the U of I]," especially after hearing a Percy Faith album of college songs that included it with more rousing numbers from other schools. Additionally, the word "corn" had taken on the connotation of something that was dated and hokey. Zacheis passed on some of his news clippings to Willson and suggested that the composer turn out a "spirited, swingy" replacement for the school. Initial versions arrived at the newspaper with the note from Willson: "I hope the Iowa boys will like it. If not, I'll try again."

After the columnist passed the music on to The University of Iowa, the school then had the manuscript inspected by the school's instrumental music head, Charles Righter. He offered a few suggestions which Willson developed into a more stirring number than its predecessor. Coincidentally, Righter facilitated the growth of instrumental music in Iowa from 1930 when he directed the first-ever national band and orchestra contest, a legacy of children playing instruments that Willson honored in *The Music Man* seven years later. Reminiscent of fans and cheerleaders at a fall football game, *The Big Show* orchestra and chorus premiered the song for the network audience on the December 31, 1950.

Righter and Willson believed the fight song to be a good fit for The University of Iowa, but the students and faculty needed to be convinced as well. After obtaining permission to use the new tune, Iowa officials allowed the fans to try it out at a basketball game against Indiana University on February 12, 1951. From that successful debut it has remained the rallying cry of the Hawkeyes.

The University of Iowa march represents an addition to Willson's canon of songs dedicated to his beloved state. "I'm From Iowa," "Iowa" and "Way Back in Iowa" had been written about the Hawkeye State early in the twentieth century. As the Mason City composer became Iowa's unofficial music laureate, songs like the "Iowa Indian Song," his hometown's "Centennial March," and the Mason City High School fight song "Mason City, Go, Go, Go," joined a list that began with his own "Iowa" in 1944. Of course, additional Iowa-related tunes joined the group after *The Music Man* became a success. Once Meredith Willson began popularizing the state with his music during the early 1940's, his songs became the preferred standard with the public.

The new march for Meredith Willson's high school alma mater resulted from his displeasure with having Mason City High School words applied to the tune "On Wisconsin." "Now don't think that I don't like Wisconsin; they make wonderful cheese, ... or the university's fight song, mind you, but Mason City is in Iowa." Every time he played the song in the band, he felt loyal to his school but uneasy about the march's origin. To solve the dilemma, he wrote his own song in 1953, during the thirty-five minutes it took to drive from his Beverly Hills home to the NBC Hollywood radio studio. He then gave the manuscript to the school that had created a seat in its instrumental groups for him, his flute and piccolo nearly forty years earlier.

Many of the songs that Meredith Willson wrote from 1948 through 1952 were the direct results of needs for radio programs or radio commercials. General Foods' JELL-O accounted for the following: JELL-O Pudding Sounds for his Talking People, the "JELL-O Shimmer," the "Old JELL-O" Theme, the "JELL-O Family Round," and the "Tapioca Polka." He also published "Wisconsin Cheese," "Florida Oranges," "Anaconda Copper" and "Canada Dry Water" as company themes. For his radio programs he wrote the themes "Ford's Out Front" and "Every Day."

Also during this time period he returned to writing popular songs. Among them was one that reflected his fondness for trains and their changeover stop in the Windy City. He wrote "Gone To Chicago" in 1948 to honor the Chicago and Northwestern Railroad's 100th birthday. Willson, who yielded to musician union work actions, temporarily suffered when this song appeared, because of a ban on recordings. However, the following year, the singing group The Pied Pipers performed this song on the RCA Victor label. Willson's 1949 novelty hit "The Peony Bush" best represents the composer's sense of humor in song. His light-hearted melody presented a solitary "peony bush there in the garden" that made his love turn around and smile. In the composer's words this more demure bud showed that it was more attractive than the brassy "zinnias or gardenias." The song counterpoints the ethereal against the loud and saucy, and was most capably handled when comedian Danny Kaye proffered his rendition. In 1951, Willson's "I See the Moon" ("and the moon sees me") appeared and though it is one of his simpler ditties it became another in his catalog of popular music successes.

In contrast to the lighter fare, Meredith Willson also composed his "Anthem of the Atomic Age" with Los Angeles' Westwood Congregational Church Pastor S. Mark Hogue. Published in 1950, the song restates the theme that God made all men in His image, and that because God created each atom, man must use the power contained therein with the wisdom that the Creator gave to those who were set above all other beings. With the Korean "police action" of 1950 evolving into the Korean War only five years after the Second World War, Willson and Hogue sought to direct their peaceful musical sermon as a plea that cool heads prevail and not use atomic weaponry as had been done to end the Second World War. To send their message, the two envisioned singers from around the world expressing their desires for freedom in thirty-four languages. Willson told one reporter, "If we would appreciate what our fellow man is all about and show him we care, we would not be in all this trouble."

During the 1950's, Meredith Willson and His Orchestra recorded a variety of songs typical of the director's preferences. Along with "The Singing People" (formerly The Talking People) he recorded a series 45 rpm singles for RCA Victor. The disks reprised "You and I" and "Two in Love," while adding his new song "Banners and Bonnets." In addition, five primarily romantic numbers rounded out the set. During the decade, when long-playing vinyl albums began replacing 78's and augmenting

45's, he reverted back to the musical style he made popular in the 1930's, when his Chiffon Swing album of instrumental selections debuted for the Decca label. For the same company he recorded *Modern American Music*, another long-playing album that offered ten classical musical forms (for example, the waltz, minuet, lullaby and barcarole) with melodies created by contemporary composers (Peter DeRose, Harold Arlen, Duke Ellington and Harry Warren, respectively). These songs originally appeared in *Good News* segments during the 1939-1940 season when Willson "challenged" his friends in the composing business to create new American songs in the older style. Finally, as a prelude to what would become his greatest theatrical achievement and best selling album, the soundtrack recording of *The Music Man*, Meredith Willson recreated Sousa's marches in "the original Sousa" style for the Capitol records 1957 release of *Meredith Willson's Marching Band*.

Because he was active writing many songs in the late 1940's and early 1950's, a natural connection to Meredith Willson's fondness for charity work created yet another opportunity to compose rallying numbers. Just prior to the Second World War, Willson dedicated himself to a variety of humanitarian projects that helped victims of war-ravaged countries. After the War, he continued his support by hosting radio programs for organizations like The Red Cross. He and his Talking People provided one of their humorous routines, as well as serious music, for a 1947 show, just before the plea was made for the audience to assist the organization that comes to the front when disasters strike. In 1952, he composed "Answer the Call" as a theme song for The Red Cross. During the same year, Meredith Willson also published "Banners and Bonnets," a tribute to the Salvation Army. Years later he received the Sally, the organization's highest honor, for his unselfish dedication to their cause. For the next two decades, he continued to write songs that inspired the public to help others to the point that even American Presidents requested his inspirational music.

In addition to recording music, Meredith Willson published music based on his recent accomplishments. He had been featured on single song sheets since his early composing days in San Francisco, but during the 1950's, collections like *Words and Music by Meredith Willson* appeared in book form. Riding high on the success of *The Music Man*, this 1958 book included songs from his statehood bicentennial compositions ("The California Story" and "The San Diego Waltz"), as well as numbers made popular on *The Big Show*.

As the second and final season began for *The Big Show*, Meredith Willson received the opportunity to write a musical tribute to the network with whom he had his longest affiliation. In honor of its twenty-fifth anniversary, NBC commissioned its longtime composer to write an appropriate commemorative number. Both as an assignment and as his own personal tribute for the years of happy and productive employment, he completed "Three Chimes of Silver" based on the famous three note trademark (G-E-C) of the broadcasting house founded by parent company General Electric Corporation in 1926. His connection to NBC began when he appeared with the New York Philharmonic on the first network program. Two and a half decades later he recalled that he and other musicians often engaged in "sidework" for the network affiliates in the early days of radio to augment their salaries. With experiences as studio musician, West Coast musical director and conductor on the last great radio program, Willson was more than qualified to create NBC's quarter century theme. He may not have realized it at the time, but the song also heralded the expansion of television, the younger medium that would take the three chimes to new heights of sound and color in the next few years.

NBC witnessed incredible growth during the second half of the twentieth century, as television supplanted radio as the primary source of advertising revenue. Network radio's final hurrah, *The Big Show* began its dissolution during its second year. In cooperation with the British Broadcasting Company, Tallulah, Meredith and company started the 1951-52 season with a European tour. Unfortunately, the anniversary celebrations and remote broadcasts were clouded with controversy. The live performance and the September 30, 1951 recorded presentation of *The Big Show* monetarily outdistanced any previously installment. So that it was truly a hands-across-the-sea venture, producers delineated the cast between English and American actors. Fresh from performing *Caesar and Cleopatra*, Vivien Leigh and Lawrence Olivier joined fellow English performers Jack Buchanan, Bea Lillie, Vera Lynn, and George Sanders. Fred Allen and his wife Portland Hoffa accompanied Willson and Bankhead as the American delegation for an intended jolly good time at the London Palladium. Tallulah had returned as the toast of the English theatre district, where she had been popular two decades earlier. Unfortunately, she upset the sensitivities of newspaper critics with her rendition of a Willson suggested number near the end of the program.

Although the in-house audience adored the performance, the public gave it a positive hearing, and even the manager at the theatre dubbed the radio show the best there in twenty years, critics panned Tallulah's spirited reading of Gene Fowler's poem "The Jervis Bay," a reprise from the show's first season. The journalists called her narrative to Willson's musical accompaniment "maudlin" and in bad taste. London's *Daily*

Express called the show "90 minutes of bad jokes, tuneless songs, witless dialogue, soapy compliments, and onion-under-the-nose emotion."

A potential problem surfaced the day before the opening curtain. Willson had received an affirmative to include in the program his "The Margaret Waltz," a song intended as a tribute to the two young Margarets of their respective countries: President Truman's daughter and King George's younger princess. Even though Buckingham Palace gave the go ahead to play the number, guest George Sanders confided with Willson that the monarchy's acquiescence to allow the song was merely political and that such a performance would not be in the countries' best interests. Wanting not to create an international incident with his music, Meredith Willson stayed up until three in the morning and rewrote the song for the show, hoping that "Let's All Do the Festival Waltz" with British sensitive lyrics was non-confrontational.

A week later, the program headed to the continent for its next European broadcast, when Fred Allen, George Sanders, and the usual members of *The Big Show* staff made the channel crossing and began setting up at the Empire Theater in Paris. Joining the cast were American ex-patriot Josephine Baker, whose singing and dancing career became legendary in France, and world-renowned British singer and comedienne Gracie Fields. Once again NBC presented the broadcast as a joint effort between itself and another foreign broadcasting company, Radio France. Unfortunately, this installment had even more difficulties than did its British predecessor. Art Buchwald lauded the show in his "Paris After Dark" column, but Meredith Willson felt that it was not promoted well to the unfamiliar audience. In another miscalculation, the sense of humor of the American and British actors did not translate well to the French audience, who responded only politely to the performance. Additionally, Willson experienced monumental directorial headaches.

Once the American musical director arrived in France, he discovered that customs had held up his scores. After this fiasco was sorted out, he discovered that he almost did not need the music at all. The sixty French musicians hired for the orchestra were not eager to stay and practice for the upcoming program, because they had other jobs and wanted to get to them quickly. After finally rehearsing for six hours on Friday, Willson told them when they were to be in their places for the Monday night recording. (Both European programs were broadcast live in the host country and played several weeks later in The United States.) Oblivious to their obligation, the musicians merely said that they were busy that night and exited the Empire Theatre. Tearfully pleading with them to return, the famed American conductor literally had to run down the street to retrieve his orchestra. Eventually they relented, and the program went on as scheduled.

As well as feeling the effects of a slipping audience share, other problems affected *The Big Show* on its return to America. During this second season, Tallulah had to confront one of her hired help with theft. In turn, the woman threatened to tell all she knew about Miss Bankhead's lavish bohemian lifestyle that included frequent overindulgences in alcohol and drugs. Even though privately the incident made Tallulah a nervous wreck, she carried on at rehearsals joking about the very public trial. The end result found the former employee guilty, but for a number of reasons, including Tallulah's pleading, the judge suspended the sentence.

Late during *The Big Show's* final season, the producers offered a tribute to Meredith Willson on March 9, 1952. His then current creative endeavor, the novel *Who Did What to Fedalia?* appeared on bookshelves that year, and the radio program presented a serious adaptation of the book as well as a parody of the same story. The performers that evening included stuttering comedian Joe Frisco, Peter Lorre, Jim and Marian Jordan (Fibber McGee and Molly), Phil Foster, Richard Eastham, and Sheppard Strudwick. They all collaborated to honor the composer who seemed to have captured the hearts of radio audiences for over two decades.

♪ ♪ ♪

Four years after his first autobiographical installment *And There I Stood With My Piccolo* debuted, Meredith Willson's first novel appeared on the nation's bookshelves. After he published the first of his three autobiographical works, Willson then turned to the comedy-mystery genre with a saga of a small town Iowan set adrift in New York City. His *Who Did What to Fedalia?* was a quasi-autobiographical/biographical farce about a young lady from the Parker family of Fort Madison, Iowa, who leaves her two brothers to seek fame and fortune in the city where Willson began his professional music career.

Fedalia Parker and her two siblings were neither coincidentally nor subtly cast after the images of Dixie, Cedric, and Meredith Willson, for the story's tribute was inscribed: "This book is dedicated to Rini, Dixie, Cedric, and George." (There is no clue as to which "George" in Willson's career is the subject of the dedication, but George Burns seems to be the most likely candidate.) Fedalia and Dixie both left their brothers behind to seek their respective fame and fortune, ultimately in New York City. Unlike Fedalia, of course, Dixie Willson succeeded in the Big Apple.

Prophetically, the story of Fedalia Parker contained numerous images, situations, and statements similar to *The Music Man* that was five years from its premiere.

Meredith Willson tested his reading audience with many autobiographical references, some of which would be used in his first musical. Early in the suspense novel he refers to numerous Iowa locations, ending with the Doerflingers in Mason City's Cerro Gordo County. Epithets such as "great honk" as exclaimed by Cousin Clell (Willson's real Mason City cousin) is used in the novel, just as it became one of the embarrassing near swear words uttered by River Cityans in *The Music Man*. Furthermore, in the novel, Willson recalled learning "The Highwayman" as he did as a child in Mason City and taking the train from Fort Madison to Chicago (Meredith took the train East to the Windy City, while Harold Hill ventured West to River City.) Finally, New Yorker Spartan Corliss bears an uncommon likeness to con man Harold Hill. He uses a strikingly similar rhythm in his sales delivery, which is most obvious just as the character is about to present his last critical shot at Fedalia before she returns to Iowa. Even another long-suffering salesman pitches his wares to Fedalia right after she comes home to a doting and patient native named Charlie Landry.

The basic story involves Fedalia Parker of Fort Madison, Iowa, who, according to the locals, is gifted with a beautiful voice. She takes the train through Chicago to her "uncle's" house in Hoboken, New Jersey from where she intends to pursue a singing career in New York City. Eventually, she makes connections with Hunter's Talent Bureau on 44th and 6th Avenues, and soon thereafter, she is lured into the confidence of a nefarious radio producer, Adelbert Wixberry. He is attracted to her and leads her on, all the while telling others that she has no talent. One day, after she overhears his pronouncement that she cannot sing, Fedalia returns to New Jersey, where she unearths some very strange findings about her supposed uncle. It seems that when the protagonist queries housekeeper Miss Broder as to the whereabouts of the widowed Uncle George, now referred to as Doctor, the visitor discovers that he is about to perform strange surgery on the family cat, Ruggy. To add to the conundrum, as the shocked Iowan looks to the cat in horror, she discovers that Broder is actually the formerly thought deceased Aunt Bernette, and Fedalia is the next to be the subject of Uncle George's scalpel!

Fedalia, of course, escapes as Doctor/Uncle George is whisked away to the state insane asylum. She boards the next train for the safety of Iowa, and upon her return, the heroine is welcomed home by stalwarts like Mr. Vance, farmer Garvey and his wife, and Mr. Gale at the drugstore. To show that things in Fort Madison do not change and represent a reliable sanctuary, a long-suffering salesman, who was present at the start of the story selling an autoharp, returns with a combination phonograph-piano.

Complimentary criticism of the book did not dominate the literary world's reaction to the story. Willson received kudos for his use of dialects, but the story's mixed messages that vacillated between a Horatio Alger saga and a trip to the macabre hurt the effort. After years of hearing accents from New York to California, a variety of voices came alive. Whatever possessed the author to include a strangely sadistic and psychotic uncle weakened the overall effort. An introspective statement by the author entered at the end of the novel when Corliss lamented the prospects of producing a musical flop. Such a disaster prevailed in Meredith Willson's mind at the time, because he was suffering periods of stagnation while writing *The Music Man*. He later said that one of his reasons for writing a musical was to disprove those who thought that he could not do it. Although the author did not know it at the time, *The Music Man* would become Fedalia's antithesis on that count, and Willson returned to his greatest project endeavoring to create a smash hit that would dispel those who criticized his prose.

Even though Meredith Willson became a success on radio through his songs, personality, and most recently through his prose, *The Big Show* folded after two seasons. The program delivered all that it promised and more, but its nearly $100,000 per episode was insufficient to mount a production that was able to compete with a weak television line-up and an established CBS Sunday night radio schedule. Television's draw came from its novelty, and *The Big Show* only had an advantage in areas where viewing was limited. However, in the large cities, where advertising revenue counted most, the four television networks (ABC, CBS, Dumont, and NBC) started to drain commercial dollars away from radio. The novelty of the visual medium, coupled with the expense of the appliance, caused the public to turn it on despite the inferiority of some programs. By 1955, what was later referred to as Old Time Radio had reached its end.

Meredith Willson's radio career did not end with the demise of *The Big Show*. During the 1952-53 season, he, as well as opera singers Robert Merrill and Margaret Piazza, collaborated for a thirty-minute Monday night program of serious music on NBC's *Encore*. Merrill's singing schedule was detrimental to the program, because people objected when he was absent. In one case he was to be replaced by a tape recording that would be accompanied by the live fifty-piece studio orchestra. (The prestigious organization included many musicians who doubled in Toscanini's NBC orchestra.) When the tape was replayed, engineers found that the recording machine had been slowed for a humorous effect on comedian Morey Amsterdam's program. A technician saved the day when he manually sped up the tape. The experience resulted in the singer and the accompaniment thereafter being recorded together.

In addition to *Encore*, Meredith Willson appeared on several of his own radio shows. *Every Day*, the fifteen-minute Monday through Friday program of piano and talk with wife Rini, which ran through the 1954 on NBC, included a feature that showcased hometown newspapers and their editorials. A similar show, *Weekday*, aired on the 1955-56 schedule. Meredith Willson's *Music Room* continued through the 1951-52 season on NBC during its 10:30 P.M. Eastern Time slot. Of course, guest appearances on friends' radio and television programs, as well as visits to conduct symphony orchestras and specials to herald favorite charitable causes continued. However, another project, his first venture into musical theatre, occupied the bulk of his creative time until *The Music Man* opened in late 1957.

After NBC cancelled *The Big Show*, an abbreviated and less costly version appeared on television starting in the fall of 1952. Originally entitled *Four Star Revue*, because of the original four rotating hosts Ed Wynn, Danny Thomas, Jack Carson and Jimmy Durante, the program name changed to *All Star Revue* in 1951. In its third season, Tallulah Bankhead and Meredith Willson recreated their famed radio roles for the live television and kinescope cameras on a rotating basis with other hosts. NBC was so confident of their performances that the duo's first joint television appearance came on the first show of the 1952-53 season on October 11, 1952. The program was thirty minutes shorter than the radio program, but it had its predecessor's flavor, starting with distinguished guests like Ethel Barrymore and Groucho Marx.

The first television program emulated *The Big Show* when it reprised standards like Tallulah's monologue followed by sketches and songs. Her opening line was "Welcome to Tallulahvision" after which the Willson song "Hallelujah, It's Tallulahvision at Last" became the first musical production number. Wonderful songs by Groucho and carefully integrated commercials for Pet Milk (Ben Grauer explained the product while Willson accompanied with "I'll Be Seeing You") preceded Tallulah's promotion of her new autobiography, *Tallulah*. A number by the Ron Fletcher dancers preceded a reprise of the previous spring's *The Big Show* sketch "Writer

Vs Critic," in which Meredith Willson moderated a panel comprised of an insulting Groucho, Ethel Barrymore, and Miss Bankhead. A final Tallulah skit, "In New York City," wrapped up the program before the cast sang "May the Good Lord Bless and Keep You." The following week Jimmy Durante hosted his trademark program. Among the Bankhead-Willson programs scheduled every fourth Saturday was a February 7, 1953 show with guests Phil Foster, Bert Lahr and Patsy Kelly, and a March 3, 1953 offering with Foster and Kelly in addition to Fred MacMurray, Wally Cox, and Cab Calloway. Unfortunately, the *All Star Revue* left television the following month. Even though the show placed a respectable twentieth in the 1952-53 television ratings, it was substituted with a weak half-hour situation comedy starring singer Ezio Pinza.

♪ ♪ ♪

In 1955, Meredith Willson published the second of his three autobiographical works. *Eggs I Have Laid* is essentially a tribute to his radio years from where his last autobiography left off five years earlier, things he forgot in that book, life with Rini, and hopes that his current project, *The Music Man*, would be a success. As a result of his happy accomplishments on *The Big Show*, the book was dedicated to "Dee, Bud and Goody" (*The Big Show* director-producer Dee Englebach, NBC vice president and associate producer Bud Barry, and *The Big Show* key writer Goodman Ace respectively.) The story often alluded to Clell Squires back in Mason City with the author wondering what his cousin might think about a variety of matters covered in the book. Starting with his "L'Embryon" to Clell, the favorite relative whom Willson admired as an estimable athlete, the writer then tendered dozens of tributes to friends and acquaintances from Mason City to Hollywood. The author spent extra time relating his undying gratitude to John Philip Sousa.

His recollections shared problems with *The Big Show* and its production. The program usually had three rehearsals between Friday and Saturday, and the final rehearsals for the program began at 9:00 a.m. on Sunday, when to his approval (he was a stickler for serious rehearsals) Tallulah and the guests took their places. While one such practice was in progress, Frank Sinatra cancelled the day of the show nine hours before airtime. By midafternoon the musical arrangements for him were replaced for the final rehearsal at 2:00 P.M. with new ones for substitute singer Frankie Laine. The cast broke at 4:00 so that they could get a bite to eat and to change into dress clothes for the show. At 5:00 final script changes were meted out. So frantic were the preparations for the third act of this particular show that it was broadcast unrehearsed. Fortunately, the program came off fine, and even President Truman called with congratulations and positive comments about the duet sung by his daughter Margaret and Fred Allen.

Other remembrances of eggs laid include a recollection of a particular guest on the *Sparkle Time* radio show. Attempting to be a genial host like his friend Arthur Godfrey on the *Talent Scouts*, Willson sought to introduce new singing voices to the listening audience. When the last show of the 1946-47 season ran out of time, one hopeful actress did not make an appearance in the last singing slot. Willson recognized her talent and regretted that Doris Kappelhoff was not given an early chance to sing before a national audience; however, the following year she started making movies as Doris Day, and during the 1950's, she became one of the top grossing film actresses.

Meredith Willson continued his second autobiography with a variety of personal anecdotes. He spent a great deal of time on his wife Rini's frequent use of malapropisms (she was one half French and one half Russian.) He also believed that Paramount pictures wanted to film his *And There I Stood With My Piccolo* with Bob Hope playing the lead. Recreating the lives of musicians had been common fodder for filmmakers before and after the War, but the idea to immortalize Willson on film soon died. The musician also described another purely Willson invention: music for people who could not sing a note or Words-Without-Song. The gimmick was a counterpoint to the Talking People, and it went nowhere.

By the end of the 1955-56 season, all of Meredith Willson's appearances as a star on major radio programs ended, for the medium was headed, and especially to consternation of the composer from Iowa, in a very hostile direction toward the rock and roll/disk jockey format. Even though he watched the medium that he called home for over twenty-five years change drastically, it was for the better, because all of his energies could be channeled to complete his greatest creative effort, *The Music Man*.

Chapter Nine
"Seventy-Six Trombones"

Meredith Willson did not recognize the great significance of the events when they were happening, but the first five decades of his life (and especially from the year 1912 onward) formed the foundation for his most ambitious and best-known project, *The Music Man*. Even though he had achieved instrumental music success when he played with the March King John Philip Sousa and philharmonic maestro Arturo Toscanini; his name had been interwoven between the origins and final days of "old time" radio; he had scored critically successful motion pictures; and he had composed music from the top hits of the day to symphonies, none of these achievements rivaled that which would occupy his time during the first half of the 1950's.

When the story of *The Music Man* began is no clearer than who Harold Hill actually was in real life. The memories of growing up in Mason City, Iowa were, of course, subconsciously filed in Willson's mind until he opened the cache of recollections and rearranged them into the idyllic scenario that became his first Broadway musical. The official spark to pen the first words of a libretto came when old crony and fellow composer Frank Loesser suggested that Willson put his typewriter where his stories were and develop his oft-told Hawkeye tales into a full-length musical play.

By the time Meredith Willson became a fixture on radio and a creator of hit songs, he amassed a number of songwriter friends, among them Harry Ruby, Johnny Mercer, and Loesser. The latter wrote numerous hit songs, like "Slow Boat to China" and "Baby, It's Cold Outside" and succeeded with his own musical *Where's Charley?* in 1948. In 1950, he gave Broadway one of his greatest achievements, *Guys and Dolls*. Willson was so impressed with his friend's musical that the December 31, 1950 installment of *The Big Show* featured a lengthy scene from the play with original Broadway actors Vivian Blaine and Sam Levine. Perhaps this gesture was in reciprocation for Loesser's suggestion that a barber, farmer or salesman might be the character on which Willson might write his own musical. A few years later, *The Big Show* head radio writer Goodman Ace added his encouragement to the project. Parenthetically, as a fitting tribute to both Loesser's and Willson's talents, when the United States Postal Service honored the two on the stamp series "Broadway Songwriters" in 1999, they were placed next to each other on a sheet that included Rodgers and Hammerstein II, Lerner and Lowe, George and Ira Gershwin, and Lorenz Hart.

For years, Meredith Willson regaled party groups with stories of this cousin or that storeowner from Mason City, just as he had with Frank Morgan on *Good News* and George and Gracie on the *Burns and Allen Show*. By the time *The Big Show* was in production, Tallulah Bankhead's on air character regarded the Hawkeye reminiscences as "nauseating" little necessities that delighted the audience, and especially those in Cerro Gordo County, Iowa. As this last major effort to keep a radio audience that enjoyed live variety show programming faded into the ether, the idea of a musical based on Iowa characters re-emerged. Loesser's earlier suggestion, coupled with Willson's desire to write a musical play, fully took wing in 1952, when a helpful partner from the past proffered the necessary protagonist to get the plot moving.

From the time he arrived in New York three decades earlier to begin his musical career, Meredith Willson frequently had his creative sibling Dixie only a few minutes away. While he was learning classical music, she was progressing with her accomplishments as a writer. When he moved to California, she contributed to his radio shows. After Loesser suggested that Willson write a musical in 1949, the nostalgic Iowan began bandying ideas about. However, he could not come up with the basic catalyst to get the project going. Three years later Dixie mentioned that a story about a music professor might be the hook that the composer sought. Her contributions not only got the project off the ground, but it also eventually netted her a generous share in her brother's financial success.

By the time Willson changed the character to a band instrument salesman, he caught the interest of potential producers Cy Feuer and Ernie Martin. (They produced Loesser's *Where's Charley?* and Willson knew Martin when the younger man was a page at NBC.) Although Meredith and Rini Willson performed the entire three hour and forty-five minute prototype entitled *The Silver Triangle* to the delight of the Feuer and Martin team, five years passed before the first stage light glowed. Shortly after the two agreed to shape the musical, the lead had a name: Harold Hill, a lovable rogue, a character that they felt was always a surefire bet in a show.

The theatrical era into which Meredith Willson entered with his new show emerged as one mixed between financial woes and artistic triumphs. In general, post World War Two theater experienced the challenges of higher production costs, rapidly increasing ticket prices (between 1944 and 1960 the prices doubled), and the same menace that radio felt: the threat from television to steal entertainment audiences. The combination of these problems resulted in Broadway hitting one of its lowest points by the middle of the twentieth century, when only fifty-nine productions debuted in New York during the 1949-50 season.

In Meredith Willson's favor, musicals remained the most popular theatrical ticket. The "new Broadway" emerged and rejuvenated what had been primarily formula productions, after the innovative staging for the premiere of *Oklahoma!* For example, instead of an ensemble opening the performance with a large production number that hearkened back to nineteenth century minstrel shows and including songs that were merely a change from the dialogue, newer musicals like *Oklahoma!* integrated songs, choreography, and sets that all flowed from the script. This Richard Rodgers and Oscar Hammerstein II adaptation of *Green Grow the Lilacs* represents the starting point for modern twentieth century musicals, when it opened with a lone cowboy singing "Oh, What a Beautiful Morning" on a near empty stage prior to narrative dance numbers that told the story through what then seemed a different art form.

As the eventually named *The Music Man* evolved in the early 1950's, Meredith Willson found several occasions to renew his old acquaintances in Mason City, Iowa. He regularly returned to his hometown after he departed in 1919 to study music in New York, but in 1953 he had a special reason to come back, the city's 100th anniversary. Because his grandfather was one of the early pioneers in the region, Meredith Willson took great pride in composing the "Centennial March" for the festivities. Singled out from a number of renowned returnees, the musician received the title of honorary mayor, a job that included naming the centennial queen. A few years prior to this event, Mason City's KGLO radio began to contact Meredith Willson to give the folks at home a direct report on their local hero. Fortunately, many program recordings, often with interviews by host Doug Sherwin, exist and chronicle the joys and anxieties that Meredith Willson experienced as he developed his musicals and other projects.

As the decade of the 1950's unfolded, Willson shared his ongoing projects with the Mason City audience. His visit to the 1948 Iowa bandmasters' conference formed the basis for the earliest recording, while reports on his *Big Show* activities, the subsequent radio and television appearances, current compositions, the second part of his autobiography, and the development of *The Music Man* and the later musicals were also chronicled. Sherwin provided the listeners with informal discussions that show insight into Meredith Willson's desires to share his bi-coastal life with his friends and cousins back home. In a broadcast made prior to the Mason City centennial in 1953, Iowa friends chatted with him on air as if there were no listening audience, and calls often ended with a "say hello to family members like Cousin Clell [Squires]."

Meredith Willson was not the only famous Mason Cityan exercising his talents in New York City's entertainment circles. During the 1930's and 1940's, Bil Baird began making inroads into national prominence as a puppeteer. He was a few years younger than Willson, and once he arrived in Mason City from his Nebraska birthplace, Baird eventually joined the Mason City High School Band and occupied the peck horn (alto horn) chair. Decades later, his Marionettes ambled across Broadway stages in productions like *The Ziegfeld Follies of 1941* and *Baker Street* (1965.) After he married Cora, who became his life partner in the business, the couple brought their creations to early television on programs like their own *Life with Snarky Parker* and *The Ed Sullivan Show*, as well as frequent stints on Jack Paar's show. Among their most memorable contributions to puppetry were the lion Charlemane, honky tonk piano playing Slugger Ryan, the television special *Peter and the Wolf* with Art Carney, and the Marionette cast for the lonely goatherd scene in the film *The Sound of Music*.

During the Willsons' and the Bairds' mutual residence in New York City in the 1950's, the couples often socialized, sharing musical performances, stage plays, and meals. Meredith Willson frequently joked about his friend that the one "l" that Baird dropped from his first name (the puppeteer said that one does not pronounce it anyway) was borrowed for the music man's last name. Interestingly, even though Willson and Baird were not close chums in Mason City because of their age difference, the Baird collection of puppets found a permanent home at the Charles H. MacNider Museum within eyesight of the memorabilia collection housed in the Willson Boyhood Home.

While he was in New York doing a variety of writing, directing and acting chores, for the next three years after their initial meeting, Meredith Wilson and the team of Cy Feuer and Ernie Martin edited, rewrote, doctored, and discussed *The Music Man* to the point that the three actually gave up hope of ever seeing it on stage. The Feurer-Martin team had produced hits such as *Guys and Dolls, Can-Can, The Boyfriend,* and *Silk Stockings,* so their credentials indicated a successful track record on Broadway. Specifically, Feurer became the director of the Willson show, and Martin assumed the role of script doctor. In order to get started, two or three of the songs came from Willson's music "trunk," but the next three-dozen compositions evolved with the show's development. Before the show was finished and pared down to eighteen numbers, at least one song, "I've Already Started in To Try To Figure Out a Way To Go To Work To Try To Get You," probably did not deserve a place in the final cut. The characters, situations, and songs came in spurts, and Willson later admitted that his own Iowa stubbornness often prevented real progress. He did not realize the significance at the time, but his own often-obstinate posture helped provide inspiration for "Iowa Stubborn," the Grant Woodesque number that welcomed Harold Hill to the bucolic residents of River City.

One engaging character based on a real Mason Cityan and one who emerged in *The Music Man* early on came from Mason City's fledgling high school band and orchestra. The two organizations had been in existence only a short time when the Willson brothers joined as instrumentalists, and the young musicians even played without a proper leader. After musing over the 1912 band photo that hung in his study and served to haunt and goad the composer in those formative years of *The Music Man*, Meredith Willson began examining the picture more closely. First, he identified peck horn player Alvin Tank, and then he recalled the group's conductor, the German teacher whose limited musical knowledge came from playing the violin. Ultimately, Willson's reminiscences carried him to Marian McGuire, who played the cello parts on her brother's euphonium. As a result, Marian the librarian, the female love interest in the play, emerged. (The composer based the character on real Mason City residents during the Willson childhood era, including librarians Lydia Margaret Barrett and Bertha Baird, as well as art teacher Florence O'Leary.)

Not only were characters from the high school band incorporated into *The Music Man*, but also their practice habits became important plot elements. Anyone who welcomed the kids and their instruments into their Mason City homes soon learned to appreciate Beethoven's "Minuet in G." This number frequently rounded out the rehearsals and performances ("the one piece we could always get through without stopping," said Willson) and was subsequently enshrined as the practice song of the fictitious River

City band. Likewise, this was the number that Harold Hill actually did direct in lieu of being carried away in irons to the River City jail.

Just as Meredith Willson recalled making significant progress that inched *The Music Man* onward in the early 1950's, diversions took him from his work. When his *Meredith Willson's Music Room*, which began as one of his post-War radio endeavors, ended until 1952, he then began his five day a week *Every Day Show* with his wife Rini. While in New York, Meredith Willson auditioned for a new television game show entitled *The Big Surprise*. This giveaway program was one of many quiz shows proliferating on the VHF dial prior to the *$64,000 Question* scandal that nearly spelled total doom for the popular small screen genre. Unfortunately, after getting his and Rini's hopes up for a regular paying job, he lost the opportunity because instead of giving the contestant the question for the grand prize of $100,000, he gave the answer. The down but not out composer returned to his home in California with the intention of moving *The Music Man* on to completion and dropping the notion of hosting any such show again.

An early sticking point in the play was the inclusion of a subplot that involved a wheel chair bound spastic boy. In Meredith Willson's words, "not exactly a character you would normally select for a musical comedy." Shortly after the producers mulled over the initial draft, they decided that the musical had to be shortened, the title had to be changed, and something had to be done with the boy. Pruning the libretto and score began right away; after all, unused songs could go back into the writer's trunk for future consideration. Feurer proposed *The Music Man* as a title with no resistance from the other parties. However, the character of the boy continually plagued the creative team.

In order to make ends meet, Meredith Willson needed to develop revenue-producing projects until he sold his musical. Royalties from songs like "May the Good Lord Bless and Keep You," "The Peony Bush," and "I See the Moon" (a tremendous hit in England) helped, as did the income from television appearances and radio programs like his daily shows *How To Listen to Long Hair Music* and *Every Day*. These endeavors generated a respectable income, but as audience tastes changed during the 1950's, opportunities for Meredith Willson's homespun humor began to dry up. And being active in broadcasting also created diversions that slowed the pace of writing *The Music Man*.

Although the process suffered from time devoted to other projects, the next time Feuer and Martin got together with Willson to hear how he had progressed, the composer delivered a one-two punch. At the time, cutting the long score was the immediate goal, yet Meredith Willson added a new tune, "Seventy-Six Trombones," and chanced upon the showstopper. Hearing the march revived the producers' enthusiasm for the musical. Besides, shortening the production could come later.

If Willson felt that con man Harold Hill could express his desires to sell the idea of a boys' band and the necessary uniforms through a rousing march, then his love interest, Marian the librarian, could likewise express herself with the same melody. "Seventy-Six Trombones" honors the composer's years with John Philip Sousa and his famous six-eight marches. Willson knew that Sousa sped up some of his own three-four waltzes and turned them into marches. If he reversed the process and cut the time of "Seventy-Six Trombones" in half, he was able to mold it into the waltz tempo number "Good Night, My Someone" to counter Hill's song. Just as this novel musical gimmick brought the two principles together melodically, later in the show, as the con man and librarian exchanged lyrics and tempos, they would inch romantically closer. After Ernie Martin enthusiastically approved the additions, he then directed Willson to revamp the whole show. Well after the success of *The Music Man*, its creator expressed his total appreciation for the producers' guidance in readying his script. He said that they moved it from "a play with music" to a "musical comedy." Fortunately, at this point in its development, Willson's story about a boys' band seemed destined to follow the new Feuer and Martin 1956 hit *Silk Stockings* on Broadway almost immediately. Nothing was farther from the truth.

Character development and situations continued as real people from Willson's hometown evolved into the residents of River City. The aforementioned Alvin Tank and a boy called Kilroy, one of many whom Mama Rosalie Willson befriended, inspired the composer to create Tommy Djilas, the rough boy who favored the mayor's daughter and whose salvation came when Hill converted him into the leader of the band. (The character's last name came from a Bulgarian ex-patriot who worked in a New York delicatessen often frequented by Meredith and Rini.) Originally envisioned as the wheelchair bound child, the lisping little boy who evolved into Winthrop Paroo was based on young Charlie Haverdegrain, and his Irish mother, Mrs. Paroo, was a characterization of the Willson's current German housekeeper, Mrs. Buehler. (By the way, she must have found a warm spot in the composer's heart, because he used her again as the non-speaking housekeeper in his third musical *Here's Love*.) The entire pool hall controversy in the musical emerged from reminiscences of Congregational Church organist Ed Patchen's sojourns to Mason City's PLEAZOL billiard parlor to play the gentlemen's game that contained no evil pockets in the table. Harold Hill's sidekick was named for Marcellus

Washburn, who was listed in the 1918 Mason City Directory as manager of the local B.F. Goodrich tire store and became the entertainment chairman for the Fourth Victory Liberty Loan drive of 1919. Constable Lock in the play was appropriately named after officer and later Mason City Chief of Police, Tom Lock. Meredith Willson borrowed the unusual first name of Mayor Shinn's wife from Mason City High School classmate Eulalie Johnson, and her "Pick-A-Little" co-singer Ethel Toffelmeyer was named for a Sunday school teacher of the same last name. Mrs. Squires' surname came from cousin Clell Squires' daughter Doris, who later became Mrs. Doris Blakesley. Gracie Squires, the lesser-known daughter in the cast is, of course, a tribute to Gracie Allen.

When Warner Brothers filmed the musical in 1962, more local names appeared. Long-time Willson friend and newspaper publisher Earl Hall witnessed his name placed on the front of the River City real estate dealer's office, while Jim Griffith's Shave and Haircut Parlour of Mason City likewise appeared on the set. (Jim's daughter Hazel played piano in the Erwin-Wells Orchestra that first hired Willson as a professional musician, and John Willson spent a great deal of time bending the barber's ear in the real shop.) Cora Sundell, nearby resident to the Willson house, had her Pennsylvania Avenue house used as the prototype for the Paroo home, the replica of which still stands on the Warner Brothers back lot. When he began writing his libretto, Meredith Willson often stated that River City was not a direct mold of his birthplace Mason City; however, from the play's inception it always certainly seemed more than just coincidentally symbolic of that north central Iowa town.

Numerous circa 1912 Mason City events likewise emerge in *The Music Man*. The gymnasium scene where the relatively sedate Virginia reel deteriorated into the spirited Shipoopi dance recalled Mason City's Jack Kohl whirling anxious local girls around to the Castle Walk. The older women in the play are a recollection of the Mason City women's club to which Rosalie Willson belonged and from whom many of her civic endeavors emanated. The Fourth of July celebration scene served as a dual recall in the musical, for Mason City did enjoy fireworks and rousing music during its Independence Day festivities, often at East Park. The fireworks display in *The Music Man* took place across the creek from the "Pest House," and Mason City's East Park put on its display close to City Detention Hospital for people with contagious diseases, a building referred to as the "Pest House." However, unlike the droplets that fell in *The Music Man*, no rain touched Mason City on July 4, 1912. On the other hand, a small footbridge in East Park really did provide romantic couples with a place to meet. The cannon in front of the courthouse square brought by a Wells Fargo Wagon in the play was placed on the south corner of the first real Cerro Gordo County Courthouse block in 1900. However, in true patriotic fashion, the residents had it melted down for a World War II metal drive. In line with Meredith Willson's numerous contributions to the military, and especially during the Second World War, he would have been proud of his town's sacrifice to the War effort and was likewise aware of the replacement that arrived after *The Music Man* encountered its long run.

The episode in the show wherein the problem of a music holder for flutes and piccolos came right from Mason City's harness maker, Mr. Bushgens. The inventive leather worker attempted to remedy the situation for the sideways instrument by making a chest mounted lyre holder that was tied on from the player's back. Unfortunately, a different problem emerged, because the device bobbed when the wearer marched. His second idea, attaching a lyre to a leather strap around the player's upper left arm, enjoyed even less success. The idea was sound, for when the musician snapped the flute or piccolo into playing position, the notes popped up in front of the player. Sadly, the holder cut off the circulation to the arm, rendering the fingers useless.

In the third installment of his autobiography, *But He Doesn't Know the Territory*, Meredith Willson shared his frustrations at making critical decisions in the musical creative process. He admitted that his trying to please Ernie Martin, out of respect for the noted script doctor, stifled Willson's own infusion of original ideas. Both men were perplexed because Willson often wrote to please Martin. They did agree that con man Harold Hill should be exposed as a phony to the audience from his first entrance, as opposed to revealing his charade late in the show. On the other hand, they did not agree on the method from which the songs would emerge. Willson argued that the songs should come out of the dialogue: the actors would just follow their spoken lines with sung ones. Martin thought that Willson was attempting to have the characters talk in a cadence that led up to a song, and that the audience did not need the rhythmic set up. The script doctor stated that people came to hear songs regardless of what brought the actors to the singing point. Willson's suggestion eventually led to the opening number of the salesmen decrying the antics of Harold Hill with a beat that mimics the train accelerating and decelerating. In short, Martin was not sold on all of the time-consuming trouble that Meredith Willson was infusing into the show. Wanting to make a profit on this project or move on to the next one, Feuer and Martin amicably and temporarily separated from Willson and *The Music Man* to work on another show.

Temporarily daunted by the departure of his production support, Meredith Willson moved headlong into rewriting the opening of the play (before he was finished he revised it over forty times). The first result was actually getting the opening train number to work. By the fall of 1955, the revolutionary start to a musical took its place with talking salesmen echoing the Talking People of ten years previous. In the meantime, when Meredith and Rini played one of their numerous personal appearances to local musical groups and colleges, Ernie Martin phoned to tell the Willsons that CBS television showed interest in broadcasting the unfinished play for $100,000. The composer welcomed the infusion of the much-needed cash at first, and besides, the two-hour special would have been the first ever Broadway premiere on television. Martin even secured a prime Sunday nighttime slot, pre-empting the *Ed Sullivan Show*, a variety program whose ratings scored as one of the top television shows in the mid 1950's. Unfortunately, the television network declined the project, because they wanted absolute control of casting. To make matters worse, because the project seemed not to be advancing toward completion, Feuer and Martin departed the show for good.

Bleakness and alternative endeavors marked the first half of 1956. After trying numerous friends, many from his radio days, who might produce the show and help finish the book, Meredith Willson dedicated himself to get the play staged, even though at the time all of his long hours of work and presentations by himself and Rini seemed futile. Encouragement buoyed the project when luminaries, including famed movie director Robert Mamoulian, Oscar-winning director Fred Zinneman, and movie mogul Jesse Lasky heard the couple present the show for a small group of Hollywood friends. After offering constructive help, they told Willson that he had a hit and should patiently continue. The composer often shared his creation with visitors and even allowed friends like Norma Zimmer to try out new songs.

During an involvement in a centennial celebration, Willson made an acquaintance who later aided in getting *The Music Man* finished. Music for *The California Story*, a two-week extravaganza presented in San Diego to honor the state's 100th birthday in 1950, came in part from Willson's "trunk" of songs. While organizing his music for the centennial production, he chanced upon Franklin Lacey, who was readying the pageant's book. After meeting again six years later and after sharing the basic story of *The Music Man*, Meredith Willson obtained an ally who had a utilitarian knowledge of script editing, as well as practical experience with spastic children, like the troublesome character Winthrop, from his own teaching experiences.

By September 1956, Willson began the rewriting that would see *The Music Man* finished. When Frank Lacey visited later in that year, the author, who had spent many long nights creating while Rini plied him with food, drink, and vitamins, revealed to his new partner "Ya Got Trouble," both a popular song from the musical and a subject matter that concerned Willson less and less during the next twelve months. The composer was so enthusiastic about the new song that he even wrote a parody to "Trouble" that the salesmen echoed back to Harold late in the show. It was, however, only used in a Philadelphia try-out performance and was dropped before the show reached Broadway. During this phase of writing, "Sadder But Wiser Girl" entered the script, and it even had a place as a counterpoint to "My White Knight," just as "Good Night, My Someone" and "Seventy-Six Trombones" did, but this idea also fell from the final score.

Ernie Martin entered Meredith Willson's life one more time during *The Music Man* project when he offered the Iowan a new opportunity. Just as the musical moved closer to its completion, which surprised Martin who thought that the project had been abandoned, the producer found a book for Willson to turn into a musical. Feeling that the story of *Indian Joe*, one based on the famed Mark Twain antagonist in Tom Sawyer, might be a suitable story to adapt, Martin suggested that the diversion might offer needed background training for Willson and future theatrical projects. Despite the fact that Willson's friends said to grab any project with the Feurer-Martin stamp, and even though famed comedy writer Norman Krasna was already writing pages for the production at MGM (the movie studio had the film rights to the story that would eventually become the forgotten film *Whoop Up*), Willson declined the offer in favor of finishing *The Music Man*. Hoping that his friend had made the right decision to continue onward, Martin tried to be helpful and said he would see the Iowa show finished and staged for 1958. Willson, whose finances were being strained and who could have used the infusion of cash from another project, remained firm and several weeks later finished his musical.

The selling of *The Music Man* began afresh. At Rini's suggestion, her husband contacted producer Kermit Bloomgarten, who was finishing a successful run with Frank Loesser's *Most Happy Fella*. A former CPA, Bloomgarten became noteworthy for producing stage hits like *Death of a Salesman*, *Command Decision*, and *The Diary of Anne Frank*. Rini and Meredith flew to New York, and for three-and-a-half hours they once again presented the show, this time for Bloomgarten at conductor Herb Greene's apartment on a "sleety, cold, blowy night" on December 19, 1956. The over four-hour performance lasted until five in the morning. Later that day Meredith Willson was in Bloomgarten's office, where the producer said, "May I have the privilege of producing your play?" One year later to the day, *The Music Man* debuted on Broadway.

Once the story was ready, the cast search occupied the next phase of Willson's energies. Of course, finding the title character was the most important challenge. Friends from Willson's radio past, which included noted song and dance men, received invitations to audition for the lead. According to *But He Doesn't Know the Territory*, the following notables were considered: Danny Kaye, Dan Dailey, Gene Kelly, Ray Bolger, Jackie Gleason, Milton Berle, Jason Robards, Art Carney, Andy Griffith, and Bert Parks. Seeking a director next required the creator to choose carefully. An early prime choice, famed scriptwriter and director Moss Hart, declined because he did not like the show. Although progress toward an opening continued, a few more bumps delayed the Broadway premiere, until Kermit Bloomgarten invited the Willsons to his New York apartment to perform the show one more time.

Many of his friends dissuaded the producer from investing his efforts in *The Music Man*, because they felt that the subject matter was too hokey for post-War sophisticated Broadway audiences. However, Bloomgarten used his natural instinct, ignored the critics and pursued the Willson project. At the next Meredith-Rini presentation, John Shubert, owner of the New York's Majestic Theatre, and director Morton DaCosta heard the show. As a result, *The Music Man* found an initial home and a pilot for its 1375 performances, as well as a director for the subsequent film version. From its initial New York performance, Meredith Willson's "speak songs" and stylistic throwbacks to music like that which the audience's grandparents enjoyed won over the crowd that included many Broadway luminaries in attendance that night.

Meredith Willson needed to solve two last main character problems before the show went into casting and rehearsals. The spastic boy subplot that never seemed right was consolidated with the introverted, lisping boy called Winthrop Paroo (who finished "The Wells Fargo Wagon" song at the end of the first act). Willson vowed to do justice with the eliminated spastic boy part in a future production, but he never did. Hill's love interest Marian showed her standoffish character in early drafts of the show and her desire for her own Lancelot to carry her away from the boredom of small-town America and life as a spinster librarian. She exhibited this character trait from her song "My White Knight," but her part was not complete. Before the summer of 1957, Willson discovered that Marian's character was merely in need of "a man who loves her, who is not ashamed of a few nice things." The admission that what she needed was a romantic counterpart who was not too stubborn to admit his intentions was all that the librarian needed to round out her character.

To make the choreography reflect the then current belief that steps should be integrated into the story as a result of plot development, the producer sought famed choreographer Michael Kidd for the show but he was unavailable. As an alternative, his untried assistant Oona White moved the characters through scenes containing dances as far ranging as the haunting "Marian the Librarian" to the raucous "Shipoopi." The critics lauded her efforts as a nostalgic return to bygone dance styles that normally would have seemed out of place with the stylized choreography so prevalent on Broadway during the post War decades.

To establish the first "miracle" of the play, as Willson referred to the casting success, an award winning barbershop quartet, The Buffalo Bills, won the right to play the role of the feuding but harmonious local school board members. Organized ten years before *The Music Man* began rehearsing, the quartet had garnered first prize in 1950 for the first international championship of the S.P.E.B.S.Q.S.A. (Society for the Preservation and Encouragement of Barbershop Quartet Singing in America.) They were subsequently featured on a number of record albums and radio and television shows like those hosted by Arthur Godfrey. Even the group's appearance exuded an appropriate pioneer flavor when they appeared in public wearing fringed costumes, despite the fact that the bison in their name actually came from their hometown of Buffalo, New York. Willson was particularly proud that his musical held perhaps the first such quartet ever, and they were the first cast members signed. Those who followed were David Burns as Mayor Shinn, Iggie Wolfington as Hill's sidekick Marcellus Washburn, Pert Kelton as Mrs. Paroo, and Barbara Cook as Marian the Librarian. Burns had been an actor in important Broadway productions as early as 1939, when he supported Monty Wooley in *The Man Who Came to Dinner*. Ultimately, he would be cast with Jack Gilford in *A Funny Thing Happened on the Way to the Forum* (1962) and with Carol Channing in *Hello, Dolly* (1964). Kelton and Wolfington appeared in many television productions in the late 1940's and 1950's, and while he made in bigger impact on the small screen, she continued primarily on stage. The female lead who rose quickly through the ranks of musical theater and continued entertaining after her Broadway debut in 1951 was Barbara Cook.

Playing the ingénue lead in *Flahooley*, a musical fantasy that also satirized the ongoing McCarthy Congressional witch hunts, gave the young Atlanta born singer the break that would start her major appearances for the next five decades. (An interesting casting connection occurred when Meredith Willson's Mason City friend Bil Baird and his wife Cora manipulated two of the puppets alongside Cook in this show.) Despite being in a musical that lost $160,000 and closed after forty performances, her opportunities continued to rise. She played Carrie Pepperidge in *Carousel*, Cunegode in Leonard Bernstein's *Candide* and Ado Annie in a revival of *Oklahoma!* After several more stage successes following *The Music Man*, Barbara Cook embarked upon a very active concert career that afforded her the chance to entertain four Presidents, perform at Carnegie Hall, sing with a number of orchestras, and travel to a variety of venues overseas. However, before any of the aforementioned qualified cast members could act in Meredith Willson's play, one very crucial part still needed to be filled.

In his third autobiographical work, Meredith Willson admitted that he learned as much as he contributed to *The Music Man*. Realizing that the entire show probably rested on a convincing lead in the part of the con man, he continued to audition in the East. At this early stage of casting the show, Meredith Willson overlooked the suggested Robert Preston, believing that the actor did not have the right credentials to play Harold Hill. Wanting to return to their home in California while hoping to lure the right person into the part, Meredith and Rini Willson flew West to talk to some old friends about the casting. The composer's heart was set on the humorous, talented, and energetic Danny Kaye, who had achieved a string of successes on radio and in films like *The Secret Life of Walter Mitty* (RKO, 1947), *The Inspector General* (Warner Brothers, 1949), and *The Court Jester* (Paramount, 1956). Believing that the part was not right for her husband, Mrs. Kaye (composer and lyricist Sylvia Fine) expressed her thanks for the consideration. Other California actors thought that the show was "too corny" or not right for them (and some later regretted the decision). Bandleader Phil Harris did not return Willson's calls, while screen musical stars Dan Dailey and Gene Kelly feigned disinterest in the project. The composer returned to New York and at the insistence of director Morton DaCosta agreed to hear Preston perform "Trouble."

Based on his previous appearances in films and on stage, Robert Preston Meservey did not seem like a potential musical lead, because most of his parts in films had been in serious dramatic roles. His biggest motion picture roles came at Paramount, where he performed in William Wellman's *Beau Geste* (1939), as well as Cecil B. DeMille's *Union Pacific* (1939) and *Northwest Mounted Police* (1940). During the 1940's, Robert Preston reprised many of his successful screen roles on the famed *Lux Radio Theater*. However, after he returned from duty in the Army Air Corps during World War II, Preston continued to be stereotyped as a tough guy in primarily westerns and war films. He decided to leave for New York in 1951, where television was opening new possibilities for actors and perhaps held different roles for himself.

Instead of finding a place on the small screen, Robert Preston starred in a variety of successful theatrical parts. After seeing him act on stage, Kermit Bloomgarten approached the actor and suggested that Preston tryout for the part of Harold Hill when the actor was performing in a Philadelphia production of *Boy Meets Girl*. The part of the con man appealed to the actor because Hill was, in Preston's words, "a slugger, a one-punch guy." Just prior to *The Music Man*'s opening, Preston shared with *The New York Times* reporter Murray Schumach: "They don't want a singer in this show. That's why I'm comfortable." He continued to explain that the part was "just an extension of my singing voice ... talking in rhythm ... wouldn't make sense any other way. The character [is] ... a cross between a gospel preacher and a con man. Besides, there's an underlying rhythm [to the show]." Not only did Robert Preston become Harold Hill and vice versa, but he also delighted audiences in the part for the first two years of the production and reprised his role in the motion picture version at the insistence of Meredith Willson.

Incidentally, for all of the people and encounters Meredith Willson borrowed and adapted from his own experiences into parts of *The Music Man*, he repeatedly refused to identify the real con man prototype. Fearing that someone might be incriminated when identified as the actual visitor to Mason City, Meredith Willson kept Harold Hill an enigma. Frank Hoare ranked among those suggested as a candidate. He arrived in Mason City after a stint as a Cornell College Conservatory violin instructor. The journeyman musician brought with him classical training and a verbal delivery that would have swayed any listener into believing that his or her child had the potential to develop both instrumental expertise and a performance personality through the new Joachim-Moser method. At the time the musical was set, on July 4, 1912, a salesman, not of musical instruments, rather of fraudulent insurance policies, and an illegal bootlegger were arrested in Mason City. Of course, Hill could have had a little bit of Squiz Hazelton, Willson's first flute teacher, Mason City music proponent W.A. Storer, or any one or part of the characters who made an impression on a young boy furthering his musical training. In his Frank Simon biography, Michael Freedland suggested that Harold Hill was Lynn Sams, long the educational director at the Conn Instrument Company and president of the Buescher Band Instrument Company.

After *The Music Man* became a hit on Broadway, newspaper reporters sought the prototype for the lead and one candidate heralded by the Mason

City paper harkened back to Willson's first foray in a boys band. James W. Jeffers not only organized boys bands in Iowa starting in 1915, but he also sold musical instruments and guaranteed that the students would be able to play a song after their first lesson and have a repertoire of twenty-five numbers when three months of lessons ended. During this era, Mason City merchants anteed up the necessary funds to outfit their town band. Jeffers completed this phase of his life, albeit more legitimate than that of Harold Hill, in 1924, when schools began organizing their own instrumental groups thus eliminating the need for a private teacher. At the time of musical's heyday, eighty-year-old Jeffers recalled that he had to convince local parents that playing in a band would be a good influence on their children's lives and keep them from nefarious activities. If any or all of the aforementioned real characters became embodied in Harold Hill, Meredith Willson of Mason City, Iowa never disclosed who he was. The composer did mention in a 1979 interview that the anonymous archetype was by that time deceased.

The last cast member to join *The Music Man* was Eddie Hodges, who played the long difficult to define character of the lisping, shy Winthrop Paroo. The ten-year-old actor was appearing on a television quiz show, *Name That Tune*, where he had been dazzling viewers with his knowledge of music, just as he had done earlier on the infamous quiz show, the *$64,000 Question*. After Rini Willson saw the boy on television, she told Meredith, "There's Winthrop." During the next several weeks, she hounded Bloomgarten and DaCosta to watch the quiz show until they relented and then finally endorsed her choice.

As the show continued to gel into a viable Broadway production, Meredith Willson carefully monitored the process. Because he was a neophyte dramatist, he watched with amazement the workings of the production staff, the directors, the musicians, and all of the others needed to take his book and music and mold them into a successful Broadway show. Likewise, as the sets moved from sketches to scenic pieces designed by Howard Bay and the costumes emerged from the colorful creations designed by Raoul Pene du Bois, the composer's enthusiasm for opening night increased. The entire ordeal of staging *The Music Man* is revealed, in Willson's now familiar Iowan style, in his book *But He Doesn't Know the Territory*, the last of the autobiographical trilogy. Among the more emotional remembrances in the recollection comes when the actors read the first words of the show in rehearsal - Meredith and Rini Willson wept.

By mid-October 1957, preparations in Philadelphia began in earnest. The show opened there on November 18, and for thirty days it played to out-of-town audiences and received last minute alterations. Meredith Willson admitted that he was apprehensive about the paying audience's role, because he was not familiar with a crowd unlike the admission-free radio audiences that he knew so well. He believed that because the radio congregation did not have to pay to see the show, they tended to laugh more readily as a result of having no financial stake in the program. On the other hand, the theater audience anted up substantial fees to be entertained and might not respond if they saw no humor in the lines.

While *The Music Man* was in rehearsal in Philadelphia, Meredith and Rini performed their duet version of the show for prospective recording companies. Capitol records won the contract, and Stu Ostrow, for whom Meredith Willson gave a recommendation to join Armed Forces Radio in 1951, managed the account. (Two years after *The Music Man* debuted, Rini and Meredith Willson recorded ... *And Then I Wrote the Music*, a Capitol records l.p. that simulated their oft-repeated rendition of the show.) Before the musical opened in Philadelphia, the singles "Seventy-Six Trombones" by the Billy Mays Orchestra, "It's You" by The Four Preps, and "Till There Was You" by Sue Rainey with the Nelson Riddle Orchestra were pressed for sales. A national audience got to hear "Goodnight, My Someone" sung by Eddie Fisher on his television program in December, and the following January on the same show, Guy Lombardo's orchestra played "Lida Rose."

The play, although complete just before its debut on Broadway, still experienced changes at the hands of Meredith Willson. One addition answered his request to get Mama Rosalie into the play by name. After taking one of his frequent walks through Central Park in New York, the composer penned "Lida Rose," a tribute to the composer's mother and her sister Lida, and the song successfully debuted at the next day's rehearsal thanks to the barbershop harmonizing of The Buffalo Bills. An early draft of the musical had Marian singing "Will I Ever Tell You?" from across the stage as an answer to their harmonizing. However, this next attempt by Willson to play one song off another did not remain, because he shelved the idea.

The rehearsing progressed at a 2nd Avenue hall, before it moved to the historically prestigious but aging New Amsterdam Roof on 42nd Street, where practices continued on a real stage. After a few more weeks of fine-tuning, rubber-stamped tickets allowed 200 friends and relatives to see a bare bones presentation of *The Music Man* at the Barrymore on 46th. Here the crowd swelled to include many of Broadway's luminaries, including directors, producers, stars, agency representatives, and television network executives. Prominent among those anticipating the trial performance was old friend Frank Loesser, the man who first encouraged Meredith Willson eight years previous and later found himself co-producing the show and the cast album. Without an orchestra, real costumes, and real scenery, the company ran through the show for the insider crowd.

Meredith and Rini clutched each other while their only child, other than their dachshund Piccolo, unfolded before the sympathetic eyes and ears of Broadway's elite. The venerable audience not only loved *The Music Man*, but when the piano broke into the "Seventy-Six Trombones" reprise at the end of the show, they were the first to engage in what would become a time-honored tradition of modifying their applause to clapping in rhythm with the march. Famed columnist Walter Kerr later referred to the phenomenon as "the rhythmic hand clapping which greeted the finale of *The Music Man* on opening night ... a single irresistible impulse ... that could not possibly have been inhibited."

Although the first reception of *The Music Man* succeeded, Meredith Willson still exercised cautious optimism for a Broadway triumph. He knew that the show's first audience, though seasoned thespians, contained many allies who wanted their friend to succeed. Real, paying patrons would be more objective, and once all of the bright scenes, costumes, and lights paraded before a full orchestra, these spectators might be distracted by the lavishness surrounding the performance and react coolly to the musical comedy itself.

The company returned to Philadelphia for its November opening. After observing the play for the first time with all of its dazzling visual elements added, Meredith Willson waited for the reviews. When the first observations trickled in, most writers except many of the all-important New York critics dubbed *The Music Man* a potential hit. Their lot questioned the critical success of a play that lacked the style of other 1950's productions and were unsure of a show that so faithfully hearkened back to simpler times. The next day, Willson went to the theater to fine tune the musical, so that when it premiered in New York a month later, the weak spots would be eliminated.

Walking around the Shubert Theatre, Meredith Willson began examining everything that could possibly distract from the performance. First, the amplification system needed to be mended, for it garbled words and projected weak sounds. A dead microphone, too few and poorly placed speakers, and consideration of what could be done to tighten the opening number were among the next alterations.

The train number suffered from being first in the show. Latecomers interrupted the concentration of those already sitting and shuffling through their programs to understand what the story was all about. He wondered if the train should be parked at the Brighton, Illinois station and then take the salesmen down the track to River City. The author objected to changing it, because he wanted the train in motion when the curtain rose. Instead, the orchestra stopped after the overture in favor of a piano accompaniment during the train scene, a surprise tactic intended to restore the audience's attention. Besides, more instruments could be added as necessity called them back.

More alterations involving the train number continued, because its position also made it the hook to grab the audience and convey them along for the ride. First, as the overture "pulled into the station," the musicians came to a halt and the salesmen took over. As the train accelerated, so did their talking. The passing lights behind the train likewise picked up speed with the action and then slowed down incrementally. A few orchestra chords were added to accent the decelerating engine. To complete the illusion, the choreography of the peddlers made them bounce along with the appropriate rhythm as if they were really riding in a 1912 passenger car and to coincide with their speech patterns.

More changes tightened the musical for the Broadway opening. Willson trimmed jokes and stage business to streamline the Main Street scene. On the other hand, he then added the naming of real Iowa towns like Mason City, Ames, and Clear Lake to end the segment. The song "Blessings" entered and later left the score, while he pared down "My White Knight." The last adjustment was the most painful to Willson, because "My White Knight" was Mama Rosalie's song, one that reflected the longings of a girl from Brighton, Illinois, who after her graduation from the Armour Institute in Chicago joined her own white knight in a small Iowa town. By the final cut, "Sincere" replaced "I Found a Horseshoe" in the first act, and in the second "Lida Rose" emerged as the favorite over "My Baby," a reprise of "Gary, Indiana" nudged out "Tomorrow," and "You Don't Have To Kiss Me Goodnight" fell from the footbridge scene altogether. Even the park name experienced a last minute revamp when Madderson became Madison at the eleventh hour.

After Meredith Willson spent many hours elevating *The Music Man* to become a prime candidate for Broadway musical success, Robert Preston created a nickname for the overly energetic composer. Willson had been constantly revising and augmenting his show in Philadelphia – thirty-eight rewrites by his estimation, and when the lead saw the opportunity, he chose an appropriate title. After Willson inserted "Blessings" as a new number, Preston observed the creator during a new plotting of the choreography for the Marian the Librarian scene. Upon seeing the unshaven and disheveled writer, he decided that he was in the presence of a biblical character who rose from the dead. Thereafter, those actors attempting to bring his story to life on the Broadway stage affectionately called Meredith Willson "Lazarus."

If any more changes could have been made to strengthen the show, *The Music Man* might have languished in Philadelphia a little longer or moved to New Haven for some more polishing time. However, Kermit Bloomgarten, Morton DaCosta, and the Willsons chose to go to New York's Majestic Theatre as scheduled. A flood of anxious emotions re-emerged in Meredith Willson, and these feelings manifested themselves at least one time when Meredith Willson of Mason City, Iowa first gazed upon the giant marquee that heralded his name and that of *The Music Man*. His return to Broadway held nostalgia; for it was there that he played in the pit orchestras in this house and many in the surrounding area. In Times Square he was christened with the nickname "Down Beat" Willson for his frequent timely arrivals just before the first note was to be heard. As the moment for the opening curtain approached, his anxieties increased, because he loved Iowa and the sentiments contained in *The Music Man*, and, he feared that hostile audiences and critics might dash their representations to pieces.

Meredith and Rini Willson did not stay in the alley on opening night as they hinted to Doug Sherwin and his KGLO audience back in Mason City prior to opening night. The couple did, however, occupy seats convenient to the exits, just in case they needed to make a hasty departure. In short, the critics hailed *The Music Man* to the point that they selected it as the best of the season over the powerful *West Side Story*. John Chapman in the *Daily News* called Willson's show "one of the few great musical comedies of the last 26 years." From the scenery to Preston's "splendid" job as the "jaunty faker," Chapman's review was echoed by Brooks Atkinson's account in the *New York Times*: Meredith Willson "has translated the thump and razzle-dazzle of brass band lore into a warm and genial cartoon of American life ... If Mark Twain could have collaborated with Vachel Lindsay, they might have devised a rhythmic lark like 'The Music Man,' which is as American as apple pie and a Fourth of July oration." Entertainment industry magazine *Variety* said of the play: "Nothing like it has ever been seen on Broadway." Famed *Herald Tribune* reviewer Walter Kerr, who had dissected hundreds of plays and films, proclaimed, "'The Music Man' is for absolutely everybody." He ended his examination by simple stating, "In short, a wow. A <u>nice</u> wow."

Before it ended its initial run, *The Music Man* played 1,375 performances. The seats at the Majestic at 44th Street and Broadway normally sold for $8.50 with a top on New Year's Eve of $10.50, but a few standing room seats were always available for $3.00. The show opened on the heels of *West Side Story* and *My Fair Lady* and was often considered the American counterpart in charm and characters to the latter show. Before Willson's play finished its initial run, it placed in the top ten most attended Broadway musicals, outdistancing *The King and I* and *Guys and Dolls*. Although its position slipped before later musicals that drew more patrons, none can compare to the popularity of this musical's life in community theater and on high school and college stages, a distinction that has never diminished. Because its inherent values and because the musical still delights audiences of all ages, *The Music Man* endures as Meredith Willson intended it, a salute to a bygone era, his hometown, and band music. During the 1999-2000 Broadway season, *The Music Man* played alongside several important revivals (including Cole Porter's *Kiss Me Kate*, the opera *Aida*, and *Jesus Christ Superstar*) and continued to entertain audiences into the 21st Century.

In a view near Central Park in Mason City, Meredith Willson proudly leads one of many bands containing "76 trombones in the big parade" at the 1958 North Iowa Band Festival. (Mason City Library Collection)

Chapter Ten
"I Ain't Down Yet"

Meredith and Rini Willson experienced a multitude of anxiety provoking moments through most of 1957; however, once *The Music Man* opened triumphantly, the two eventually basked in the glory of its resounding success. All of the sacrifices made to get the show finished and staged for the December opening were supplanted with praises and packed houses.

The years of accepting a variety of jobs to support the couple, while the musical developed, paid off immediately after the show's first successful performances. *The Music Man* initially grossed $70,000 per week and with his 7% take, the Iowa creator netted nearly $5,000 of the total. A month after the show's opening in December of 1957, advanced tickets went on sale through January of 1959. One investor in the show, who contributed $2,000, sold half of his interest when his wife disliked the musical when it was being tried out in Philadelphia. He was heartsick when he learned that what he thought might have been the waste of his hard-earned money actually would have grown ten fold.

Immediately after the play's initial success, television networks and motion picture companies began eyeing the property - to the horror of CBS. Originally, the network could have had 40% of the play for a $300,000 investment, but they remained firm about controlling the casting of the show that some of their executives dubbed "too corny." The same broadcasting giant did ante up $400,000 to support Meredith Willson's *Here's Love* in 1963. Much to their own embarrassment, the television network eventually paid over one million dollars to broadcast the motion picture version of *The Music Man* in 1966. The cost to acquire the rights to film the musical started at $1,000,000, and a line for this honor soon formed.

The media nurtured further interest in *The Music Man* when the songs played on television and radio, and as favorable newspaper articles and columns appeared. Even a small but vocal anti-*Music Man* faction appeared in New York to decry what they believed to be the over-attention that the folksy musical was receiving at the expense of other worthy shows. As a result, Brooks Atkinson returned to visit the production in September of 1958 and reiterated his original accolades. After his second visit, the famed critic proclaimed Willson's show "as fresh as it was last December" and laid praise at the feet of Robert Preston for "not losing the vibrance of his early performances." Famed columnist Walter Winchell quipped that *The Music Man* was the "only show on Broadway to which you can take a nun with no fear of embarrassment," a universal appeal that caused ticket shortages for theatergoers. In the extremely popular *Life* magazine weekly of January 20, 1958, the young musical success story jumped off the pages of the periodical, with the actors, costumes and sets lavishly printed in full color, and where the show was proclaimed "a rousing, oom-pah delight."

Cloning of the fledgling show began in March of 1958. The American touring company of *The Music Man* with Forrest Tucker in the title role quickly went into rehearsal. In order to ensure a quality road company, the choreography by Oona White, sets by Howard Bay, and costumes by Raoul Pene du Bois, were faithfully recreated to give remote audiences an accurate taste of the Broadway show. Even musical director Herbert Greene came West to oversee the production and to conduct the 1958 Los Angeles premiere. That August opening consisted of Hollywood's elite, including long-time Willson friend Dinah Shore and her husband George Montgomery, as well as Judy Garland and her spouse Sid Luft. The profits from the stellar West Coast premiere went directly to one of Meredith Willson's favorite philanthropic ventures, The Big Brothers chapter of Los Angeles. By October 1958, the road company headed to Dallas and added $75,000 per week to the financial success of the Broadway show. When the musical moved to Austin, it opened at the Texas State Fairgrounds with an advanced sale of $200,000 and where it grossed $271,000.

To appease those who wanted to hear the music but could not get into the sold out shows, the Capitol cast album temporarily sufficed. The recording came on the heels of the relatively new long-playing vinyl $33\frac{1}{3}$ RPM records that gradually augmented the then popular 45 singles. The forty-five minute abridged version of the story in high fidelity immediately accelerated the album to the top of the bestseller charts in New York City. Just as CBS passed initially on the broadcast rights, record companies like RCA Victor and Decca (both of whom had recorded Willson music before), as well as Columbia, had had a chance to record the soundtrack for the unfinished *The Music Man*. Unfortunately, all three speculated that the musical would be a failure and chose not to invest in the project. Not only did the cast album sales soar during the run of the show, but also the recording of *The Music Man* continued in popularity through changes in the recording industry that saw the musical recorded on open reel tape, cassettes, and compact discs. In addition to the recorded offerings from the musical, Meredith Willson also penned a novelization of the story in the spring of 1962.

Just as *The Music Man* became a financial success, it likewise continued to receive critical acclaim. Meredith Willson originally anticipated the New York theater reviewers as potentially merciless critics; however, much to his surprise they praised his play and even selected it as the best Broadway musical of 1957-58. In a very competitive season, *The Music Man* tied *West Side Story* on the first New York Critics Circle ballot before the Iowa tale won the title in a tie-breaking vote. The following year, the recording industry created a new award, and Meredith Willson literally received the first Grammy for his cast album. In 1959, Willson returned as emcee for the second installment of the honors, where he presented Grammys to pianist Van Cliburn and singer Bobby Darrin.

Foreign road companies, that would eventually adapt the musical for audiences as far away as mainland China, started when motion picture musical star and leading man Van Johnson won the opportunity to head the London company's opening on March 11, 1961. After playing Harold Hill in England for a year, Johnson returned to Hollywood where the show appeared for the first time in a nightclub setting at the famed Coconut Grove. This special event also represented the first musical to be presented on the Ambassador Hotel's renowned stage, one that had to be enlarged to accommodate the cast. Even though the April 20, 1962 opening date was usually a time when many celebrities enjoyed their desert homes in Palm Springs, a number of Willson's West Coast friends attended this premiere. The luminaries included Los Angeles Mayor Sam Yorty, Rosalind Russell, Jack Benny, George Burns, Spike Jones, Milton Berle, and Peter Lawford, as well as Ozzie, Harriet, and Rick Nelson. Of course, Meredith and Rini Willson nervously attended the performance, as *The Music Man* once again played before a prestigious crowd.

As early as 1965, the first Broadway revival of the show opened with Bert Parks creating his own version of Harold Hill, and in 1980, Dick Van Dyke grabbed the instrument salesman's suitcase in another very successful incarnation. Incidentally, original cast member Iggie Wolfington reprised his role as Marcellus Washburn in the latter of these two productions. In addition to its stateside success story, *The Music Man* often became the first new American musical on a number of Iron Curtain stages when it played in then communist countries like Czechoslovakia in 1970 and Poland in 1972. In 2000, *The Music Man* once again successfully ran on Broadway to another generation eager to learn about the inhabitants of River City, Iowa. On February 16, 2003, *The Wonderful World of Disney* presented a made-for-TV installment of the musical on ABC. Fresh from his award-winning role in Mel Brooks' *The Producers*, Matthew Broderick offered yet another rendition of Harold Hill. *The Music Man* never seems to grow old and never ceases to enthrall new audiences from high school productions to the Broadway stage.

After the accomplishments of the original stage production and its spin-offs on the road, serious negotiations began afresh for the film rendition of *The Music Man*. Motion picture versions of popular Broadway musicals drew audiences to motion picture theatres in the 1950's, because they offered several unique opportunities to the viewer. Until the road company of a popular Broadway show came to a fairly large city or if one were fortunate enough to see the musical on Broadway, spacious movie houses provided an admirable alternative ticket. Although television and its phenomenal growth changed American entertainment habits during the 1950's, during this decade TV set owners viewed the medium generally on a small, usually black and white screen with an inadequate speaker set in its side or front. Conversely, films of Broadway musicals like *South Pacific*, *West Side Story*, *My Fair Lady*, and *Oklahoma!* enjoyed vivid colors, a wide screen, stereophonic sound, and the intimacy of a big house that mirrored the integrity of the original live performance.

Casting the film version of *The Music Man* did not run as smoothly as Meredith Willson had hoped. As for volunteers to play the cinematic Harold Hill, popular singer and film star Frank Sinatra, fresh off his musical success *High Society*, hastened to offer his services for a part that none of his Hollywood cronies wanted several years earlier. However, before signing movie actors began, studio details for the filming needed to be ironed out. Besides, for all of the trouble that Meredith Willson went through to secure his male lead in the first place, abandonment of Robert Preston in the part was not yet a consideration. Two and a half years passed between the stage play's opening and filming began on its cinematic counterpart.

♪ ♪ ♪

Early in the musical's developmental stages, Meredith Willson usually explained that Mason City, Iowa was not the prototype for fictitious River City. Perhaps if the show would have been the flop that some rejected as "too unsophisticated" to make it on a refined Broadway stage, then a non-attachment to Willson's hometown was the better choice. When the musical took that same theater district with a vengeance, the creator affectionately and deliberately affiliated Mason City as the original home of the "Iowa stubborn." The north central Iowa town would be forever, whether directly or indirectly, assigned as the real River City of *The Music Man*. Willson even approached then Iowa Governor Herschel C. Lovelace about building a 1912 River City motion picture set somewhere near Mason City. After the company completed its filming, the period buildings could have been turned into a representation of bygone Iowa, a tourist attraction like Michigan's Greenfield Village or Virginia's Colonial Williamsburg. Unfortunately, instead of the Iowa politicians voting first on what would have been a major state expenditure, they took to the 1960 campaign trail. Unable to wait until after the end of the political season, Warner Brothers needed to start filming and did so on a California back lot.

During the annual North Iowa Band Festival in June of 1958, Meredith Willson returned triumphantly to his hometown to visit old friends and relatives, but on this occasion he donned a plumed hat to champion long suffering music directors. At the bandmasters' luncheon, where Willson had visited several times before, the man who was currently the toast of Broadway theater exuded no big city airs before the 300 directors who gave him a special presentation. Tipping his hat to the region's devotion to instrumental music, the composer proudly exclaimed that he could imagine no place else where so many kids in uniforms could be brought together in such a musical aggregation. The conductors then presented him with a golden piccolo prior to his leading the first of many bands inflated to seventy-six trombones in honor of the man who immortalized their instrument. Also appropriate for this unique meeting of bandmasters was a special visit by the Mason City barbershop quartet, The Rusty Hinge, which was forever preserved by The Buffalo Bills as the harmonizing school board in *The Music Man*. And to continue their coverage of Willson's successes, *Life* magazine sent a photographer to document how the real River City appeared when Meredith Willson returned for his 1958 visit. Likewise, the weekly's sister publication *Time* adorned its cover with images from *The Music Man* on its July 21, 1958 issue.

Meredith Willson directs a group of North Iowa high school band members past the Congregational Church in the 1958 North Iowa Band Festival parade. (Mason City Library Collection)

Leading abnormally over-sized music sections like the one immortalized in the song "Seventy-Six Trombones" became a regular occurrence for Meredith Willson when he appeared in public. In the fall of 1958, he led 600 musicians playing "Seventy-Six Trombones" and a 2,500-member chorus singing "Lida Rose" and "Will I Ever Tell You" at the Cotton Bowl football game. The following year he conducted the University of Iowa band at the 1959 Rose Bowl and led 12,500 Michigan high school musicians with 1,076 trombones during half-time show at the Southern California-Michigan football game.

Once Meredith Willson experienced the adoration of the hundreds of bandmasters and band members in his hometown, the die was cast for a love affair with the first person to honor marching bands in a musical and whose magnitude in the band music field approached that of John Philip Sousa. As a lucky coincidence, when Elkhart, Indiana, the band instrument capital of the world, decided to celebrate its centennial in 1958, their obvious choice for a grand marshal was the man who thought that bands kept kids out of trouble. Securing Meredith Willson for the gala may have helped this Indiana river city escape its own troubles, for a 1957 recession threatened to force the layoff of many Conn instrument workers. However, the newfound interest in musical instruments as a result of *The Music Man* may have saved some jobs, an ancillary benefit of the musical for which the composer was forever proud.

Meredith Willson – America's Music Man

According to one Conn official, "America needed this show ... it symbolizes the American band instrument movement." From the first successes of *The Music Man*, journals like the company's newsletter as well as other band industry and director publications praised the musical for one of Meredith Willson's important themes: the salvation of wayward youth through music. During this period, Conn began promoting its instruments with links to the composer and the musical, cleverly declaring that "Meredith Willson says: 'The Music Man' is a Conn man." According to ads in the company's *Instrumentalist*, Willson proclaimed that he knew that the company's flute was the industry leader as early as 1921, when he used such an instrument while playing with Sousa's band. To further expand connections to the popular musical, Conn instrument salesmen gave out paper *Music Man* hat reproductions with their names stamped under the "simulated gold crepe plume." When they opened their special *Music Man* sales kits, the images recalled for potential customers the valise that a different "con" man, Harold Hill, dragged into River City. Not surprisingly, the result was the largest sales increase in the company's history, with the greatest demand coming from the trombone production line.

In typical Willson fashion, the composer borrows a piccolo to show proper playing methods at the 1958 band festival. (Mason City Library Collection)

At this juncture in his career, Meredith Willson enthusiastically participated in festivals like the one held in Elkhart. While in north central Indiana, the city honored him and six other celebrated musicians during the local high school football game halftime show. The local newspaper even pictured Rini holding the first sousaphone, which was built by Conn employee Edwin Pounder for Sousa in 1898. Of course, part of the pageant included what would become an obligatory portion of any such celebration, the chance for Meredith Willson to direct seventy-six trombones and one hundred and ten cornets. All things considered, the Indiana visit was a major triumph for the city, and Willson's affiliation with the company that legitimately put instruments in the hands of idle children continued for years. As a later tribute to *The Music Man*, Conn unselfishly gave 1,076 trombones to underprivileged musicians after a 1997 production of the musical in Nappanee, Indiana.

♪ ♪ ♪

Although it was no secret that Meredith Willson believed that participation in a band might be the salvation of wayward youth; conversely, he made public his belief as to what kind of music he thought could be detrimental to responsible child development. He hated rock and roll. Shortly after he and Rini began touring and basking in the success of *The Music Man*, the composer loudly labeled the current teenage craze as "garbage ... a creeping paralysis." He condemned the big record companies for making the loud and simplistic "plague" readily available and for "prostituting the music business" just to make money. Not content to echo criticism that it was "lascivious" with "suggestive dancing," he denounced it as only "two chords," requiring "no craftsmanship, no natural ability." Sadly, he admitted that parents could do little to create an interest in composers like Brahms or Beethoven and placed the blame on the record companies. In his forward to fellow classical music lover Sigmund Spaeth's book *Fifty Years With Music*, Meredith Willson closed with: "I am grateful for every scathing word he [Spaeth] has written or spoken about the rape of the blues, that mewling, babbling destroyer of craftsmanship, that scaly corrupter of taste known as Rock 'n' Roll."

Meredith Willson's resolute opinion about the popular musical genre of the 1950's and 60's may have been altered somewhat when one of rock and roll's most popular groups, the Beatles, scored a hit with their rendition of Willson's own "Till There Was You" in 1963. Even though his diatribes against rock music continued publicly, he did defend this particular group in a rather backhanded way a year later when he said, "They have to be four brilliant young guys perpetrating the biggest hoax in show business. They are essentially satirizing the whole teen-age idol phenomenon and no parody could be more biting."

Ironically, one of rock and roll's greatest tragedies happened just a short distance from Meredith Willson's home, a little over a year after *The*

Music Man opened. "The Big Bopper" (J.P. Richardson), Richie Valens, and Buddy Holly played at Cedar Lake, Iowa's Surf Ballroom, a popular night spot just ten miles west of Mason City, as part of their 1959 three week tour. After their February 3rd performance, the singers drove back toward the Mason City municipal airport. Opting to fly in a small plane rather than take a long, overnight trip in a converted school bus, they and their pilot crashed and perished shortly after taking off. The bitter winter weather that froze up their regular tour bus a week earlier caused the plane to falter in sub-zero temperatures.

Despite the phenomenal incursion rock and roll music achieved in the popular music scene during the late 1950's, numerous opportunities honoring the success of *The Music Man* presented themselves to Meredith and Rini Willson in 1959. In March they appeared as guests on the Garry Moore television variety show with the composer recreating "Trouble" and his wife singing "Till There Was You." The couple also acted in several skits. During the fall of 1960, Meredith Willson joined Boris Goldovsky as the two played pianos to illustrate Giuseppe Verdi's use of bands in the opera *Aida* on the twentieth anniversary broadcast of the Metropolitan Opera on CBS radio. The Willsons also took a twenty-city visit to schools and civic organizations, where they shared the story of *The Music Man* and promoted Meredith's third autobiographical work, *But He Doesn't Know the Territory*, the story of getting *The Music Man* on Broadway. During 1960, Meredith and Rini Willson started taking annual tours to recount the making of *The Music Man* and *The Unsinkable Molly Brown* in formal settings like colleges and universities, as well as at impromptu stops like the Iowa School for the Blind in Vinton and Mason City's Hoover School for crippled children.

The following year, Meredith Willson took time from his busy schedule to pen the words to a new fight song for Newman High School. The Mason City parochial school received the lyrics to fit famed bandmaster Paul Yoder's tune "The Band," after superintendent Fr. William Powers made the request. As has already been mentioned, Willson had already written songs for schools, like the fight song for his own high school, one for the University of Iowa, another for Iowa State, and "in remembrance of the jewel-box campus" the melody to "Hail, Alma Mater" for Hanover College in Indiana. Appropriately, the 2000 North Iowa Band Festival opened its festivities with barbershop and instrumental music in the Newman basketball court that had been symbolically transformed into River City's Madison gymnasium. This gala event occurred the day before the opening of The Music Man Square, an area in downtown Mason City that honors Willson's boyhood home and the adjacent multipurpose building designed primarily for musical activities.

♪ ♪ ♪

During the late 1950's and early 1960's, decisions on the motion picture version of *The Music Man* progressed, while plans continued on Willson's next theatrical venture. By the spring of 1960, the filming of *The Music Man* began as part of a one-two musical punch at the Warner Brothers studio that also included the 1959 Broadway hit *Gypsy*. Once again Meredith and Rini Willson made the unenviable commute between their home in California where they oversaw the filming of *The Music Man* to New York where their new stage production, *The Unsinkable Molly Brown*, was staking its claim on Broadway. The only major sticking point for the motion picture was Willson's insistence on Robert Preston in the lead. Conversely, because film musicals require such an enormous investment, Warner Brothers desired a more bankable and recognizable screen name. One such potential singing star came to Willson's rescue. After seeing the stage play, Frank Sinatra re-entered the casting quandary, this time to help convince Jack Warner that Preston was the best choice in the role of Harold Hill, even though the Hollywood mogul preferred a better box office bet like Cary Grant in the role. Bing Crosby's agent brother Everett lobbied for his sibling to take the film part that the "crooner" had turned down when Willson sought his Broadway lead, but the singer also agreed after watching Preston create his magical role that no one else could play the movie part.

Hollywood set a precedent many years earlier when studios often cast more profitable names and often non-singing stars in a film musical leads, but Meredith Willson remained Iowa stubborn and thankfully convinced Warners to let Robert Preston recreate Harold Hill on film. The only other key players who came from the Broadway production to the film were The Buffalo Bills and Pert Kelton as Mrs. Paroo.

Morton DaCosta reprised his Broadway role as director and successfully molded a cast that included Shirley Jones, fresh off successes in several film musicals, to undertake the part of Marian the Librarian. Not quite twenty years old when Richard Rodgers heard her first audition for Laurie in the film version of *Oklahoma!* Jones' untried abilities prohibited her from being cast immediately. After listening to her audition, the composer asked if his partner, Oscar Hammerstein, Jr., could hear her sing. She agreed and replied, "Of course, and what is *your* name." The famous songwriter did not overlook Shirley Jones' talent based on her knowledge of Broadway legends but did allow the young singer to prove herself on stage before placing her in the much-anticipated Rodgers and Hammerstein film. Starring in *Oklahoma!* and later *Carousel* enhanced her reputation as a motion picture musical star and created the opportunity for her to appear in another Broadway-to-film venture, *The Music Man*. Incidentally, to keep from being typecast as the lovable heroine in film musicals, in 1960, she played a prostitute in the drama *Elmer Gantry* and won the Best Supporting Actress Academy Award for her effort.

As for the supporting cast of *The Music Man* film, an all-star group assembled from a variety of directions. Comedy film and television stalwarts Paul Ford and Hermione Gingold played the cinema Mayor and Mrs. Shinn, while rising comedy success Buddy Hackett became Harold Hill's partner Marcellus Washburn, and *The Andy Griffith Show* child star Ronnie Howard created a convincing Winthrop Paroo. After touring in the national company, Harry Hickox reprised his role as Charlie Cowell, the anvil salesman who constantly plotted to expose Harold Hill's chicanery. Susan Luckey as Zaneeta Shinn and Monique Vermont as Amaryllis also moved from the road company to their motion picture counterparts. The prognosis for the film's success seemed eminent with this talented assortment of players who would be guided by Morton DaCosta.

After Robert Preston returned in his role as Professor Harold Hill, the first real Meredith Willson motion picture became almost as successful as the stage play. Just as the creator wished, the Technicolor, wide screen, 151 minute version received an A1 rating, hence, morally objectionable to no one. Entertainment trade magazine *Variety* christened the picture "the big one for '62 ... as irresistibly corny as an Iowa landscape." In its April 12, 1962 appraisal, the trade weekly echoed a common sentiment when it predicted that just as " '76 Trombones' led the big parade, and so will 'The Music Man' - back to motion picture theatres." By the time the film opened at Radio City Music Hall in New York City, it had been grossing over $300,000 per week in the twenty-one cities where it was already playing. In London, the British press hailed the film no less enthusiastically. Especially praising Robert Preston, Dilys Powell reported for *The Times* that "To an English cinema audience the performance ... is still astonishing."

Because the show experienced few changes (the key one being "My White Knight" dropped in favor of the new number "Being in Love"), the accolades for *The Music Man* movie continued to follow those awarded the stage version. The Golden Globe of 1963 dubbed the film the year's best musical at a time when motion picture musicals made a temporary box office recovery. The genre's success in the early 1960's came alongside popular musical films like *Camelot*, *West Side Story*, *Bye, Bye Birdie*, *My Fair Lady*, and *Mary Poppins*.

Unfortunately, the Motion Picture Academy did not present as many Oscars as did its East Coast theatrical award counterparts. Only the Best

Score award went to Ray Heindorf for his music adaptation. Neither Robert Preston nor the film even received a nomination during a year that recognized more serious dramatic motion pictures like Gregory Peck's performance in *To Kill A Mocking Bird* and best film *Lawrence of Arabia*. The Writers Guild did present the film its Best Screenplay Award that year. Although Hollywood's elite rejected the public appeal and critical praise for *The Music Man* and Robert Preston, an immense tribute came from the people when the film premiered in Mason City, Iowa in June of 1962.

♪ ♪ ♪

As a result of his success as Harold Hill in *The Music Man*, new opportunities presented themselves to Robert Preston. Between his initial stint in the show's first 882 stage productions and before filming of the musical began, Preston returned to the Hollywood that earlier typecast him primarily as a rugged, dramatic, non-musical star. After his triumphant return to film *The Music Man*, he then starred in the critically acclaimed *The Dark at the Top of the Stairs*, ironically at the request of studio head Jack Warner.

Unfortunately, for most of his career, Robert Preston was often reviewed in light of his stellar performance in *The Music Man*. For example, when he attempted to play the elder statesman Benjamin Franklin in Broadway's *Ben Franklin in Paris* in 1964, *New York Times* reviewer Howard Taubman proclaimed that "neither the wig nor the fine 18th century waistcoat, breeches, and boots can fool us ... [he] is really our friend selling band instruments in Iowa." And although Preston knew that his very successful character would be difficult to shake, he hoped that the very different Franklin role would finally stop people from identifying him with Harold Hill. Eventually, time created distance from the comparison, and before the actor completed his body of work, Robert Preston starred in the 1966-67 stage musical *I Do, I Do* with Mary Martin, films including *How the West Was Won* (1963), *S.O.B.* (1981), *Victor-Victoria* (1982), and *The Last Star Fighter (1985),* and television productions like *"The Man Who Corrupted Hadleyburg"* before his death in 1987.

As for Shirley Jones, a variety of entertainment opportunities presented themselves after her appearance in *The Music Man*. However, her appearance in a situation comedy gave her the most audience recognition. After ABC television successfully created the family comedy *The Brady Bunch* for the fall of 1969, the network attempted to repeat its triumph the following year with *The Partridge Family*. Based on the premise that a widow and her children could get together and form a successful rock band, the half-hour comedy stayed on the evening schedule for four years and even produced hit songs like "I Think I Love You." The following decades witnessed Shirley Jones continuing her work acting and singing in films, on television, and on stage.

Ronnie Howard and Shirley Jones accept the key to Mason City from Charles MacNider at the press premiere of the film The Music Man in 1962. (Mason City Library Collection)

♪   ♪   ♪

Just as a train carried Meredith Willson to fame in 1919, and just as surely as that same mode of transportation brought scores of enthusiastic audience members to view River City on stage and in movie houses, a newer mode of transportation, the airplane, brought Robert Preston and the major players of the motion picture version of *The Music Man* to Mason City, Iowa for the film's world premiere. The renowned North Iowa Band Festival represented the most appropriate occasion - a high school band festival in the real River City. Moreover, the residents of the prototype Hawkeye town in the musical delighted at the chance to play host to a once-in-a-lifetime Hollywood style opening night that somewhat overshadowed the hundreds of teenagers who came to town for the band competition. Fortunately, because of the uniqueness of this particular festival, the band members did not mind taking a back seat to the activities that transpired.

Iowa put great credence in Meredith Willson's oft-touted support of municipal and especially youthful instrumental organizations. Appropriately for Willson, former New York Symphony conductor and musical counselor of NBC radio, Walter Damrosch, proclaimed on February 10, 1928, "Iowa is the most musical State in the Union." He based his remarks on the residents' responses to his classical programming that often witnessed Meredith Willson playing the flute or piccolo in the orchestra's woodwind section. Shortly after Meredith and Cedric Willson helped establish the Mason City High School band as a viable organization, musicians who followed the two brothers' footsteps elevated the organization to the extent that it performed admirably at national competitions.

As the band flourished during The Great Depression, Carleton L. Stewart, a nationally recognized director, and local businessman Lester Milligan, helped encourage Mason City to become a hub of instrumental activity in the area. In conjunction with the 1936 Iowa Bandmasters Association meeting, the first North Iowa Band Festival occurred. Except for the War Years between 1943-1945, the annual assembly grew in participants and prestige from 770 band members for the first meeting to thousands by its peak years in the 1960's. Once Meredith Willson made his mark as a nationally famous music personality, he frequently returned as the festival's guest of honor. Despite his joy at returning to his hometown, no other appearance exceeded his 1962 visit for the press premiere of *The Music Man*, and, fittingly, both Stewart and Milligan also attended the celebration.

Incredible preparations for the weekend evolved to ensure success for the 1962 North Iowa Band Festival. Popular radio and television personality of the 1950's and 1960's, Arthur Godfrey, who delighted at the kind of wholesome work that Meredith Willson turned out, agreed to emcee the festivities in Mason City. His variety shows often heralded the hometown values espoused in *The Music Man*, and one of his favorite guest groups was The Buffalo Bills. Both the film's world premiere and the band competition invited so much interest that residents had to open their homes to visitors. Mason City and its surrounding area held about 30,000 inhabitants, but on this weekend it would swell to an estimated 125,000. Among those who needed to be accommodated for the annual musical competition were 3,500 band members, many from out-of-state who were vying for a first prize of $10,000 in musical instruments. To make this special edition of the annual June event a success, the municipality raised $35,000 to augment the quarter of a million dollars invested by Warner Brothers, Richards Music Corporation and the visiting bands. The band festival that located in Mason City out of a competitive spirit to better Cedar Falls for the honor in 1936 became the focus of a worldwide audience twenty-six years later.

Realizing the special attention derived from a location premiere, the studio pulled out all publicity stops and invested its money and energy second only to MGM's output for its 1939 *Gone with the Wind* Atlanta premiere. Stars Robert Preston, Shirley Jones, The Buffalo Bills, Ronnie Howard, director Morton DaCosta, and Hollywood columnist Hedda Hopper rode in the parade that delighted thousands. On the night of June 19, 1962, the citizenry of Mason City, Iowa experienced their second major electric thrill of being associated as the home of *The Music Man*, when a worldwide audience heard the premiere festivities broadcast over the Voice of America. Likewise, 104 visiting journalists "from Portland, Maine to Portland, Oregon" reported back to their home newspapers. Enjoying typical Iowa hospitality, the visitors to Mason City were as overwhelmed with the locals' cordiality as the residents were with the celebrities' presence and the chance to host a Hollywood premiere.

In order to guarantee that the weeklong celebration was first class, long-time Willson friend and local newspaper editor Earl Hall chaired the events. Hall closely followed the development of the musical from its early days when it still bore the name *The Silver Triangle*. When he and his wife traveled East or West to see the Willsons, Meredith played many of the show's first songs for the Iowa visitors. As Earl Hall continued to gather information on a variety of Willson projects during the 1950's, he made sure that the *Globe-Gazette* reported on their progress. Subsequently, the Halls proudly attended the premiere Broadway performance of the play and visited the sets at Warner Brothers during the filming of the musical.

Robert Preston and Hedda Hopper are welcomed to Mason City by Mayor George Mendon and Vicki Ross, the 1961 North Iowa Band Festival fair queen. (Mason City Library Collection)

During the 1960's, the North Iowa Band Festival reached an impressive following, and to combine it with the movie premiere took a Herculean effort. With Mayor George E. Mendon's unequivocal support, the program, complete with a massive parade led by Meredith Willson himself included: the minting of a special gold coin honoring the composer, the Lockport (Illinois) High School band winning the competition from ninety others, the crowning of Miss North Iowa, the dedicating of the Meredith Willson footbridge over Willow Creek, and celebrities eating meals ranging from a chicken luncheon to a formal dinner at the Indianhead home of local military hero General Hanford MacNider. One example of the extensive coverage the festival received came from the *Chicago Daily News*, which reported on the success of the winning band and how the musicians took the prize money back to Lockport by climaxing their show with music from *The Music Man*. The media and those in attendance pronounced the exhausting festivities a phenomenal hit. Following the precedent set at Mason City, other openings of *The Music Man* in cities like Des Moines, Iowa, involved area bands to appropriately herald the arrival of the film.

♪ ♪ ♪

So popular was Willson's first musical that entertainment luminaries began courting the composer for their chance to work with him. The savvy Iowan took the advice of fellow Broadway composer Oscar Hammerstein, II, who encouraged Willson to reject the numerous offers that would probably come flooding in, until one presented itself, which was so powerful that it could not be refused. Months passed before such a story arrived on Willson's desk. Among the interesting few were the chances to adapt the 1937 screenplay *Saratoga* and Eugene O'Neill's 1933 stage hit *Ah, Wilderness!* into musicals. Appearing to be in harmony with Willson's style, O'Neill's play held a variety of vintage 1906 popular songs from which Willson's writing talents and personal desires to preserve such songs of the past might have found a starting point. The story also bore an enticing comedic plot involving a small town American family with the opening scene set during one of Willson's favorite holidays, The Fourth of July. Although a press release announced the O'Neill-Willson collaboration, such a show never materialized. However, the drama did see the light of day as the fairly successful 1959 Broadway musical *Take Me Along,* which starred Jackie Gleason. After careful consideration, Willson opted for a more alluring story.

Television offers likewise came to the overwhelmed Iowa native son. In 1961, Dave Kaufman, formerly of Mason City and then an NBC television producer, offered Meredith Willson his own series at $125,000 per show for fifty installments, an estimated one million dollars for record albums on a proposed series, and three million more for three years in a subsidiary income. Although the proposal of a $38 million deal seemed inviting, Willson rejected the money first from NBC and a similar one from ABC, because he "felt like an arrogant know-nothing ... you do what you think is best, what you are spiritually and emotionally involved in. I felt I was too far obligated mentally to Broadway to accept the TV deal." NBC even countered with an offer to broadcast a Willson special; all he had to do was to notify the network. Eventually, he signed with CBS television to host *The Star Parade* (CBS), a three part series with Rini.

The next Meredith Willson theatrical project after *The Music Man* came as a result of a Hollywood writer finding an intriguing tale during a 1955 vacation to Colorado. Screenwriter Richard Morris returned home to draft a preliminary story based on local legends about Johnny and Maggie Brown and then molded the ideas into a stage play. With the help of The Theatre Guild and its leader Dore Schary, whose credits included sharing an Oscar for co-writing the film *Boys Town* and a Tony for his *Sunrise At Campobello*, Morris engaged in a two-year search for a credible composer-lyricist. "If you'll take the cussin' out of there and be mindful of beautifying the love story, I'm your boy," Meredith Willson offered. And when the three parties agreed, the Iowan helped to create *The Unsinkable Molly Brown*, a project that continued to evolve until the show opened on Broadway almost exactly three years after *The Music Man* premiered.

The rags-to-riches Cinderella story of Irish chambermaid Maggie Tobin and her husband Johnny Brown appealed to Meredith Willson. This basically real story later created some problems with some critics who disbelieved the improbable tale set forth. Re-named protagonist Molly, "who was born in a cyclone in Hannibal, Missouri," really did seek her fame and fortune in Colorado, and after a series of mercurial triumphs and tragedies, unfortunately found herself on the deck of the ill-fated *Titanic* ocean liner in 1912.

The actual events that evolved into the libretto panned out in two acts. The first half chronicles Molly's early questionable social status as an unpolished backwoods yokel who works her way from a barroom hostess to the wife of successful miner Johnny Brown of Leadville. The second presents Molly and Johnny rising from the stigma of outcasts from snobbish Denver social circles to the toasts of Europe. A number of the facts in the show, like the accidental burning of $300,000 in a wood stove, were among those stretched in the name of literary license to glamorize her life. However, even the real Margaret Tobin Brown would have supported such inventions, because, in her words, "It's a damn good story." On the other hand, because she really did endure incredible hardships, like being on a ship that caught fire on the Atlantic Ocean and on another that struck a floating mine missed by World War I minesweepers, her real life does not pale in comparison to her theatrical legend. The climax of her brushes with fate in the musical occurs when, on her way back from the European continent, Molly secures for herself a $4,350 stateroom on the "unsinkable" White Lines *Titanic*. In a small lifeboat she establishes herself not only as a survivor of the ill-fated ship's maiden voyage, but also as a hero and leader.

In a year when non-musical Broadway productions with renowned stars like Bette Davis, Lucille Ball, and Henry Fonda could not stimulate audience interest, the musicals of the 1960-61 season fared somewhat better. Not only did many weak plays fold, but also for the first time since 1919, Broadway theatres closed for nearly two weeks in the summer of 1960, because of a dispute between actors and producers. The musical *Bye, Bye Birdie* succeeded as well as any that season, with *Camelot* and *Irma La Douce* also reaping a respectable return. In addition, Rogers and Hammerstein's *The Sound of Music*, which opened in 1959, successfully continued its run of 1,443 performances. One off-Broadway show, *The Fantastics*, made box office inroads into mainstream musical respectability.

Meredith Willson worked on the words and music for *The Unsinkable Molly Brown* at his home in Santa Monica, California until it opened in Philadelphia on September 26, 1960, at the same Shubert Theatre where *The Music Man* premiered. He often composed mentally on his daily long walks. Upon returning from one such three-mile stroll, he grabbed his wife and sang to her Johnny's song "If I Knew." Likewise, after another trip he penned the beautiful love song "Dolce Far Niente." However, not all of the songs came from Meredith Willson's amblings: "I'll Never Say Never Again" resulted after chewing on a Morris line in the libretto and a subsequent swim in a pool. Even though the songs progressed via the usual strolling of the composer, Molly's showstopper, "I Ain't Down Yet," did not completely gel until the second week in Philadelphia.

As was the case for the success of his first musical theater venture, Willson's new play required a strong main character. Like Robert Preston, Tammy Grimes had little experience in musicals, and also like her Preston counterpart, numerous critics praised her performance as the quintessential tomboy and society lady rolled into one. After a little less than a decade on the stage, she auditioned for *Molly Brown* by singing "Melancholy Baby." She believed that her rendition of the song won her the title roll in what was the most expensive Broadway musical to date. Nearly four months after the show opened, investors saw their $520,000 stake begin to show a profit. The star in the title role played the girl from Hannibal for over a year and then transferred her portrayal to a road company.

In similar fashion to Robert Preston's lead performance in *The Music Man*, Tammy Grimes provided the necessary enthusiasm that was required to transform her character from an unpolished stone to a gem. Generally, if a reviewer favorably analyzed the musical, he sometimes did so because he liked her performance. Such was the case for Walter Kerr, who suggested that her somewhat bizarre character might have emanated from an Edgar Allen Poe story and her attraction came from the way she mesmerized her audiences, including this venerable critic. Others like Richard Cooke for the *Wall Street Journal* and Whitney Bolton for the *New York Morning Telegraph* offered praise for the star's exuberant work. The latter proclaimed just what the patriotic composer might have wanted to read in a review: Willson "writes Americana into his music the way Betsy Ross sewed a flag. ... It is star-spangled, Yankee Doodle music, home-brewed and home-bottled." At the end of the theatrical season, the critics' poll of musicals proclaimed Tammy Grimes the best female lead over worthy competitors like Elizabeth Seal in *Irma La Douce* and Julie Andrews in *Camelot*. Harve Presnell won the best male honor for his portrayal of Johnny Brown.

Like its Willson predecessor, *Molly Brown* had its trial run in Philadelphia in the fall prior to a winter holiday opening on Broadway five weeks later. The New York reviewers generally praised the three-hour show; however, even seasoned critics were unable to avoid comparing this new theatrical venture to *The Music Man*. Such analyses continued during the play's run. For example, *Newsweek* magazine made comparisons between the two plays and added that this second venture deserved a "fanfare from the brass section." The appraisal from the magazine *America* stated that Meredith Willson's "score [was] reminiscent of the John Philip Sousa marches that were popular when Molly was assailing the ramparts of Denver society." Hollywood columnist Louella Parsons liked both the show and Tammy Grimes in the lead, adding that Marilyn Monroe had already expressed interest in the inevitable film version.

For those few who called *The Music Man* too corny and laid back, *The Unsinkable Molly Brown* offered a raucous biographical ride that should have pleased such thrill-seeking reviewers. However, many of those who wanted more rowdiness in Willson's first play named the composer's premiere outing as superior to his second and ignored their own initial inclinations. Meredith Willson was correct in his apprehensions about the press's evaluations of his shows and found himself in the same position of contemporaries Alan Jay Lerner and Frederick Loewe, whose *Camelot* was unjustly compared to their immensely popular earlier collaboration, *My Fair Lady*.

Shortly after *Molly Brown*'s opening, Capitol records released the cast album and a variety of companies offered singles. Unlike *The Music Man*, no *Molly Brown* recorded songs or performances on television appeared before the show premiered on Broadway. The intention was to allow the musical to open and create a desire for the songs. The Willsons' new Rinimer Corporation in conjunction with Frank Loesser's Frank Music Company then allowed eight different record companies to press albums and singles. Capitol held the greatest number of releases by singers like Dinah Shore, Tex Williams, and Nat King Cole. Perhaps the most unusual release was a quartet comprised of band and orchestra leaders Stan Kenton, Billy May, Nelson Riddle, and singer Ray Anthony singing "Belly Up to the Bar, Boys" with Guy Lombardo's orchestra. On other labels the performances ranged from Andre Kostelantez's orchestra providing an instrumental album of the score to Aretha Franklin singing "Are You Sure?"

To the creators' credit, *The Unsinkable Molly Brown* ran for 533 performances, not close to *The Music Man*'s tenure on Broadway but respectable enough to place just ahead of Victor Herbert's *The Red Mill* and Alexandre Breffort's *Irma La Douce* on the list of all-time box office runs. A more impressive statistic comes from the realization that both of Willson's shows ran on Broadway concurrently. Having a Broadway show receive the necessary backing and then actually debut in New York's theatre district is a monumental achievement, but only a few of the caliber of, for example, Richard Rogers and Oscar Hammerstein II ever witnessed multiple shows experiencing success in that neighborhood. After *Molly Brown* opened at the Winter Garden, New York's second largest house, *The Music Man* left the Majestic and removed to the Broadway, then the city's largest capacity theatre.

Soon after the Broadway opening of *The Unsinkable Molly Brown* on November 3, 1960, Meredith and Rini Willson left for Mason City to pay a tremendous honor to Rosalie Willson, a major addition to the Congregational Church in her name. With a $50,000 financing from the composer ("You might say that the annex represents Mama's well-deserved cut from a number of things that have turned out nicely for me.") and especially the royalties from "May the Good Lord Bless and Keep You," the size of the church building nearly doubled. The dedicatory service on November 20, 1960, included a challenge to those present to honor not

Meredith Willson – America's Music Man

only the new wing with Rosalie Willson's name, but also to continue her legacy of teaching the scriptures to all ages. Many residents who received her training and departed the church with her blessing "May the good Lord bless and keep you till we meet again" attended the ceremony.

After the stop in Iowa, the composer and his wife left for California, where filming started on *The Music Man*. Three years later Willson repeated the process by adapting *Molly Brown* into a screenplay. Like its predecessor, the new Willson musical was to have been filmed at Warner Brothers with Morton DaCosta as its director and Shirley MacLaine in the lead. However, because of legal problems MGM released the musical in 1964. Charles Walters directed the film that starred Debbie Reynolds, who was making her musical comeback. Walters' previous cinematic musical chore was Billy Rose's *Jumbo* (1962), while Reynolds assumed the role of Molly Brown after a lead role in the MGM epic *How the West Was Won*. She later expressed her appreciation for the chance to play the part, because it symbolized many of the ups and downs in her own personal life. Harve Presnell was fortunate enough to reprise his role as Johnny.

Debbie Reynolds performs "Belly Up to the Bar, Boys" for the 1964 MGM film of The Unsinkable Molly Brown. (Mason City Library Collection, MGM Studios, Inc.)

♪ ♪ ♪

With Meredith Willson's penchant for composing music to honor communities on their one hundredth birthdays, his third and perhaps most ambitious state centennial venture took place during the summer of 1959. As a result of working with producer Wayne Dailard on *The California Story* in 1950 and *The Oregon Story* in 1959, Meredith Willson contributed the music to *The Kansas Story* in 1961. After co-coordinating dancers from the Chicago Opera Ballet with folk songs representative of the Sunflower State's origins, director Vladimer Rosing melded Willson's "The Kansas Story," "American Anthem," and "My Kansas, My Home" into a musical four hundred year state history lesson.

Frank Allen Hubbell became Willson's writing counterpart, and the two formed a pageant that played to capacity crowds. With the exception of an occasional postponement as a result of summer thunderstorms, the extravaganza ran from June 13th through the 25th at Topeka's Mid American Fairgrounds and for the first two weeks in July at Wichita's Veterans' Field. As a result of helping to create the centennial history lesson that musically evolved from a Spanish conquistador's search for gold to a renowned twentieth century Kansas military hero and United States President, Dwight David Eisenhower, the state honored Meredith Willson at a governor's ball.

Essentially, *The Kansas Story* followed the format of its predecessor, *The Oregon Story*, as it wove a tale from explorers' dreams in Europe to the present day. With the exception that *Oregon* began at the court of Queen Elizabeth I of England and her intrepid Sir Francis Drake, and *Kansas* started with Charles V of Spain and explorer Francisco Vásquez de Coronado, the two state pageants traced the struggles of early pioneers, statehood, wars, and the hope for a bright second century. Set in two parts and including hundreds of participants, both spectacles integrated professional and local singers and dance groups performing original Willson songs and his arrangements of American favorites from "My Darlin' Clementine" to the "Charleston." Willson used his "American Anthem" in both, while the original "My Kansas, My Home" debuted in the Kansas festival before he reused it in his next musical *Here's Love*. Featuring 1,000 players and led by Chicago Opera Ballet singer Lucille Norman, *The Kansas Story* provided its audiences with tremendous entertainment for the top price of four dollars. So immense was the production that it took two main stages and six smaller ones to hold the performers during the two-and-a-half-hour presentation.

After Meredith Willson experienced the greatest successes of his life, the Mason City *Globe-Gazette* paid him a brief but poignant honor in its June 6, 1962 edition. The newspaper reprinted an interview by Doc

Quigg, a United Press correspondent, who queried the Iowan as to why his home was so prevalent in the composer's life. "I've thought and puzzled over why Iowa sticks with me," he recalled. "I can still hear the back screen door closing ... can see the grass in the backyard ... can hear the sound of the cold air register at the entrance of the First Congregational Church as we kids ran across it with snow on our shoes." He finished his recollections with times when he joined his brother under the pieplants in the summer and how the two would get rock salt from the barn, grab a pieplant leaf, and then grind "it down into the palm of your dirty hand where the salt was, and it was about the finest thing a fellow could eat."

Such idyllic scenes derived from a carefree childhood in Mason City, a place he departed perhaps too early but stayed entrenched in a special place in his heart. The magnitude of those images grew with the passing years yet were never displaced by his later homes. As a result, recalling his Mason City and recreating the year 1912 became the inspiration for his greatest artistic endeavors.

Chapter Eleven
"Thoughts While Strolling"

Before filming actually began on *The Unsinkable Molly Brown* and while the play was still enjoying its initial Broadway run, Meredith Willson continued writing newspaper and magazine articles, an avocation he had been nurturing for over a decade. The topics often included his personal beliefs on a variety of topics. For example, after the success of *The Music Man* on Broadway, he envisioned organizing fifty high school bands to tour European capitals as part of a goodwill gesture. Even though the ultimate gathering never fully materialized, he expounded on the idea when he visited with Doug Sherwin on KGLO the day after *The Music Man* motion picture premiered on June 21, 1962. The concept reflected Willson's life desire to occupy the time of wayward youth with wholesome diversions like a band. At the same time, he reasoned, such musical organizations could bring Willson's happy message of kids and instruments even behind the Iron Curtain that ideologically divided Eastern from Western Europe.

After *The Music Man* film premiered in his hometown, Meredith Willson once again shared his faith in band members and small towns in a newspaper column entitled "A Special Tribute to a Pennsylvania Band." In this missive he expressed pride in all band members who departed the 1962 band competition as winners, because when the instrumentalists returned home, proud communities welcomed them back regardless of how the school fared. The band in the title of the article came as a result of one lady from Lebanon writing to the composer about the jubilant residents who waited for the school buses to arrive at this southeastern Pennsylvanian town at two o'clock in the morning. Moreover, Meredith

Willson wrote of his own hometown, and how the locals opened their homes "just like in the good old days." So committed were these Iowans that when one family was summoned away to be with their daughter in Florida after the birth of her first child, they merely tacked a note on the front door that told the total strangers: "The key is under the mat. The refrigerator full of food. Have a good time."

Throughout his endeavors on Broadway, Willson contributed several columns to New York newspapers; however, the *New York Herald Tribune* and its affiliated papers nationwide frequently welcomed both Willson the subject and Willson the author to its pages. Once *The Music Man* enjoyed success on Broadway, he recalled in print the path that led him to the pinnacle of Broadway's elite. For the Herald Tribune Syndicate's "New York Theater Letter" column printed on August 25, 1958, he wrote of the proudest moments of his life from his days watching the stereopticon projection at the Congregational Church Christmas pageant to his first musical's opening. On February 1, 1959, he offered a treatise on why "Playing in a Band Instead of a Gang" helped keep him on a righteous path toward a successful career. In another column the composer came straightforward when he substituted for vacationing Walter Kerr with "TV Is Just Not Show Business." Blasting television, he said that the one-eyed medium presented specials that "stink," because they are tailor-made to meet deadlines and contain segments designed to fit between the all too predictable commercial breaks. He preferred "real show business" like radio and the theater. Even though he enjoyed his numerous guest visits to the medium, he proclaimed that he "can't stand television."

In a very timely column shortly after *Molly Brown* opened, Meredith Willson shared with readers his inability to understand "the mysterious phenomena of show business." He empathized with theater owners who tried to unravel why a certain play seemed destined for success, only to have an audience reject the notion. By the same token, he likewise did not understand unpredictable crowds that became enthralled with what those in the theatrical know determined might be a potential dud. More specifically, in "New Shows, New Woes: The 'Biz' Is Mysterious," Willson analyzed the placement of jokes near his ballad "Chick-a-Pen" and explained how he had to move the song to the second act and then back to the first act to shore up some weak spots in the show, changes needed to appease the audience's reaction.

In another column on a musical theatre topic, the music man attempted to explain his most asked question, "Do you write the music or lyrics first?" Before he committed, the composer segued into the similarities between lyrics and poetry and why "The Star Spangled Banner" is a "thrilling poem" but a challenge to a singer. He reluctantly offered that it is "easier to fit music to words than vice versa." In typical Willson fashion, he reverted to band music and explained that sticking words into someone else's fight song, like a "seventeen syllable High School [sic.] into 'On, Wisconsin'" requires a lyrical contortionist. After proffering his view on what he wrote first, he then stated apologetically that it was his social obligation to answer the question. He also added that the questioner might get the complete opposite response the next time.

♪ ♪ ♪

During the early 1960's, a variety of conflicts changed the face of Broadway. Overseas hostilities that grew with the Cold War in the 1950's escalated to the point that a third world war might become a reality. At the same time Meredith Willson endeavored to get his third musical staged. Just as the composer believed that band music might mollify those whose ideologies seemed destined for conflict, the barriers to such a tour became more pronounced and insurmountable. Not only did international tensions deliver anxieties for the American public, but also several forces at home severely harmed traditional musical productions in New York's theatre district. In short, rock and roll continued its phenomenal acceptance as the popular music force, few shows enjoyed long runs, and for three and a half months newspapers, the conduit through which the public learned of new productions, closed because of a strike. Meredith Willson continued to craft his next musical despite the uncertainties and opened it amid such obstacles in the fall of 1963.

A press release from the fall of 1961 announced that the next project for Meredith Willson after *The Unsinkable Molly Brown* would be a musical entitled *The Understudy*. After rising quickly in the ranks of musical theatre production, Stuart Ostrow planned to produce the third Willson show after Ostrow's first venture into Broadway musicals. *We Take the Town,* which debuted in March 1962, bore a hopefully prophetic title, and the show seemed destined for success with Robert Preston leading the production after the actor's triumphs in both *The Music Man* on stage and in film, as well as his second musical venture in 1963, *Nobody Loves An Albatross*. The story was based on MGM's *Viva, Villa!* and after analyzing Wallace Beery's performance as Pancho Villa in the 1934 film, Preston created his own Mexican hero-villain. Unfortunately, *We Take the Town* opened weak in New Haven and died in Philadelphia. The primary backer, Columbia Pictures, offered to invest more money in the show and see it made into a motion picture, but Ostrow declined and instead turned to Willson for the next project.

The next merger of the talented Willson and Ostrow seemed to destine *The Understudy* as their next successful musical. The intriguing concept evolved as Willson envisioned male and female leads for this backstage story similar in strength to those played by Robert Preston and Tammy Grimes. However, just as Ostrow's first production did not succeed, this first planned vehicle with Willson did not materialize either. Instead, by the end of 1961, the two announced that they would create a musical version of *The Miracle on 34th Street*. Before the team got started, the composer returned to see *The Unsinkable Molly Brown* filmed.

Numerous attempts had been made by others to secure the rights to *The Miracle on 34th Street*, a story that seemed a natural for musical theater adaptation. Twentieth Century Fox created an enduring and very successful film version of Valentine Davis' book in 1947. However, it took the golden name of Meredith Willson to convince the film company that the Ostrow production was in capable hands. Originally entitled *The Wonderful Plan*, this musical version of *The Miracle on 34th Street* was supposed to precede *The Understudy* on stage. However, the renamed *Here's Love* took two years to complete and opened its pre-Broadway run during the heat of August in Detroit. Ten days after the show's initial opening, Stuart Ostrow took over the reins as director. The musical traveled to Washington, D.C. and Philadelphia before opening at the Sam Shubert Theatre in New York on October 3, 1963.

Early reviews were mixed, with Louis Cook of Detroit proclaiming that *The Music Man* might be topped by the success of the latest Meredith Willson offering. After recounting the popular motion picture about a man named Kris Kringle who thinks that he is Santa Claus and a little girl who tries to believe in him, the production overwhelmed the critic. From the opening march representing Macy's Thanksgiving Day Parade scene through the legitimization of Kris Kringle in the "That Man Over There" reprise near the end of the show, the Michigan analyst raved about the new musical. Fellow *Detroit Free Press* reviewer Judd Arnett likewise praised the show saying that it contained "the genius for being tender without resorting to schmaltz" and proclaimed that Meredith Willson "belongs in the Hall of Fame reserved for those who possess ... 'The All-American Touch' ... [like] John Steinbeck, Walt Disney, Johnny Mercer." Early reviews expressed the concern that the basically solid show might be able to have its rough places worked out, and if this were done, *Here's Love* would probably enjoy a long run in New York. Before the show debuted on Broadway, it earned the distinction of breaking all records for road tryouts.

After watching the opening on the road, critics noted a number of weak points in the musical. *Variety* reviewer "Tew" observed that the musical had potential but cautioned that "Willson's music and lyrics, plus casting errors" might scuttle chances for the Iowan's third hit. The critic likewise condemned the musical for having too little music and too much talk, as well as poor singing from good actors. The last comment seemed directed at the vocal abilities of the love interests played by Craig Stevens, who was better known as the star of the popular late 1950's television detective series *Peter Gunn*, and Janis Paige, who achieved Broadway success in the 1954 musical *The Pajama Game*. Tew continued that he was unable to give an objective opinion of the music in *Here's Love* because of the "poor voices" and a "lackluster quality about them."

Janis Paige and Craig Stevens contemplate falling in love during the first act of Here's Love. (Mason City Library Collection)

Anticipation was high for Paige, who was featured in a November 9, 1963 *Saturday Evening Post* article after her nine-year absence from New York theater. Her last successful stage role on Broadway had been *Pajama Game*, before she left for Hollywood to make several movies and television appearances. Because of personal problems, she took four years off to recover. However, when Meredith Willson called her to assume the lead in *Here's Love,* she used the opportunity to make her comeback. She signed an eighteen-month contract to appear in the show but left before it closed during the summer of 1964.

Even though the two characters destined to fall in love seemed miscast, a few others showed more promise. "Lawrence Naismith as Mr. Kris Kringle is Santa Claus in sight and spirit," reported *Variety*, which was quick to include that early on he too struggled "with his acting chores." Fred Gwynne, who had just finished his role as one-half of the dimwitted police team of Toody and Muldoon in the Emmy winning television show *Car 54, Where Are You?* drew praise as Macy's assistant promotional director Marvin Shellhammer. Others singled out for their admirable performances included: Paul Reed (Charlie Cowell, the anvil salesman in the motion picture cast of *The Music Man*) as R.H. Macy, Cliff Hall (former straight man to radio star Jack "Baron Munchausen" Pearl) as Judge Martin Group, and David Doyle (later the manager of *Charley's Angels* on television) as the neurotic psychologist Mr. Psawyer.

Newspapers in Washington, D.C. (as well as those in Philadelphia) echoed the sentiments of the other mixed pre-Broadway appraisals after the show premiered at the National Theater. The common negative remark was that unlike other Willson efforts no memorable songs emerged. The writers must have overlooked "It's Beginning to Look A Lot like Christmas," a popular Willson Christmas song that had been written over a decade earlier and was fused to the new song "Pine Cones and Holly Berries." On a positive note, while a great deal of the Washington newspaper copy space reported on the civil rights marches in the city, it credited the casting of *Here's Love* as in harmony with then current trends to create an integrated cast. Some columnists pointed out that the play's supporting players mirrored the faces of real New York City and contained about ten percent African-American actors. On a humorous note in a volatile racial climate, the *Wall Street Journal* published a 1963 article entitled "Behind It All - Roosevelt, Reds, and Meredith Willson." The tongue-in-cheek story told of how these three might have spawned the civil rights movement. The link to Willson occurred because a nineteen-year-old Chicago student incorrectly identified the creator of "Seventy-Six Trombones" as the person who "tried to get into the University of Mississippi." Of course, the reporter mistook the sixty-one year old Iowan with James Meredith, the first African-American to integrate the formerly segregated school.

When *Here's Love* opened on Broadway on October 3, 1963, the famed theatre district found itself in the depths of its worst years outside of The Great Depression. Television's growing popularity, escalating production costs, and increasing flight to the suburbs contributed to the downward spiral. Out of the ordinary shows began to emerge as producers attempted to lure audiences back to live theatre. During the spring of 1961, the motion picture *Lili* made the transition to the stage as *Carnival*, a story of a lame puppeteer who falls in love but can only express himself through his puppet. The following fall, long-time Willson friend Frank Loesser scored another hit with his satire on big business, *How To Succeed in Business Without Really Trying*. However, the season after that saw virtually no American musicals enjoying sustained success. Instead, two British shows, *Stop the World I Want to Get Off* and *Oliver*, captivated audiences just as their rock and roll countrymen, The Beatles, were doing in the popular music world. When Meredith Willson's *Here's Love* opened, it represented just one of nine new productions on all of Broadway that played over 200 performances, a dismal season that witnessed dramatic improvements the next year. Despite the dark financial cloud that hung over the famed theatrical district in the fall of 1963, *Here's Love* premiered at the Shubert Theatre with the best opening week in its then fifty year history. The Christmas musical enjoyed a one million dollar advance sale.

Like those in Detroit, Washington, and Philadelphia, New York reviewers offered mixed opinions of *Here's Love* that often contained similar praises and complaints about the new Broadway show. The unanimous concern was how to pan Santa Claus, a seemingly impossible task, especially in lieu of the main theme of the play and because of Lawrence Naismith's convincing portrayal. Hence, the role of Kris Kringle seemed relatively safe from negative scrutiny. Michael Kidd's spirited choreography, especially the opening Macy's parade, often faired better than Alvin Colt's costumes, which were sometimes noted as louder than the singers. Howard Taubman of the *New York Times* felt that the show was well "engineered" and "efficient," but "the fantasy in the plot is not matched in the telling on the stage." Ending with a qualified endorsement that proclaimed the musical good family fare, Taubman continued saying that few surprises were to be found in the unraveling of the tale. *Saturday Review* critic Henry Hewes echoed these sentiments, calling Willson's third venture "tamely routine and undistinguished ... suitable for children, and for want of competition, should run until the day we all throw out our Christmas trees."

As a novel sidelight to a Broadway opening, Macy's department store, the primary location for the scenes in the musical, offered an unusual tie-in to the show. In early August, two months before *Here's Love* opened in New York, costume designer Alvin Colt visited the Seventh Avenue flagship store. Feigning the usual creative license to originate all of his own costumes, he instead used outfits off the store's racks from commonly manufactured lines. Once the clothing was identified with the musical, the sales promotion and public relations head advertised the Macy's connection, noting that patrons could purchase the same outfits from the popular department store.

Unfortunately, a great pall fell over early performances of *Here's Love* when, at the end of the second month of its Broadway run, an assassin took the life of President John F. Kennedy. The loss was particularly devastating to Willson, because the President had been one of the musician's devotees, and the Chief Executive had presented the music man with a cherished award two years earlier. As the winter holiday season approached, a very busy time for theater audiences, the depression of losing the nation's young leader forced the show to regroup and regain its momentum.

Despite the lackluster reviews, *Here's Love* continued as a modest success and completed a respectable 338 performance run. Before it closed on July 25, 1964, the most distant time for audiences to be thinking of Santa Claus, several cast changes occurred. Film star John Payne replaced Richard Kiley, who had taken the male love interest from Craig Stevens. Likewise, Lisa Kirk ended the show in the female lead. Naismith continued as Kris Kringle. On August 3, the Los Angeles Civic Light Opera Company, which would debut Meredith Willson's next and final musical, presented the West Coast version of the show. Unfortunately, a movie version of the show never materialized. However, on October 3, 1963, Columbia recorded a cast album, which Sony records deemed worthy of transfer to compact disk thirty years later. Additionally, *Here's Love* continues to re-emerge in local productions.

♪ ♪ ♪

Shortly before *Here's Love* closed, Meredith and Rini Willson hosted three CBS television specials for Texaco. The hour-long shows, rich with anecdotes about Iowa, began on June 4, 1963, with special guest Robert Preston. Rebelling against traditional television fare (offering the predictable), instead of the obvious offering of Preston singing "Trouble," Willson decided to perform the number himself as he had done dozens of times before when he tried to sell the play in New York or just share it with a variety of audiences. Typical of a Willson-conceived production, the first show emphasized folksy topics and positive images.

The entire program series exuded all of the benchmarks that epitomized the composer's beliefs and writings. For example, during this first show one segment spotlighted Meredith's recreation of John Philip Sousa leading a band. On a more somber note, he chose this program to publicly introduce his new song, "Ask Not," a tribute to the late John F. Kennedy. Initially, the musician attempted to have Frank Loesser write the number based on the late President's famous speech. Nonetheless, the Iowan capitulated when his old friend believed that Willson could do a better job. The project remained secret until its debut on the television special. Essentially, the words "Ask what you can do for your country" and an additional verse listing the thirteen colonies shaped the framework of the lyrics, which resembled "the form of a Negro spiritual." Motion picture and television columnist Bob Thomas predicted that it might "endure as long as '76 Trombones.'"

Meredith and Rini Willson sing a duet on their summer series for CBS television in 1963. (Mason City Library Collection)

Representing good, wholesome popular singers of the day, Caterina Valenti, Sergio Franchi, and The Young Americans joined the Willsons in a down home setting, and in the finale the ensemble gathered around the piano to eat popcorn and sing. "That's the way we did it back in Mason City," announced Meredith Willson as he shared the fun he experienced in his home state. Years later Cousin Doris Blakesley recalled that her father, cousin Clell Squires, and Meredith always loved cooking up a pile of popcorn that covered the kitchen table, enjoying the stack and family fellowship until the last kernel was gone.

Debbie Reynolds joined the Willsons on the second show on June 30 to reprise some of her *Unsinkable Molly Brown* numbers from the film, while popular singers Vicki Carr and Jack Jones headed another patriotic assemblage on July 28. From Willson's "Chicken Fat" song written to encourage America's youth to exercise to The Young Americans singing his "My Kansas, My Home" and an original commercial, the last program represented a smorgasbord of the Iowan's best creations. At the end of this show, producer George Schlatter organized an impressive tribute to Willson in appreciation for the composer's unwavering support for the American Armed Forces. The producer stationed 1,000 marines from Camp Pendleton on top of the CBS building to stand at attention as the U.S. Marine Drum and Bugle Corps played "Seventy-Six Trombones."

♪ ♪ ♪

Throughout the early 1960's, Meredith Willson's efforts as a leader in philanthropic and humanitarian endeavors netted him nearly as much recognition as his musicals garnered. In 1961, President Kennedy presented Willson the Big Brother of the Year Award for the composer's "deep and abiding interest in the welfare of youth." The honor was particularly significant, because in 1955, Meredith Willson organized the Los Angeles chapter of this group that helped pair men with fatherless boys. The year before Willson's national recognition, he and friend Walt Disney gave the greater Los Angeles Big Brother of the Year Award to then Vice President Richard Nixon. The National Fathers' Day Committee likewise awarded Willson their Humanitarian of the Year Award of 1962 for his activities with the Los Angeles Big Brothers, while music groups like the American Guild of Organists also presented him with their highest honor.

In the 1962, the composer wrote the "Chicken Fat" song for President Kennedy's youth fitness program. The new march was intended as a rallying call for children to encourage their families to start exercising. In an attempt to have its workforce get into physical shape, executives at the Young and Rubicam advertising agency created an exercising program for its 1,600 employees. After the company committed to the healthful program, an executive contacted Willson to create a composition that would inspire exercise and become a theme song for an active lifestyle. Distributed free to elementary schools by the U.S. Jaycees, the Capitol single instructed youth to "give the chicken fat back to the chicken" and included one version by Robert Preston.

Appropriately, in 1963, Meredith Willson was named honorary chairman for National Library Week and was given a Gold Library Card from the librarians of Los Angeles (the Marians). He also received recognition from the Illinois Association of Broadcasters, the Parents Magazine Award, a citation from the Los Angeles City Council, the first annual Music Award of Texas, a fellowship in the International Institute of Arts and Letters, the Annual Award of Masquers (Hollywood's oldest show business club), and in recognition of his efforts to bring people together through song, he was the featured speaker at a meeting of The National Conference of Christians and Jews. During the next several years, Meredith Willson received many awards, but two epitomized the heights to which the composer had ascended. In January of 1966, Willson became the National Honorary Christmas Seals Chairman, and President Lyndon Johnson appointed the composer to serve on the newly formed National Foundation on the Arts and Humanities.

With Rini looking on, Meredith Willson accepts The Big Brother of the Year Award from President Kennedy in 1961. (Mason City Library Collection)

From the late 1930's onward, Meredith Willson concerned himself with preserving musical creations and performances that he felt might not survive the test of time. His radio shows frequently included "forgotten songs" and his plays echoed music and dance styles of earlier ages; therefore, in 1963, he donated his entire Armed Forces Radio Services Programs to the Hollywood Museum. Not only do these recordings capture the enthusiasm that the entertainment community fostered unselfishly during the Second World War, but they also represent many one-of-a-kind performances that were often destroyed after disk jockeys and television replaced the type of radio on which Meredith Willson performed. Similarly, in 1965, he outbid a Hollywood music dealer for what was "the largest private collection of sheet music in America." After anteing up $6,100 for the 400,000 pieces, some dating before the Civil

War, he announced plans to donate the entire collection to the University of California at Los Angeles, where the pieces would be preserved.

Prior to the Texaco specials in the summer of 1964, Meredith Willson began his fourth musical, a tribute to his wife Rini. Intended to be a biographical study of her experiences as a concert artist in Europe, the project was never completed. Instead, the woman who was to be embodied as a new protagonist in a musical met an antagonist that the composer had never considered and which unfortunately created a tragic ending to their love story.

Chapter Twelve
"My White Knight"

Meredith Willson continued composing after his triumphant television series in 1964, but his desire to persevere was burdened by the knowledge that his beloved Rini had a short time to live. He abandoned plans to write a musical based on his wife's early life, and in October 1964, announced that his next theatrical venture would be *1491*, a show about Christopher Columbus that was to be ready for the 1967-68 season. However, his creativity was slowed because the woman, who encouraged him to complete his first theatrical success and then helped him sell the show to dozens of potential producers, directors, and theatre literati, faced terminal cancer.

A 1960 *American Home* magazine article focused on the residence built from the Willsons' accomplishments in music. The feature story chronicled their lives from their first meeting in 1938, when she was a guest on the *Good News* radio show. According to the report, they dubbed an office in the house the "words room" and another room the "music room." Although two grand pianos stood back to back near an organ in the living room, Meredith instead chose to do his composing on a less impressive spinet. There he positioned himself in a modified armchair in front of a composing board that took the place of the traditional music rack. Mementos from the Sousa days and the philharmonic concerts, a clock given to him when he visited the Elkhart centennial, the gold piccolo he received at the 1958 bandmasters convention in Mason City, a Grammy, and a gold cast album of *The Music Man* also decorated the room.

The daughter of a Russian father and French mother, Ralina Zarova came to the United States in 1927 at age fifteen where she continued her musical training. After playing in nightclubs and on stage, she made her first network appearance on NBC radio in the late 1930's. Zarova, as she was often billed, stayed in Mexico during the Second World War and then returned to become a United States citizen. After her arrival, she acted in New York and Los Angeles and scored some successes in motion pictures and with the Pacific Opera Company. Her path once again crossed Meredith's at the time his first marriage to Peggy officially ended in 1948. Both Cedric and Dixie Willson joined the new couple at their wedding the same year.

Rini usually accompanied Meredith to a variety of venues, such as their SRO appearances at the Hollywood Bowl. On one occasion, when she returned home with a cold, a minor disaster occurred. Performing their two-person show by himself, Willson fell off the stage. Bruised but not seriously hurt, the still sick Rini rushed to his side so he could finish the tour. By the fall of 1966, this time traveling as the National Honorary Chairman of Christmas Seals, he announced at the organization's fall kick-off program in Des Moines that his wife was seriously ill. After riding along with Meredith on his meteoric rise during the 1950's and 1960's, Rini left a void in his life when she died at age 54 on December 6, 1966, not just because he lost a beloved marital partner, but also because he lost the person who struggled with his greatest creations. It was she who lovingly criticized him along the way, sang the female parts of his latest creation, and helped him sell his shows during his most productive years.

When Rini died, notes of sympathy, flowers, and telegrams came from hundreds of friends and relatives who enjoyed their lives. Among the correspondents were dozens of chapters of the American Tuberculosis Society; the Salvation Army; colleges where Meredith and Rini performed; Hollywood directors, producers, actors, agents, and studios; the SPEBSQSA; Mamie Eisenhower; long time friend Abe Meyer; old friends from the military, music industry, and radio; and cousins from Iowa.

Two hand-written notes typified those received, yet were especially significant. Ex-wife Peggy (now VanBomel) expressed, "Am so very sorry about Rini. I always liked her because she was a good wife to you." Long-time friend Frank Loesser poignantly shared: "There are no lyrics or music for this time now." He continued by recalling the wonderful times spent with the Willsons, of raw cauliflower, dachshund Piccolo chasing the cat into the piano, and his friend Meredith announcing from out of nowhere at a party that Rini was his darling. Loesser recalled his pride in identifying the implacable "Iowa style" that was Meredith Willson in the good times with Rini and reminded his friend "how beautifully good you have had it."

To carry on with the work that he and Rini so loved together, Meredith Willson returned to complete *1491*. By the time of his wife's death, he had already spent time researching all he could find on Christopher Columbus at the explorer's European starting points in Spain and Italy, in the Library of Congress, and at UCLA. After attempting to clarify muddy uncertainties about the explorer's early life, Willson decided that because there were few tangible facts, the composer could exercise his literary license and fabricate some. The one fact established early in the project and which experienced no changes was the production company that would premiere the musical, the Los Angeles Civic Light Opera. The composer intended to tryout the production in Los Angeles, move on to San Francisco, and then open on Broadway ten years after *The Music Man* debuted; however, the time frame changed when Rini became ill.

A half-year after Rini's passing, Meredith Willson recalled his ex-secretary Rosemary Sullivan and wondered if she was still unmarried. Having worked in film studios like Monogram after she moved west from her Michigan home, the career girl was still available. She endeared herself to him nearly thirty years earlier when she came to California for a vacation and to take in a Willson-directed radio show. Rosemary first met the conductor backstage in her hometown of Detroit, where he was guest conducting on the *Ford Sunday Evening Hour.* She was a tremendous fan of his musical style and especially of his then popular hit "You and I." After he offered her a chance to join the audience of the *Maxwell House Show* in 1941, she and a girlfriend headed to Los Angeles to accept his proposal.

After the two disembarked in the film capital, they left a call at NBC announcing their arrival. Their initial joy became quickly overshadowed because they could not contact conductor Meredith Willson. As the time to leave for home grew closer, the chance to watch him and a network show first hand diminished. The young women believed that the experience might not materialize, but fortunately, a timely message left at their hotel indicated that they should come to the NBC studio. Upon arrival they were ushered to very special seats. Unable to obtain places in the studio audience for the last show of the season, Meredith Willson did find space for them in the sponsor's booth. The visitors were delighted to be watching a Hollywood network radio program, although they felt somewhat awkward next to the nattily dressed General Foods executives.

After making his acquaintance before the Second World War, Rosemary kept up with the composer over the years. She eventually returned to California, where she found employment with the movie studios. When Meredith and Rini moved back to the Los Angeles area after *The Music Man* opened in New York, the couple found themselves in need of a secretary, because their current one chose not to make the trip West. The Willsons remembered Rosemary, contacted her, and offered her a job. She left her studio position, but when the Willsons departed for Europe in 1964, she decided that she needed to establish permanent employment. Until the music man called on her three years later, Rosemary Sullivan worked at Universal and Paramount pictures.

The once fan of Meredith Willson became his wife on Valentine's Day 1968, and although she admitted that her musical knowledge was not as strong as that of Rini's, Rosemary provided the love and support that carried the composer through his final years. She even witnessed him hosting the popular Garry Moore daytime show in June of 1968. Early on, Rosemary realized that her husband's creative habits involved an early rising and concentrated composing until he took his afternoon walk. It was on this two to three hour stroll that he ruminated over the morning's writing: he played out the songs in his head until he was ready to return and do the necessary editing. While he was in the music room built with the proceeds from *The Unsinkable Molly Brown*, his new wife soon learned that she should not knock on the door when she wanted the composer. The tapping disrupted his thought process, but a light scratching on the door informed him that a message was at hand. It was his option as to whether he responded or not. Among his compositions in 1967 was a tribute to the fiftieth anniversary of The American Legion, a march for drum and bugle that was a six-eight throwback to his Sousa years.

♪ ♪ ♪

Los Angeles Times writer Ed Ainsworth originally put the germ of an idea for a story in the composer's ear after the columnist returned from a trip to Spain. Believing that the origin of the guitar in 1491 might be the spark to start a musical, Willson and Ainsworth agreed that the instrument's story might not be as interesting as what else was happening on the Iberian Peninsula that year. In the interim of getting the now guitarless script about Christopher Columbus completed, Meredith lost his second creative partner when Ainsworth died in 1968. When Willson returned to composing again after Rini's death, he sought to do justice to her memory and Ainsworth's by finishing the musical with help from writers Richard Morris and Ira Barmak.

Taking liberties with history, Meredith Willson assumed that one element carefully omitted from other biographies was that Christopher Columbus had a mistress. It was from this illicit relationship, as well as that of the seemingly stagnant relationship between King Ferdinand and Queen Isabella, that the singing and dancing before the big voyage to America originates. With a twinkle in his eye, Willson defended his story as unprovable, and the composer's literary license allowed him to fabricate a prediscovery character based on post discovery writings. For example, because Columbus wrote volumes, when far less information was needed, Willson assumed that the explorer was a prototype for later verbose New World politicians. Because of the adventurer's power of persuasion, Willson surmised that Columbus talked the queen into selling some of her jewels and other valuables to fund a trip by a fairly non-scientific explorer. The Italian adventurer was, indeed, an historical predecessor of super salesman Harold Hill. The character of Columbus even emulates his theatrical forerunner of the first Willson stage production when the Harold Hill method of speak-singing convinces the Spanish audience that the world might not be flat.

Willson explained that his three main characters essentially formed a love triangle, the nucleus of his show. He portrayed Queen Isabella and mistress Beatriz as being in competition for the explorer's affections. Columbus loved Beatriz, but Isabella had the resources to fund the trip. Because the mistress loved him so much, she was willing to give up anything so he could pursue his goals. King Ferdinand was mostly in the show to offer comic relief and money for the trip. Willson easily suggested that life with Ferdinand did not fulfill the passion of the outgoing queen and that Columbus might provide her with the desired excitement.

Progress on *1491* resumed during the summer of 1969 on the heels of another great adventure, the first landing on the moon. The musical with exploration as its theme seemed likely to capture the attention of a nation excited about the greatest exploration since Columbus' journey and weary of Vietnam War news. In anticipation of the long-awaited Willson show and in celebration of the safe return of the first American lunar crew, Meredith Willson attended a gala diner with the astronauts a few weeks before his new show opened.

With the exception of a West Coast road premiere instead of tryouts in the East, the production continued with the enthusiasm and quality of Willson's previous shows. Before the rehearsals began, an admirable company assembled. Richard Morris, formidable creator of the Molly Brown libretto, contributed to Willson's story and directed the production. Fresh off successes as Laertes in Richard Burton's *Hamlet* and the male lead in *On A Clear Day You Can See Forever*, John Cullum emerged as an estimable choice as Columbus. Coincidentally, Cullum, who made his Broadway debut in *Camelot*, also played opposite Robert Preston in *We Take The Town* seven years earlier. Jean Fenn as the queen was likewise qualified, as was Broadway's fiery Chita Rivera as Beatriz. Talented Gino Conforti capably portrayed the ineffectual King Ferdinand. With such a stellar cast in the Los Angeles Light Opera's final season production, what went wrong?

The show opened September 2, 1969, at the Dorothy Chandler Pavilion in Los Angeles, with the full intentions of moving to San Francisco before a Broadway opening. However, the musical barely made it out of Southern California. Perhaps an omen of the course that the show would take came when Steven Arlen (Don Esteban, the nefarious bounder who attempts to scuttle the explorer's plan to discover America) found that he might not carry out his role because the local Actors Equity believed that he was ineligible to perform. Arlen sued the opera company to prevent anyone else from taking his part, and the opening one week after the suit was initiated seemed in question. Ultimately, participation in the show did little to enhance his theatrical reputation.

The *Variety* review of *1491* decimated the production, calling it an "unbelievable bore." It liked neither the book nor the score and noted that the musical only exhibited an iota of life at the end of the first act. The main complaint stemmed from the lack of a sense of coherency between the musical's three stories: the plan to outfit ships for the New World, the love story between Columbus and Beatriz, and the interest Isabella shows in the explorer. The reviewer lauded the acting and singing, but completely panned the second act as "ridiculously melodramatic." He continued by lambasting the portrayal of Ferdinand as completely historically inaccurate and felt revulsion at the king being portrayed as a bi-sexual lecher, licentiously eyeing Columbus on the one hand, while bragging about the bastard children that he fathered under the pseudonym Tio Paco on the other. The costumes and sets received the most praise. The reviewer concluded that aside from a complete rewriting, the show would not be ready for Broadway rehearsals several weeks hence.

Other reviews of Willson's "romantic speculation" were just as severe. Winfred Blevins reported for the *Herald-Examiner* newspapers that the serious parts were funnier than those intended as humorous. Her key objection to the show was that the authors made the lead look foolhardy and only pretending to be heroic. Her greatest approval came for the song "The Queen and the Sailor," the primarily spoken number wherein Columbus poses his case for financing before the solicitous Queen. Dan

Sullivan of the *Los Angeles Times* simply stated that the improbable story could have been fun, but it ended up simply dull. He added that Cullum's Columbus was a poor Harold Hill "selling maps instead of trombones" in a comparison to *The Music Man* that was echoed by other reviewers. To confound matters, on opening night Jean Fenn experienced vocal troubles.

A rare, poor quality, and unprofessionally recorded audiotape, gives the listener a fair impression of a typical performance. Harkening back to Willson's passages from his *Missions of California Symphony* and the opening number used in *The Kansas Story*, the composer starts his show with similar regal Spanish melodies. A rousing number to a drum cadence, "Gloryland" represents Columbus' challenge to the sailors that he hopes will start them marching into his exploration camp. Great applause follows the spirited tap-dancing troops, who agree to the leader's call to make the trip in uncharted waters "for God and country." Another favorable audience response resulted from Beatriz' "Why Not?" late in the second act. However, even though the audience seemed to be having a good time, their enthusiasm waned as the show wore on.

In his own appraisal, as the musical was readied for its opening at the Curran Theatre in San Francisco on October 28, Meredith Willson explained his new project in a dramatic column for the Bay Area audience. He espoused his historically indefensible position that inevitably Columbus and Isabella "wittingly or unwittingly would fall in love with each other." The composer continued to explain that his job was to wrestle with the cast, "their strengths, their weaknesses, and their unwitting involvements in an adventure." After Meredith Willson explained his case, he likened the adventuresome spirit of the show to the unreal quality of Columbia's earlier journey to the moon. Ironically, the city that held so many wonderful memories early in his career also represented the unsatisfying final chapter of his theatrical endeavors.

♪ ♪ ♪

After *1491* closed in San Francisco, the now sixty-seven year old Meredith Willson continued composing and appearing with his one-man show. At the request of the governor of Iowa, the Mason Cityan composed "Iowa - A Place To Grow" to stimulate development in the state. He also created a three-part *Mass of the Bells*, which included the invocation "Lord, Have Mercy," praise sections "Glory to God" and "Holy, Holy, Holy," and the benedictory "Lamb of God." Dedicated to his sister Dixie who died in 1974 and with a footnote that the composer was a well-traveled flautist (he lists a representative sampling of virtually everyone he joined in musical groups from his teen years to NBC), he published his nostalgic *A Suite for Flute* in four parts. The piece that moved from the moderately fast opening section to two graceful parts and then back to a quickly paced tribute to John Philip Sousa's summer home includes "The Second Flight of the Bumblebee," "Gracefully, Please, Not Fast," "Would You Believe E^b?" and "The Whippoorwill in Willow Grove Park." The last section contains a few notes of "Whose Dream Are You" and "Seventy-Six Trombones" to bring the flautist full circle and back to The March King. Also during that year, the composer who was always answered the call to write for American Presidents wrote the inspirational song "W.I.N." His call to "Whip Inflation Now" came after a request from President Ford to create an inspirational song to help solve the country's economic woes. One final musical tribute from Meredith was his "Nocturne for Piano," which was published in 1977 and dedicated to Rosemary Willson.

Walt Disney, Meredith Willson and Vice President Richard Nixon enjoy the first "magic kingdom" opening day ceremonies at Disneyland in 1955. (Mason City Library Collection)

As an honor to his fellow Midwesterner, Meredith Willson was on hand to help Walt Disney open both of his famous family amusement parks. Walt Disney and Willson became friends when their paths crossed in Los Angeles before the Second World War. Born in Chicago, Disney's teething years in animation paralleled Willson's formative years in New York in the 1920's. By the time the two established themselves in Southern

California during the next decade, their similar small town, Midwestern values created mutual interests. During the War, they both dedicated their talents to the American military effort. Meredith and Rini were especially delighted to be on hand for their friend's 1955 Disneyland opening day ceremonies. The modern amusement park reflected the musician's love of wholesome family entertainment starting with its Main Street decorated to look like America shortly after the start of the twentieth century. Of course, Willson loved the family setting right down to the parades and strolling barbershop quartets. Willson and Disney helped promote The Big Brothers Los Angeles Chapter in the 1950's, and the great filmmaker even empathized with Rini by sharing his own serious illness with her just a month and a half before the two died within days of each other.

Disney expanded his dream for a new generation of amusement parks on October 25, 1971, when Florida's Walt Disney World opened. Meredith Willson reprised his role as an honored guest at the opening ceremony as a tribute to his late friend. On the occasion of the park's debut and at the climax of the ninety minute television special heralding the grand opening, he led 1,076 band members down Main Street for the first parade of what became a daily occurrence in The Magic Kingdom.

After Rini's death and often with Rosemary by his side, Meredith Willson resumed his visits to symphonies, colleges, and universities. These solo concerts often included his ascending the podium to direct the evening's entertainment. When he appeared at a typical performance, like the one at Indiana State University on May 13, 1970, most of the program included his own work. He spent three days in Terre Haute for rehearsals with the orchestra, a luncheon with local music teachers, a formal gathering so he could be inducted into the local chapter of Phi Mu Alpha Sinfonia, and a meeting with university officials and the press. By the time the performance was at hand, the genial wit of the Iowan had created a rapport with many in the community, providing the town with a once only experience.

After host conductor Dr. Earle R. Melendy opened the program with Von Suppe's "Light Cavalry Overture," Willson took the baton to direct Gounod's "Ballet Music From Faust," which was followed by Sousa's "Washington Post March" and Herbert's "Love Scene From Serenade For Strings." The next section included the director's own music: highlights from *The Unsinkable Molly Brown*, "San Juan Bautista," "The Band," "The American Legion March," "Prelude to America," and a medley from *The Music Man*, an all-Willson chain broken only by Von Suppe's "Poet and Peasant Overture." For the university, the performance marked the last of their long-running guest conductor appearances, in Dr. Melendy's words, "with a bang" for an auditorium audience of 1800 and an overflow group watching in an adjacent room via closed circuit television. To punctuate the concert's finale, by this time the now obligatory seventy-six trombones and 110 cornets made up of local high school juniors and seniors marched in from the back of the hall to the delight of the crowd. For all of Meredith Willson's accomplishments, this moment of enjoying the youth of America parade before him as band members never diminished. For an encore he sat down at the piano and led the assemblage in "May the Good Lord Bless and Keep You." The song did not seem to fit the mood of many protesting campuses during that era, but for those gathered at ISU that night the nostalgia that the song held was the exact reason they came.

Willson surveys the brass section of the Indiana State University orchestra at a rehearsal for the May 13, 1970 concert. (Earle Melendy collection)

Late in Meredith Willson's career, he continued on projects that had been near to his heart. He even began a sequel to his third autobiographical work, *Eggs I Have Laid*, with the new installment intended as *More Eggs I Have Laid*. He examined Irving Stone's biography of Jack London, *Sailor on Horseback*, and envisioned the adventuresome novelist's life as the subject of a new musical. Among his projects in the 1970's, he composed the music for Hanover College's alma mater, worked on a fight song for Florida Tech University, and created new lyrics for "Seventy-Six Trombones" in honor of America's bicentennial.

Throughout Meredith Willson's final years, and even after his death, he received numerous accolades for his career. As a result of writing the school's fight song, he became the first honorary life member of The State University of Iowa Alumni Association in 1951, and one of three recipients (another was Willson friend Earl Hall) of the Distinguished Service Award by UI President Virgil M. Hancher in 1963. His first honorary doctorate came from Coe College in Cedar Rapids, Iowa in 1959. He also received honorary doctorates from Parsons College and the Indiana Institute of Technology. However, when the honor was repeated in 1979, at Wartburg College in Waverly, Iowa, he was so touched when he received the degree that the Iowan was nearly unable to speak. After he fought back the tears, he exclaimed, in his best Harold Hill voice, "Yeah, I'm crying! What else?" When asked by reporters if he became more emotional at honors bestowed in his home state, he tapped his chest and said, "It always hits you right here."

Among other recognition received late in his career were accolades from charitable groups, from those who appreciated the decency Willson portrayed in his works, from libraries, the military and civic organizations. He was also awarded an induction into the Songwriters Hall of Fame and the Carbon Mic Award from the Pacific Pioneer Broadcasters. The American Bandmasters association also gave him the rarely conferred Edwin Franko Goldman Award. Perhaps the most prestigious national award came posthumously when his wife Rosemary accepted the Presidential Medal of Freedom on her husband's behalf from President Ronald Reagan in 1986. The President recalled to her that the cavalry, in which the Chief Executive served during the Second World War, did not have its own song until Meredith Willson composed it. To the surprised and delighted audience, the President sang "Hit the Leather" at the ceremony, a tribute to the many unheralded songs written by the distinguished Iowan and perhaps as a thank you for Willson's fervent support proffered during the 1980 presidential race when he loaned "Seventy-Six Trombones" to the Republican candidate. Two years later another honor, which probably would have created a flood of emotions for him, occurred when Meredith Willson joined a very august group as he received the eleventh Iowa Award for his devotion to his home state. On May 10, 1992, the Julliard School of Music dedicated an entire dormitory floor to one of its most famous "non-graduates." Upon disembarking from the elevator to the area, the first image to greet the hopeful students is a large picture of the genial Iowan whose contributions to popular American music continues to lend encouragement to similar promising musicians studying in New York City.

Newspaper obituaries generally chose two things that earmarked the life of Meredith Willson, who died June 15, 1984: he created some of the most enduring pieces of musical art, and he was always the quintessential Iowan. Even though he was advancing in years and many of his friends and relatives had gone to their rewards, he never ceased delighting in returns to his hometown and engaging in activities as simple as sitting in the park and listening to a band. He returned for the last time on June 22, when he was eulogized in the familiar First Congregational Church before burial in Elmwood Cemetery. In his opening prayer, Pastor Robert Stone bade a farewell to Rosemary's husband, "our friend, our hero, our COUSIN -- Meredith Willson." Then he urged the congregation to "belt out" the hymns, as Willson would have wanted. Later in the service, the clergyman added that the music man "was a sucker for anyone who asked him for help ... He was Iowa stubborn," and also that he generously supported the addition to the church named in his mother's honor by continuing to send money for its maintenance. Mason City Mayor Kenneth Kew offered his remembrances on behalf of the community. Those who attended the services came from as far away as California, Texas, and Florida, and included Iowa Governor Terry Branstad, men in three piece suits, teenagers, the elderly, members of the local police force, and children bedecked in their summer finery - an appropriate cross section of America.

Those who enjoyed Robert Meredith Willson's music lined up by the hundreds to bid farewell to the man who made Mason City famous and so many people happy with his musical talents. Dozens stood along the funeral route dressed in costumes from *The Music Man*. As the cortege passed in front of the Willson home on South Pennsylvania Avenue, a quartet stood on the lawn and sang "Lida Rose, I'm Home Again Rose," and then doffed their straw hats to the appreciative widow and out of respect for their champion. After a brief ride, Meredith Willson rejoined Mama Rosalie, Papa John and sister Dixie in their beloved Mason City, Iowa.

Many reporters often ask a prolific composer what is the musician's favorite composition. When Meredith Willson responded to one such query, he thought awhile and gave a somewhat surprising answer. Averse to actually picking a favorite from his hundreds of songs, his children as he called them, he cautiously pronounced "Iowa" as his favorite. Written in 1944 and sung by masters like Bing Crosby, the loving tune about Willson's home state was a modest success. If he would have chosen "Seventy-Six Trombones" over any other song in *The Music Man*, he might have done his greatest success a disservice. Had he done the same with "I Ain't Down Yet" from *Molly Brown*, "It's Beginning To Look a Lot Like Christmas," "You and I," or even "May the Good Lord Bless and Keep You," all of the other orphaned wonderful songs would have paled by their exclusion. However, when pressed for a choice, he picked the one song that represented what took him to all of the rest and then brought him back again time after time to his beloved state. If Meredith Willson of Mason City, Iowa had to choose, he made an appropriate choice. The song meant the family homestead on Pennsylvania Avenue, Mama's five fingered exercises and Sunday school kids, Sousa, Toscanini, NBC, Armed Forces Radio, George and Gracie, Tallulah, seventy-six trombones, a brass bed, and pinecones and holly berries. It also represented the place where he excitedly walked Rini or Rosemary from street to street, pointing out familiar landmarks until they too felt at home.

Several years after Meredith Willson died, Governor Terry Branstad contacted Rosemary Willson to see if she would help cut some red tape so that the state could use "Iowa" as a theme song for an important motivational campaign. In the early 1980's, the state suffered from a myriad of farm foreclosures and economic calamities, and the governor believed that using music by its favorite son might rally the people and lift their spirits. Whether or not the song was instrumental in reversing Iowa's disastrous financial tailspin is of less importance than its representation of the fortitude that resulted, a kindred pioneering spirit like that which brought Alonzo Willson to north central Iowa one hundred and thirty years earlier. Thankfully, the state recovered and returned to its prominence as an agricultural, industrial, and cultural leader. In Willson's words:

> I-O-WA, it's a beautiful name
> When you say it like we say it back home,
> It's the robin in the willows,
> It's the postmaster's friendly hello.
> I-O-WA, it's a beautiful name
> You'll remember it wherever you roam;
> It's the sumac in September,
> It's the squeak of your shoes in the snow.
> It's the Sunday school and the old river bend,
> Songs on the porch after dark;
> It's the corner store and a penny to spend
> You and your girl in the park.
> I-O-WA, it's a beautiful name
> When you say it like we say it back home,
> It's a promise for tomorrow
> And a mem'ry of long, long ago.
> ("I-O-WA," Variety Music, Inc, 1944)

Mason City, Iowa did not forget its fabled native son. Appropriately, a later version of the town library immortalized in *The Music Man* became a repository of Willson family information, and a place where parties interested in their lives, as well as other important people and events of the north central Iowa municipality, could study. Of more recent interest to the visitor is the Willson boyhood home, which sits across the street from the present library. After volunteers worked hundreds of painstaking hours, the home has been restored to look as it did in 1912, a very happy year for the Willson family and the setting for *The Music Man*. As the centennial birthday of Meredith Willson approached, The Mason City Foundation spearheaded the development of the block adjacent to the family home as a cultural area devoted to the city's native son. By 2002, Music Man Square, complete with ice cream parlor, music lessons, and a museum dedicated to the accomplishments of Meredith Willson and his family became a focal point for cultural gatherings in Mason City. And for those who visit his hometown in search of its music man, one need look no further than the many signs and banners that herald the annual band festival, for their cartoon trombonist "Mr. Toot" bears an intentional resemblance to the bespeckled composer whose life story revolved around kids in bands.

Looking very much like a cartoon Meredith Willson playing a trombone, Mr. Toot adorns the oversized drum that annually travels in the North Iowa Band Festival. (author's collection, Mr. Toot symbol used with permission granted from the Mason City Foundation)

Appendix A
Meredith Willson's
Musical Compositions

The compositions below are listed by copyright date if known. If the copyright date is unknown, then it is listed under its first appearance. This list is definitely not complete and probably never will be, especially because Meredith Willson wrote many pieces for radio which may remain lost until a certain program on which "new" Willson music appears is unearthed and identified.

1927 Two

1928 Parade Fantastique
      My Cavalier (with Hugo Riesenfeld)
      American Fox Trot

1929 Skyline
      The Tornado
      The Seige
      The Phenomena
      Aramis March
      Defiance
      Odalisque

1930 The Jamboree March

1931 One Day of Love
      Woe Is Me

1933 Show Us The Way, Blue Eagle

1934 The Song of Steel
O.O. McIntyre Suite: Thingamabobs, Thoughts While Strolling, Local Boy Makes Good

1935 Radio City Suite

1936 Smile With Me
contributed music to Republic serial Undersea Kingdom

1937 House of Melody (John Nesbitt lyrics)
Our Destination Is Heaven (music to Edna Fischer's lyrics)

1938 Wings on High

1939 Rhapsody in Green

1940 Silly Dilly

1940 (The Liberty Bell - arrangement of Sousa march)
Rock-a-Bye Your Baby with a Long Underwear Song (for Maxwell House Coffee Time)
The Great Dictator piano score (ten items)
The Great Dictator cues
The Great Dictator - The Incident
Zigeuner (with Charles Chaplin)

1941 Falling Star (with Charles Chaplin and Eddie Delange from The Great Dictator)
Never Feel Too Weary To Pray (from The Little Foxes)
Little Foxes cues
You and I
Two in Love

1942 America Calling
Remember Hawaii
My Ten Ton Baby and Me
And Still the Volga Flows
The Tuscarora
Gangway, You Rats, Gangway

1943 Fire Up – Carry On To Victory
Yankee Doodle Girl
Mind If I Tell You I Love You?
KC-Toky-I-O

The Jervis Bay

1944 Iowa
Hit the Leather
Mail Call March

1945 Whose Dream Are You? (from "O.O. McIntyre Suite" 2nd Movement)
The Same Little Chapel
Happy, Happy, Happy (+8 more) Wedding Day (for Command Performance)

1946 The Missions of California (also 2nd Symphony)
Pi Phi Sweetheart
There Must Be Little Cupids in the Briny
Moon, Moon
Canada Dry Show cues
Radio Suite: Gracie, George, Postman, Postman Visits the Burns House, Bill

1947 I'd Like a Memory
Canada Dry and I
Ford Summer Series cues
Oh, I Wanna Go

1948 Symphony of San Francisco
Iowa Indian Song
Just Becuz
San Gabriel
Symphonic Variations on an American Theme
Cow Ponies Always Weep Just a Little
All Puckered Up For Love

1949 Gone To Chicago
Every Day (radio show theme)
The Peony Bush
Memories I'll Never Forget
JELLO Pudding Sounds
JELLO Shimmer
Old JELLO Theme
JELLO Family Round
Willson Tag
Tapioca Polka

1950   An American Anthem
        The California Story
        May the Good Lord Bless and Keep You
        Derry-Up, Derry-Down Dey
        Anthem of the Atomic Age (with Pastor Mark Hogue)
        The Falstaff Meredith Willson theme song
        This Is It
        While We Were Young
        And There I Stood With My Piccolo
        The Big Show incidental music
        Iowa Fight Song
        Till I Met You/Till There Was You (The Music Man*)

1951   I See the Moon
        Let Freedom Ring
        It's Easter Time
        Any Town Is Paris When You're Young
        Here Comes the Springtime
        It's Beginning To Look A Lot Like Christmas (Here's Love*)
        Laura Lee (lyrics and waltz adaptation of Aura Lee)
        Don't Put Bandanas on Bananas
        The Little Hours Music
        Hullabaloo (for The Big Show)
        How I Love the Music of a Band (for The Big Show)
        You Can't Have a Show Without Durante (with Sammy Cahn for The Big Show)
        Three Chimes of Silver
        Zing Zing, Zoom Zoom

1952   I Take a Dim View
        Banners and Bonnets (for The Salvation Army)
        Answer the Call (for The Red Cross)
        I Got News
        The Margarets' Waltz (for The Big Show)
        Let's All Do the Festival Waltz
        Who Needs What Moonlight?
        Hallelujah, It's Tallulahvision at Last (for All Star Revue)
        It's Half Past Kissin' Time and Time To Kiss Again
        Fedalia
        Chords

1953   Practice Makes Perfect
       Music Across the Waters
       Mother Darling
       Piccolo Polka
       I Take Just as Much Pride in My Dear Little Bride
       Finagle
       A Child's Letter
       Ignore Dior
       I'll Never Say Goodbye to You Again
       Cherokee Kid
       Thirty-two Bars of I Love You
       Nylons
       Politely
       The World's Your Oyster
       You Will Hear It Soon
       My Little Bird
       Lawn Mower Waltz
       Sneezing Violins
       Ike's Golf Game
       Annaconda Copper
       Arkansas
       We're Spending Our Honeymoon in Escrow
       A Chuckle a Day
       Indian Music
       Centennial March
       If There Were No Women at All
       If There Were No Men in the World
       Chestnut Street
       I Know It and You Know It
       My Grandmother's Grandfather's Clock
       Husband
       It's Good For You
       My Signature
       Afraid
       Dining Car
       Mule Horse Sense
       Running Water
       The Last Word
       Magic Valley
       Fan Mail
       I Love You

Old Fashioned Waltz
Spindletop
Passengers Will Kindly Step to the Back of the Bus
Callico Square Dance
Fillamaroo
Occupancy of this Building is Limited to 382 Persons by Order of the NY Fire Department
Three Ways Up
Lift Up Your Voice
I'll Sing No Duet with You
Baie Verte La
Timbuctoo
Crypto-Vestimenta-Cyclo-Furo-Mania
The World Famous Horseshoe Curve
Rosalie
At the Junction of the Chenango and Susquehana Rivers
Boy Meets Girl
Bluestem Bowl
Blue Ridge Mountains of North Carolina
Palmy Pinellas Peninsula
Green Bay, Wisconsin
Chuck Wagon Gang
Everybody Knows Everybody
Toot-a-Loor
Gold Rush Towns
Waukegan Was a Thriving and Prosperous Town Before Jack Benny Came Along
Dynamite Blasting
Blue Ridge Mountains of North Carolina
Timpanogos Glacier
The Doors of the World Swing on New Britain Hinges
Bowbells, North Dakota
Cadenza
Blue Ridge Mountains (Tennessee style)
Florida Oranges
Complexities of Radio
Two Famous Words
To Shorten or Not To Shorten
Twenty-First Century
The City (background music)
A Song Coming On (for All Star Revue)

        Mason City, Go
        Green Bay, Wisconsin

1954   Alabama Christmas
        Blow
        Wisconsin Cheese
        Jamboree
        Gary, Indiana (The Music Man*)
        Canada Dry Water
        Ford's Out in Front
        On The Big Red Letter
        God Bless the One I Love
        Roving and Dreaming
        Hi Lee, Hi Low
        We're Going to Schenectady
        Wonderful Plan
        Eat, Drink and Be Healthy
        I Want To Go To Chicago
        Kiss the Girls Good Morning
        For I For S Forever
        Florida Fresh Frozen Concentrate

1955   Freedom Song

1956   Share the Luck (for the Red Cross)

1957   (The Music Man – see also above for additional titles*)

        Rock Island
        Iowa Stubborn
        Ya Got Trouble
        Goodnight, My Someone
        Seventy-Six Trombones
        Sincere
        The Sadder But Wiser Girl for Me
        Pick-a-Little, Talk-a-Little/Good Night, Ladies
        Marian the Librarian
        My White Knight
        The Wells Fargo Wagon
        It's You
        Shipoopi
        Lida Rose
        Will I Ever Tell You?

1960 (The Unsinkable Molly Brown)
  Belly Up to the Bar Boys
  I Ain't Down Yet
  I'll Never Say No
  Are You Sure?
  Leadville Johnny Brown
  My Own Brass Bed
  Dolce Far Niente
  Chick-a-Pen
  Bon Jour
  If I Knew
  Happy Birthday, Mrs. J.J. Brown
  Bea-u-ti-ful People of Denver
  I've A'Ready Started In
  Keep-A-Hoppin'
  The Denver Police

1961 My Kansas, My Home (Here's Love*)
  Newman High School Fight Song (lyrics to Paul Yoder's "The Band")

1962 (from The Music Man motion picture)
  If You Don't Mind My Saying So
  Being in Love

1963 (Here's Love)
  Parade
  The Big Clown Balloons
  Arm in Arm
  You Don't Know
  Adeste Fidelis March (arranged by Meredith Willson)
  The Bugle
  Here's Love
  My Wish
  Plastic Alligator
  Pine Cone and Holly Berries
  Look, Little Girl
  Expect Things To Happen
  Dear Mister Santa Claus
  Love, Come Take Me Again
  She Hadda Go Back
  That Man Over There

1964 (from The Unsinkable Molly Brown motion picture)
Colorado, My Home
Star Parade cues
He's My Friend

1968 The American Legion March

1969 (1491)
Pretty Girl
Get A Map
The Silken Song
Birthday ...
The Siege at Loha 3
I For My Glory Land
Sail On
Woman
Every Woman Is A Queen
But I Will Never Say
Tio Paco
Isabella Catholica
The Trastamara Rose
The Queen and the Sailor
The Wonderful Plan
Genius
With Love
Why Not?
Lady
Lash the Wheel
What Does A Queen Have?

1970 Iowa - A Place To Grow
Mass of the Bells
Alma Mater Hanover College (music)

1971 Ask Not (first played on CBS television 1964)

1974 A Suite for Flute
W.I.N. (Whip Inflation Now)
Songs with unknown or unverifiable copyright dates:
And That Is That
Answer Me
British Grenadiers
Buffalo Fight Song

Cabadaster
Cadence
Christmas Presents
Complaint Fanfare
Country Tune
Do Sol Do
Dosi Dos
Fiddle Iddle Up
For A Song
Fourth, The
G Minor Is My Favorite Key
Gay Friends Are Essential
Gentle and Sentimental
Gentleman Tramp Cues
Goodnight, My Darling
Haffner
Heart Fund Valentine Cues
Here Comes the Queen
Horse Sense
I Know Why
I May Never Fall In Love With You
It Is G It Is Minor It Is Mozart
Josephine
Just Like A Song
Just Like A Woman
Melody Man, The
Mule, The
Now We Sing
Number Four
Oh, Where Can There Be
Oh, Where Oh, Where
Polonaise Militaire
Rakoczy March
Remington Rollamatic March
Riverside Drive
Robert Schumann
Scherzo, The
Sequence
Sing Fiddle Sing
Summer Breeze Song
This Concerto Has It

This Is the Song
Toodelso
Up Where People Are
Up Where The Joke's Going On
Very Giacoso
What A Wonderful Song
Where's The Third One?
Yuma and Fun

Appendix B
List of Radio and
Television Appearances

The following is a comprehensive but definitely not a complete record of all of Meredith Willson's appearances on radio and television. Not all information is available to complete the entries, but this author believes that even fragmented references are helpful to the reader and may be perfected as the information comes to light. The programs are listed as they appeared in the evening in the Eastern Time Zone unless followed by PT for Pacific Time or otherwise noted. All of the shows are radio appearances unless designated as TV.

1926   1st NBC network broadcast w/Walter Damrosch & NY Philharmonic (November 15)

1928-29   (at KJR in Seattle) orchestra leader

1929-1935   (at KFRC, KGO, and KPO in San Francisco) orchestra leader

1929   Blue Monday Jamboree (KFRC frequently on Monday nights) orchestra leader

1932   The Heckler Surprise Party (CBS Thursday 12:00 PT) orchestra leader

1932   Waltz Time orchestra leader

1932   Concert in Rhythm orchestra leader

1933-34   Captain Dobbsie's Ship of Joy (NBC) orchestra leader

1933-35   Captain Dobbsie's Ship of Joy (NBC Monday 8:30 PT) orchestra leader

1935   Meredith Willson Show (NBC Monday 8:30) host

1933-39   Carefree Carnival (NBC Sunday 2:00 PT) orchestra leader

1930's   The Big Ten orchestra leader

1930's   The Wandering Minstrel orchestra leader

1930's   Melody Masquerade orchestra leader

1930's   Stars in the Afternoon orchestra leader

1936   San Francisco Symphony (KPO Sunday 2:00 PT) guest conducts his "Symphony in F Minor"

1936   Magic Key (NBC April 24) guest conductor

1936-37   Meredith Willson Orchestra (NBC Tuesday 9:00 and Wednesday 10:30 PT) host

1937   Maxwell House Show Boat (NBC October 12) orchestra leader

1937-38   Good News (NBC Thursday 9:00) orchestra leader

1938   National Infantile Paralysis Program (KPO January 6) orchestra leader

1938   Ford Sunday Evening Hour (CBS Sunday 9:00) guest conductor

1938   Armistice Night Program (NBC November 12) orchestra leader

1938   National Rededication Movement (NBC December 14) orchestra leader

1938-39   Good News (NBC Thursday 9:00) orchestra leader

1939   America Calling (NBC June 14) orchestra leader

1939-40   Good News (NBC Thursday 9:00) orchestra leader

1941   10th Anniversary Salute to Radio Guide (NBC) guest

1939   The March of Dimes (NBC January 20) Franklin Delano Roosevelt's birthday – orchestra leader

1940   Fibber McGee and Molly (NBC June 25) guest

1940   Meredith Willson's Musical Revue (NBC Tuesday 9:30 July through September) summer host

1941   CBS Symphony Orchestra (CBS August 10) Meredith Willson conducts his Missions of California symphony

1940-41   Maxwell House Coffee Time (NBC Thursday 8:00) orchestra leader

1941   The March of Dimes (NBC) (16parts) Roosevelt's birthday – orchestra leader

1941   America Calling: Greek War Relief (NBC and CBS February 8) orchestra leader

1941   How To Write a Script (NBC March 17) orchestra leader

1941   USO Program (NBC June 30) orchestra leader

1941   Ford Summer Hour (CBS Sunday 9:00) guest conductor

1941   Rexall's Parade of Stars (NBC November 2-8) guest conductor

1941-42   Maxwell House Coffee Time (NBC Thursday 8:00) orchestra leader

1942   Horace Heidt's Treasure Chest (NBC January 20) guest conductor

1942   The President's Diamond Jubilee Birthday (NBC January 30) orchestra leader

1942   USO Program (NBC May 30) orchestra leader

1942   Three Thirds of a Nation (NBC series during June and July) orchestra leader

1942   Fibber McGee and Molly (NBC June 23) guest

1942   Victory Parade (NBC June 7 and August 23) orchestra leader

1942   Meredith Willson's Musical Revue (NBC Tuesday 9:30 June through September) summer host

1942-45   Mail Call, At Ease, Command Performance, Jubilee, Front Line Theater, G.I. Jive, Music Shop, Concert Hall. (AFRS) Meredith Willson headed the military network that produced hundreds of shows for service personnel

1944   Army Hour (NBC April 16) guest

1944 Three Thirds of a Nation (NBC 11 shows) orchestra leader

1944 5th War Loan Drive NBC Day (NBC June 13) guest

1944 6th War Loan Drive (NBC November 23) guest

1944 The Show Is On (NBC December 6) guest

1945-46 The Burns and Allen Show (NBC Thursday 8:00 Eastern)

1945 Stars in the Afternoon (CBS September 29) promotional show for the new CBS season

1945 Hollywood Salutes FDR (NBC April 15) Meredith Willson conducts "San Juan Bautista"

1945 Victory Day (NBC September 2) guest

1945 Bird's Eye Open House (NBC May 2) guest

1946 Request Performance (CBS January 27) guest

1946 Meredith Willson Show (NBC June through August) summer host

1945-46 Sparkle Time (CBS Friday 7:30) host

1946 Here's to the Veterans (NBC October 16) guest

1946-47 The Burns and Allen Show (NBC Thursday 8:30) orchestra leader

1946-47 Sparkle Time (CBS Friday 7:30) host

1947 Command Performance (AFRS) guest

1947 Here's to the Veterans (NBC February 9) guest

1947-48 The Burns and Allen Show (NBC Thursday 8:30) orchestra leader

1947 The Ford Show Room (CBS Wednesday 9:30) host

1947 Mail Call (AFRS August 19) guest

1947 Christmas Seals Show (distributed for Christmas Seals) guest

1948-1949 Meredith Willson Show (ABC Wednesday 10:30) host

1948 Standard Symphony Hour (NBC Sunday) guest

1948-49   The Burns and Allen Show (NBC Thursday 8:30) orchestra leader part of the season

1948   At Ease (AFRS June through July) summer orchestra leader

1948   Mary Margaret McBride (NBC June 29) guest

1948   Command Performance (AFRS October 5) guest

1948   The Burns and Allen Show (NBC December 30) guest

1948-49   Meredith Willson Show   (ABC Wednesday 10:30)

1948-49   The Aldrich Family (NBC Thursday 8:00) talking people commercials

1949   Meredith Willson Show (NBC Sunday 8:30 August through September) summer host

1949 Concert Hall (AFRS March-April) orchestra leader

1949   The Meredith Willson Show (NBC TV Sunday 8:30) host

1949   Hallmark Playhouse (CBS March 3) radio version of And There I Stood w/My Piccolo

1950   The Meredith Willson Show (NBC Tuesday, Wednesday, Thursday 9:30) host

1950   Lewis-Howe: Starlight Concert (NBC) guests and directs his "Anthem of the Atomic Age"

1950-51   The Big Show (NBC Sunday 6:00) orchestra leader

1951-52   The Big Show (NBC Sunday 6:30) orchestra leader

1951   Al Goodman's Musical Album guest

1951-52   Meredith Willson Music Room (NBC Wednesday 10:30) host

1951-52   The Name's the Same (ABC TV Wednesday 7:30) panelist

1952-53   The Name's the Same (ABC TV Tuesday 10:30) panelist

1952   Meredith Willson Music Room (NBC Sunday 8:00) host

1952-53   Every Day (NBC Monday through Friday 9:45 AM) host

1952-53   Encore (NBC Monday 10:00) orchestra leader

1953   Meredith Willson's Music Room (NBC Saturday 10:30) host

1952-3 The All Star Revue (NBC TV September 27) orchestra leader

1952 Answer the Call (distributed for the American Red Cross February 2) orchestra leader

1952 Stars in Khaki & Blue (distributed for the Armed Services April 27 and May 18)

1952 NBC Special Christmas Eve Program (NBC December 24) orchestra leader

1953 Meredith Willson's Music Room (NBC Saturday 10:30) host

1953 NBC Heart Fund Show (NBC February 13) host

1952-54 Every Day (NBC Monday through Friday) host

1954 Two in the Balcony (September 6) guest

1955 How To Listen to Long Haired Music (NBC) host

1955 Make the Connection (NBC TV) guest

1955-56 Weekday (NBC) host

1957 The NBC Bandstand (NBC December 19) Willson and the cast of The Music Man

1958 Nightline guest

1958 Grammy Awards (NBC TV) recipient

1959 Grammy Awards   (NBC TV Nov 29) emcee

1959 Garry Moore Show (CBS TV March 31) guest

1961 Army of Stars (distributed for Salvation Army) guest

1961 The Dinah Shore Show (NBC TV) guest

1963 The Tonight Show (NBC TV11:30 Monday through Friday) guest

1964 The Star Parade (CBS three Thursdays 10:00) host of summer show

1968 The Garry Moore Show (CBS daytime) guest host

Appendix C
Selected Meredith Willson Recordings

The listed numbers are a brief sampling of typical Meredith Willson recordings. Because so many of his songs were recorded by a variety of artists, attempting to list them all would certainly result in an incomplete study. Instead here is a brief representation of a few titles.

... and then I wrote The Music Man (Capitol l.p. #T1320) Meredith and Rini Willson "sing and tell their story of THE MUSIC MAN."

"Banners and Bonnets" and "Unseen Rider" (RCA 45 47-4761) Meredith Willson, his orchestra and chorus

"Chicken Fat" (Capitol 45 #LB738) Robert Preston

Chiffon Swing (Decca l.p. #DL5074) instrumental selections by Meredith Willson and His Orchestra

Collector's Choice/Time-Life Music: AFRS "Swingin' 'Round the Clock – New Year's Eve 1944 "Adjutant's Call" Major Meredith Willson and the AFRS Band

Decca series of Meredith Willson conducted numbers (Decca 45's) "Kiss Me Goodnight" and "WhileWe're Young" (#9-24625), "The Dream of Olwen" and "Similau" (#9-24626), and "Two in Love"and "You and I" (#9-27854)

Here's Love (Sony CD ASIN #B0000027W8) Broadway soundtrack

"Iowa" (Decca 78 #18912A) Bing Crosby

"Iowa Indian Song" (Decca 78 #24800) Bing Crosby

"It's Beginning To Look a Lot Like Christmas" (Decca 78 #DL8128) Bing Crosby

"May the Good Lord Bless and Keep You" (RCA l.p. #AHL10793) Jim Reeves on Sacred Songs

Modern American Music (Decca l.p. #DL8025) A collection of American songs written in classical styles. Meredith Willson conducts.

"Thoughts While Strolling" (Decca 45 #28286B) Meredith Willson flute solo

"You and I" (Decca 78 #3840B) Bing Crosby

"Two in Love" (RCA Victor 76 #27611) Frank Sinatra

The Music Man (Warner Brothers CD ASIN #B000002K9Y) Broadway soundtrack

"The Peony Bush" (Decca 78 #24784) Danny Kaye

The Unsinkable Molly Brown (Emd/Angel CD #B0000025NL) Broadway soundtrack

Works Cited

Please note: many of the newspaper articles below are from a variety of sources. Not all had authors, titles, dates, and page numbers. This is especially true of the *Mason City Globe-Gazette* articles clipped for Rosalie Willson's scrapbook and *the* Willson family archives.

"A Flattering Offer." *Mason City Globe-Gazette* July 1909: n.p.

"About John Philip Sousa." Posted on 17 November 1999. http://www.dws.org/sousa/about.htm.

Adams, James Truslow, ed. *Dictionary of American History*. New York: Charles Scribner's Sons, 1940.

"Affair of the Follies, An." *The New York Times* 28 November 1926: 22: 2.

"All Artists Engaged for Mason City Summer Band." *Mason City Globe-Gazette* 7 June 1920: 1.

"Amazing Rise of Authoress of Quaint Stories." *The New York Times* 28 November 1926: VIII, 7:3.

"And There I Stood With My Piccolo." *Hallmark Playhouse*. NBC. 3 March 1949.

Anspacher, Carolyn. "S.F. 'Lives' in Music." *San Francisco Chronicle* 12 April 1936: 5.

ASCAP motion picture cue sheet collection. New York City.

Atkinson, Brooks. ... *The New York Times* 20 December 1957: 31.

Atkinson, Brooks. "'Music Man' Reprise," *The New York Times* 28 September 1958: II,1:1.

Author's old time radio collection (300 titles with Meredith Willson as conductor or guest from 1935 to 1969.)

Author's video collection (Meredith Willson appearances on television during the 1950's through the 1970's.)

Aylesworth, Thomas G. *Broadway to Hollywood.* Greenwich, CT: Bison Books Corp., 1985.

"Bakery Stock Transferred." *Mason City Globe-Gazette* 14 May 1927: 6.

Balio, Tino. *United Artists: The Company Built by the Stars.* Madison, WI: The University of Wisconsin Press, 1976.

Barnouw, Erik. *A Tower in Babel.* New York: Oxford University Press, 1966.

"Ben Over, Call Me Stoopid," *Life* 20 January 1958: 108.

Bender, Marylin. "Fashions for a Musical Will Be Sold at Macy's," *The New York Times* 6 August 1963: 24.

Bergan, Ronald. *The United Artists Story.* New York: Crown Publishers, Inc., 1986.

Bergen, Candace. "'I Thought They Might Hiss,'" *Life.* 21 April 1972: 90.

Berger, Kenneth. *The March King and His Band.* New York: Exposition Press, 1957.

"'Big Brother' Award To Willson," *Mason City Globe-Gazette* 10 April 1962: n.p.

Bil and Cora Baird puppet collection. Charles H. MacNider Museum, Mason City, Iowa.

Blakesley, Doris. Personal interview. 3 June 1995.

Blevins, Wilfred. "Deperate Situation in '1491,'" *Los Angeles Herald-Examiner* 4 September 1969: n.p.

Blum, Daniel and John Willis. *A Pictorial History of the American Theatre 1860-1980.* New York: Crown Publishers, Inc., 1981. Fifth edition.

"Bob Preston Is Oscar Contender for 'Dark at the Top.'" Warner Brothers Studio press release March 1961.

"Book Willson Shows in Two Largest Broadway Theaters," *Mason City Globe-Gazette* 30 August 1960: 15.

Brady, James. "A Tip of the Hat in Farewell to The Music Man," Wheaton, Il: July 1984: n.p.

"Brilliant Opening at New Paramount." *The New York Times* 20 November 1926 3:2.

Brockett, Oscar. *History of the Theatre*, 4th ed. Boston: Allyn and Bacon, Inc., 1982.

Brooks, Tim and Earle Marsh. *The Complete Directory to Prime Time Network Television Shows*. New York: Ballantine Books, 1979.

Buckley, Tom. "'Music Man's Music Man at 78," *The New York Times Biographical Service* 5 June 1980: n.p.

Buehner, Kristin. "Dixie." *Mason City Globe-Gazette* 11 September 1994: S1+.

Burke, Kathy. "L.A. Composer Whips Up Inflation Fight Song," *Los Angeles Times* 30 November 1974: I: 23.

Byrne, Dan. "Meredith Willson Blasts Rock 'n' Roll as 'Garbage,'" *Mason City Globe-Gazette* 14 June 1958: 14.

CBS press releases 15 June 1964 and 10 July 1964.

Capaldo, Chuck. "Showmanship Came in 2nd," *Ottumwa Courier* 20 June 1962: 10.

"Cedric Willson Building $5,000,000 Cement Plant at Corpus Christi, Texas." *Mason City Globe Gazette* 4 January 1947: n.p.

Chaplin, Charles, dir. *The Great Dictator*. With Charles Chaplin, Jack Oakie, and Reginald Gardiner. United Artists, 1940.

Chaplin, Charles. *Charles Chaplin: My Autobiography*. New York: Pocket Books, 1966.

Chaplin, Charles, Jr. *My Father, Charlie Chaplin*. New York: Random House, 1960.

Chapman, John. "'The Music Man' One of the Best Musical Comedies of Our Time," *New York Daily News* 20 December 1957: 60.

Christensen, Richard. "Lockport's Band Jumps in Triumph," *Chicago Daily News* 20 June 1962: 6.

Collison, Jim. "Publicity Drums Beating for River City's 'Music Man,'" *Mason City Globe-Gazette* May 1962: n.p.

Cook, Louis. "Willson's 'Here's Love' Called A Happy Package," *Detroit Free Press* 10 August 1963: n.p. reprinted in the *Mason City Globe-Gazette* 11 August 1963: n.p.

Crowther, Bosley. "'The Great Dictator' by and With Charlie Chaplin, Tragi-Comic Fable of the Unhappy Lot of Decent Folk in a Totalitarian Land, at the Astor and Capitol." Review of *The Great Dictator*, by Charles Chaplin. *The New York Times*, 16 October 1940: 29.

Csida, Joseph and June Bundy Csida. *American Entertainment*. New York: Watson-Guptill Publications, 1978.

Currie, Phil. "No. 1 Band Honor Goes to Illinois," *Mason City Globe-Gazette* 20 June 1962: 1.

DaCosta, Morton, dir. *The Music Man*. With Robert Preston and Shirley Jones. Warner Brothers, 1962.

"Debbie Reynolds," *Biography* Host Jack Perkins. A & E 3 December 1996.

Department of Defense WebSite. "AFRTS Broadcast Center: History." Posted on 8 April 1999. http://www.afrts.osd.mil/history.htm.

Dick Tracy in B-Flat. Curtain Calls No. 100/1. Rerecorded from *Command Performance*. Armed Forces Radio Services 15 February 1945.

"Directs 126 Programs a Weeks." *Mason City Globe-Gazette* 20 December 1944: n.p.

"Dixie Willson Proposes 'Friendship' Peace Plan." *Mason City Globe-Gazette* n.d.: n.p. Mason City Public Library clipping.

Du Brow, Rick. "Boom in Film Musicals Spurs Movie Recovery." Mason City Public Library clipping August 1961: n.p.

Dunning, John. *The Encyclopedia of Old Time Radio*. New York: Oxford University Press, 1998.

"Durable Iowa Boy." *Time* 14 May 1951 47-48.

Eames, John Douglas. *The Paramount Story*. New York: Crown Publishers, 1985.

E.A.N. "$5,000 a Week," *Mason City Globe-Gazette* 16 January 1958: 12.

E.A.N. "Million Minimum, A," *Mason City Globe-Gazette* 18 January 1958: n.p.

"Equity Exploits Gov't Red Tape; Actor Sues CLO," Variety 26 August 1969: n.p.

"Elkhart To Celebrate 'Meredith Willson Day,'" *Indianapolis Star* 6 September 1958: 5. (Press release from Arthur Cantor, Press Rep., THE MUSIC MAN: "Elkhart, Indiana To Celebrate Mammoth 'Meredith Willson Day' Sept. 12.")

Engleback, Dee, prod. *The Big Show*. Host Tallulah Bankhead. NBC, New York, 11 March 1951.

Erwin, Hazel. "Willson Began Pro Career in Erwin-Wells Orchestra." *Mason City Globe-Gazette* 28 July 1962: n.p.

Evelove, Alex. "Willson Announces Original Musical for Broadway," Beverly Hills, CA: Publicity-Public Relations press release for 26 September 1961: 1-3.

"Famous Recipes of Famous Radio Stars." *San Francisco Chronicle* 12 November 1929: n.p.

Fernett, Gene. *Hollywood's Poverty Row*. Satellite Beach, CA: Coral Reef Publications, 1973.

"Fireproof House of $5,000." *Ladies Home Journal*. April 1907: 24.

Fischbeck, Arthur. Personal interviews. 4 June 1993 through 23 December 2004.

Flamm, Jerry. *Good Life in Hard Times: San Francisco's '20's and '30's*. San Francisco: Chronicle Books, 1977.

1491 Program printed for the Civic Light Opera Association for performances at the Dorothy Chandler Pavilion, Los Angeles, CA beginning 2 September 1969.

Frankenstein, Alfred. "Symphony Introduced by Willson." Review of *Symphony No. 2 in F Minor ("A Symphony of San Francisco")*, by Meredith Willson. *San Francisco Chronicle* 20 April 1936: n.p.

Freedland, Michael. *The Story of Frank Simon*. Portland, OR: Vallentine Mitchell, 1994.

Fromwood, C.D. "No Deal, Said Willson-Until He Got His Star." *Mason City Public Library* clipping, 1962: n.p.

Gaver, Jack. "Along the Great White Way." *Los Angeles Daily News* 15 November 1951: 26.

Gaver, Jack. *Broadway*. United Press International column clipping, October 1958: n.p.

Gaver, Jack. "Busy Year Ahead for Meredith," United Press International wire service column 12 November 1960: 1-3.

"Giant Band Festival Civic Spirit in Action," *Mason City Globe-Gazette* 16 June 1962: n.p.

Glenn, Larry. "76 Trombones Are Problem in Movie," *Mason City Globe-Gazette* 10 August 1961: n.p.

"Godfrey To Be Emcee at 'Music Man' Show Here," *Mason City Globe-Gazette* 26 June 1962: n.p.

Good News of 1938. NBC 4 November 1937.

Good News of 1939. NBC 11 May 1939.

Good New of 1939. NBC 18 May 1939.

Good News of 1939. NBC 29 June 1939.

"Grand Mixup, A," *Mason City Globe-Gazette* 6 September 1963: n.p.

Gray, Nancy. "A Fabulous Career That Started in San Francisco," *San Francisco Examiner* (n.p: n.d.) reprinted in the *Mason City Globe-Gazette* 31 July 1962: n.p.

Gray, Michael. "Jennings Recalls His Friendship With Buddy Holly 40 Years After 'The Day The Music Died.'" Posted on 14 July 2000. http://www.country.com/article/mus-news-new/waylon-jennings-99feature.html.

Greene, James, W. "The Meacham Family of Early Colonial Times." *New York Genealogical and Biographical Record, The* 65 (April 1934): 107-114.

Gross, Ben. "Triple Threat 'Music Man' Hits Jackpot the Hard Way." *New York Sunday News* 23 February 1958: n.p.

Gross, Ben. "Willson Made 40 Drafts and 70 Revisions of 'Music Man,'" *New York Sunday News* (n.p.: n.d.) reprinted in the *Mason City Globe-Gazette* 6 June 1958: C5.

Grummon, Helene. "Meredith Willson To Guest Conduct." *Mason City Globe-Gazette* 7 June 1929: 2.

Guest Mail [guest-mail@ccmsmpt4.online.Disney.com]. "Disney Archives." Private email message to Bill Oates, [boates@gte.net]. 4 February 1998.

"Happy Oom-Pah on Broadway, A," *Life* 20 January 1958: 103-106.

"'Here's Love' Breaks All Records for Musicals," *Mason City Globe-Gazette* 18 September 1963: n.p.

"Here's What 'Music Man' Says," *Mason City Globe-Gazette*, 1962: n.p. Mason City Public Library clipping.

Hewes, Henry. Review of *Here's Love*, *Saturday Review* 2 November 1963: 18.

Hirschhorn, Clive. *The Warner Bros. Story*. New York: Crown Publishers, Inc., 1979.

History of Franklin and Cerro Gordo Counties, Iowa. Springfield, IL: Union Publishing Company, 1883.

"History of the Los Angeles Philharmonic." Posted on 6 June 2000. http://www.laphil.org/about/history.cfm

Houdek, Richard. "Meredith Willson and '1491,'" Mason City Public Library clipping, 1969: 25+.

"House That Music Built, The." *The American Home*. July 1947: 28-29.

Hovelson, Jack. "'Music Man' Chokes Up in Iowa," *Des Moines Register* 7 May 1979: 1.

Jackson, Arthur. *The Best Musicals*. New York: Crown Publishers, Inc., 1977.

Jewell, Richard B. and Vernon Harbin. *The RKO Story*. New York: Arlington House, 1982.

"John Weston Bell." Obituary. *Sousa Band Fraternal Society News*: 13. University of Illinois John Philip Sousa archives.

Kane, Martin. "Meredith Willson Tells of His Music World Career." *Mason City Globe-Gazette* 19 October 1940: 3.

"Kansans Applaud Opening of 'Story,'" *The Wichita Eagle* 5 July 1961: 1+.

Kaufman, David. "Meredith Willson, Composer of Hit Song, Writes Sequel." *Mason City-Globe-Gazette* 30 August 1941: n.p.

KEB. "Beatlemania," *Mason City Globe-Gazette* column "Standing on the Corner" 17February 1964: n.p.

Kerr, Walter. "New York Weekly Theater Letter," *New York Herald Tribune Syndicate* 24 December 1957: 1-2. (Also Kerr, Walter. "First Night Report," *New York Herald* 20 December 1957: 14.)

Kew, Ken, host. *Band Festival 1988*. KIMT aircheck, Mason City, Iowa 4 June 1988.

Knox, Melissa, compiler. "Books That Shaped My Life." *Family Weekly* 28 December 1980: 18.

Krueger, Miles. *Showboat – The Story of A Classic American Musical*. New York: Oxford University Press, 1977.

Kuchwara, Michael. "Tony Nominations Celebrate Old Favorites," *Post-Tribune* 9 March 2000: A2.

Langley, Ken. Meredith Willson," *Bulletin National Tuberculosis Association* October 1966, 9-11.

Laufe, Abe. *Broadway's Greatest Musicals*. New York: Funk and Wagnalls, 1970.

Liffring, Joan. "The Many Lives of Hanford MacNider." *Iowan* March 1965: 38.

Liston, Jim. "At Home with the Willsons," *American Home* September 1960, 24-26.

"Local By Contributes to New De Forest Invention." *Mason City Globe-Gazette* 21 November 1923: 2

"London Press Lauds 'Music Man' Film," *Mason City Globe-Gazette* August 1962: n.p.

Mader, Vinton I. "Mason City's Other 'Music Man' Heads Top Bandsmen's Convention," *Mason City Globe-Gazette* 9 March 1961: n.p.

Magill, Frank N., ed. *Magill's Survey of Cinema*, first series, vol. 2, Englewood Cliffs, NJ: 1980.

Maksian, George. "3 Specials for Willson," *New York Daily News* 31 march 1964: n.p.

"Manufacturer Donates Band Instruments," *UMI Elkhart* archives 29 August 1997: 2.

"Margaret Tobin Brown." Posted on 2 February 1998. http://www.mollybrown.org/intro.html.

"Massed Bands Honor Men Of Music At Rice Show," *The Elkhart Truth* 13 September 1958: 1.

Mason City Globe-Gazette. Mason City Public Library clipping.

McCabe, John. *Charlie Chaplin.* Garden City, NY: Doubleday & Co., 1978.

McGrath, Della. "The University of Iowa Remembers Meredith Willson." The University of Iowa, 2001.

McLeod, Elizabeth. "Local Voices: The Don Lee and Yankee Networks." 1998. Posted on http://www.midcoast.com/~lizmcl/regional.html.

Mendelsohn, Jennifer. "The Musical, Man!" *USA Weekend* Jan. 31-Feb. 2, 2003: 10.

"Meredith Willson Back Home Again After Second Triumph on Broadway,' *Mason City Globe-Gazette* 18 November 1960: n.p.

"Meredith Willson Brings Happy 'Trouble' to TV," *Mason City Globe-Gazette* 1 April 1959: n.p.

"Meredith Willson Divorced by Wife." *Mason City Globe-Gazette* 5 March 1948: n.p.

"Meredith Wilson [sic] Makes Good; Art Diploma His Aim." *Mason City Globe-Gazette* 27 October 1920: n.p.

Meredith Willson papers. Kinney Pioneer Museum, Mason City, Iowa. Requested 4 June 1994.

"Meredith Willson Prefers Own Film of 'Music Man,'" *Mason City Globe-Gazette* 24 June 1958: n.p.

"Meredith Willson Residence Hall, The." Brochure obtained at Juilliard, New York City 30 June 1996.

Millstein, Gilbert. "That Brassy Music Man Returns To Broadway As Poor Richard," *Saturday Evening Post* 17 October 1964: 87-89.

"Molly Brown's Family History in America." Posted on 2 February 1998. http://www.mollybrown.com/molly-history2.html.

Morgan, Patricia. "'Music Man' Comes Home," *Globe-Gazette* 23 June 1984: 1.

Moritz, Charles, ed. "Tammy Grimes," *Current Biography Yearbook 1962*. New York: The H.W. Wilson Company, 1963.

Mulligan, Hugh A. "'Music Man' Nears Top in Cast Album Record Sales," *Mason City Globe Gazette* 12 March 1958: n.p.

"'Music Man' Follows Money Record Hit in Music Hall." Mason City Public Library clipping, 28 August 1962: n.p.

"'Music Man' 'Greatest Show on Earth,' Says Los Angeles," *Mason City Globe-Gazette* 19 August 1958: n.p.

"Music Man Is Conn Man," *Conn-vention* News 21 July 1958: 1.

"'Music Man' Performed at Nightclub," Associated Press clipping: 20 April 1962: n.p. Mason City Public Library.

"'Music Man' Rated Best on Broadway," *Mason City Globe Gazette* 9 April 1958: n.p.

"*Music Man, The*." Review of the film in *Variety* 12 April 1962: n.p.

"'Music Man' Willson To Appear with ISU Orchestra Tonight," *Terre Haute Tribune-Star* 12 May 1970: n.p.

Musical Merchandise Review advertisement May 1958: 25.

NBC Hollywood Studio Opening. NBC 7 December 1935.

"New Girl in Town, *Newsweek* 14 November 1960: 61.

"New Stage Play for Willson," *Mason City Globe-Gazette* 29 November 1961: n.p.

New York Philharmonic archives. Lincoln Center, New York City.

Nichols, Lewis. "They Hope One 'Miracle' Will Lead To Another," *The New York Times* 29 September 1963: II: 3.

Nichols, Lewis. "Willson at Bat Again," *The New York Times* 30 October 1960: II: 1,3.

Nineteen Eighteen Masonian, The. Mason City High School yearbook. 1918.

1919 Masonian. Mason City High School yearbook. 1919.

"O.O. McIntyre." *Mason City Globe Gazette* 30 May 1942: n.p.

"O.O. McIntyre Dead; Columnist Was 54." *The New York Times* 15 February 1938: 25.

"Offers Criticism, But Predicts Success of 'Here's Love,'" *Mason City Globe-Gazette* 7 August 1963: 27.

"104 Newsmen at Festival To Publicize Mason City, *Mason City Globe-Gazette* 4 June 1962: n.p.

"Organists To Add Their Honor To Meredith Willson," *Mason City Globe-Gazette* 5 July 1962: n.p.

Osborne, Robert. *50 Golden Years of Oscar.* La Habra, CA: ESE California, 1979.

"Our Family Album." *Ladies' Home Journal.* November 1925: 31.

Owens, James R. "Willson Plugs Home Town Again in Razzle-Dazzle, Successful TV Special," *Mason City Globe-Gazette* 5 June 1964; n.p.

Pack, Harvey. "The Meredith Willsons - TV's Newest Team." Mason City Public Library clipping, n.d., n.p.

"Papers Love Willson's 'Here's Love,'" *Mason City Globe-Gazette* 29 August 1963: n.p.

Parker, Katharine McAfee and Meredith Willson. "Hail, Alma Mater." New York: Frank Music Corporation - Rinimer Corporation, 1962.

Petersen, William J. "Historical Beginnings," *Palimpset* The State Historical Society of Iowa June 1968: 209-219.

"Play First Flute and Bassoon on U.S. Tour." *Mason City Globe-Gazette* 20 November 1922: n.p.

Poirier, Normand, "Jubilant Janis Is Back on Broadway," *Saturday Evening Post* 9 November 1963: 35-36.

Quigg, Doc. "Pieplant Good With Rock Salt," *Mason City Globe-Gazette* June 1962: n.p.

Quimby, Quinella. Interview with Rosemary Willson. KCMR radio, Mason City, Iowa. 2 June 1988.

"Radio Front, The." *Movie-Radio Guide* 6-12 June 1942: 10.

"Real 'Music Man' Began Iowa Bands," *Mason City Globe-Gazette* 21 July 1958: 14.

Recording Academy Website. "Grammy Search: Results." Posted on 15 April 1999. http://www.grammy.com/awards/search_results.php3.

"Recordings of 'Unsinkable' Out Monday," *Mason City Globe-Gazette* 18 November 1960: n.p.

Review of *1491*, *Variety* 10 September 1969: 118, 120.

Review of *The Unsinkable Molly Brown*, *America* 3 December 1960: 353-4.

"Rini Willson Spirit Remembered Here," *Mason City Globe-Gazette* 7 December 1966: 1-2.

Rogers, Richard and Oscar Hammerstein, II. *Oklahoma!* Director Fred Zinnemann. Angel Records album notes 1993.

"Robert Preston, B'way 'Music Man,' Longtime Film Star, Dies At 68." *Variety* (25 March 1987); reprinted in *Variety Obituaries*, Vol. 10. eds. Chuck Bartelt and Barbara Bergeron. New York: Garland Publishers, 1987.

Rosing, Vladimir, dir. *The Oregon Story*. Program printed by The Oregon Centennial Commission for performances at the Centennial Exposition Arena, Portland, OR 3-17 September 1959.

San Francisco Symphony Orchestra archives. Center House Building, San Francisco, CA.

Santi, Joseph M. "East West South and Northern Exposure," *Show Music* summer 1995: 51-54.

Sargeant, Winthrop. *Genius, Goddesses and People*. New York: E.P. Dutton, 1949.

Schneider, John. "History of KFRC San Francisco and the Don Lee Networks, The." Seattle, 1998. Posted on 14 July 2000. http://www.adams.net/~jfs/.

Schumach, Murray. "From Leading Man to 'Music Man,'" *The New York Times* 15 December 1957: II, 3: 5.

"Sentiment without Schmaltz in New Willson Musical," *Mason City Globe-Gazette* 16 August 1963: 12.

"Seventy-Six Trombones Lead the Big Parade," *Conn Chord* March 1958: 9.

Sharbutt, Jay. "First Grammy Winner Rests on Laurels," Mason City Public Library clipping, 1977: n.p.

Sherwin, Doug. Interviews with Meredith Willson. KGLO radio, Mason City, Iowa. 21 March 1953 through 13 August 1969.

Sherwin, Doug. Interview with Rosemary Willson. KGLO radio, Mason City, Iowa. 1 June 1994.

Sloman, Edward, dir. *Lost Zeppelin, The*. With Richard Cortez and Virginia Valli. Tiffany-Stahl, 1929.

Snider, Dick. "Composes Music for the Nation's Health," *Topeka Capital-Journal* reprinted in the *Mason City Globe-Gazette* 15 June 1962: n.p.

Sousa program. 1923 season. University of Illinois John Philip Sousa collection.

Sousa, John Philip. *Marching Along*. Boston: Hale, Cushman and Flint, 1941 (reprint of 1928 book.)

Spaeth, Sigmund. *Fifty Years with Music*. New York: Fleet Publishing Corporation, 1959.

Spong, Richard. "Sure-fire Success 'Here's Love' Has A Special Integrated Cast," *Mason City Globe-Gazette* 18 September 1963: n.p.

Steif, William. "Something for All." *The San Francisco News* 3 July 1958: 9.

Steinberg, Jack. "Meredith Willson, Walter Slezak, Sponsor's 20th Anniversary Are Features of Season's Premiere Met opera Broadcast," New York: Cunningham and Walsh press release, 1960.

Strauss, Janet. "The Real Me." Shirley Jones Website. Posted on 18 May 1999. http://www.shirleyjones.com/therealme.htm.

Sullivan, Dan. "CLO's '1491' An Expensive Voyage to Nowhere," *Los Angeles Times Calendar* 21 September, 1969: 30.

Summers, Harrison B. *A Thirty-Year History of Programs Carried on National Radio Networks in the United States*. Salem, NH: Ayer Company, Publishers, Inc., 1986.

"'Summery Note' from Band festival Hits LIFE Pages," *Mason City Globe-Gazette* 10 July 1958: n.p.

Surf Ballroom Website. "History of the Surf." Posted on 14 July 2000. http://www.surfballroom.com/HTML/history.html.

Swanson, Pat. "Willson Says U.S. 'Forgetting English,'" *Topeka Daily Capital* 14 June 1961: 1+.

Taubman, Howard. Review of *Ben Franklin in Paris*, *The New York Times* 28 October 1964: 52.

Taubman, Howard. Review of *Here's Love*, *The New York Times* 4 October 1963: 28.

Taylor, Markland. Review of *Here's Love*, *Variety* 9 December 1991: 85.

"This Is NWB Land," *The Northwestern Bell Magazine* July-August 1962: 2-3, 46.

Thomas, Bob. "New Willson Song May Outlast '76 Trombones,'" *Mason City Globe-Gazette* 6 June 1964: n.p.

"Three Thirds of a Nation." Photo and caption from the Prints and Photographs Division of The Library of Congress, Washington, D.C. Requested 19 August 1994.

"Trombones," *Mason City Globe-Gazette* 29 September 1958: n.p.

"24th North Iowa Band Festival, The." Mason City Chamber of Commerce brochure, 1962.

"Vacationing in Mason City." *Mason City Globe-Gazette* 22 November 1932: n.p.

Van Gelder, Robert, "Chaplin Draws a Keen Weapon," *The New York Times* 8 September 1940 ; reprinted in *The New York Times Encyclopedia of Film,* Vol. 3. ed. Gene Brown. New York: Times Books, 1984.

"Voice of America Will Give Band Festival World Coverage," *Mason City Globe-Gazette* 7 June 1962: n.p.

Walters, Charles, dir. *The Unsinkable Molly Brown*. With Debbie Reynolds and Harve Presnel. MGM, 1964.

"Well Known Violinist Locates Here." *Mason City Globe-Gazette* ca. 1914 n.d.: n.p. Mason City Public Library clipping.

Williams, Clare. "Oklahoman Recalls 'The Music Man.'" *Oklahoma City Times* n.p.: n.d. reprinted in *Mason City Globe-Gazette* 30 December 1960: n.p.

"Willow Grove Park Soon To End Season." *Philadelphia Record* 3 September 1922: n.p. Mason City Public Library clipping.

"Willson Buys American Sheet Music Collection," *Mason City Globe-Gazette* January 1965: n.p.

Willson, Cedric. *Cedric Willson Symposium on Expansive Cement* (1977: Mexico City, Mexico). Detroit: American Concrete Institute, c1980.

Willson, Dixie, "The Man Behind 'The Music Man.'" *The American Weekly* 4 May 1958: 18.

Willson, Dixie. "Felt It Increased the Quality of Her Town." *Mason City Globe-Gazette*, 27 February 1964: 12.

"Willson Donates Transcriptions to Museum," *Mason City Globe-Gazette* 16 March 1963: n.p.

Willson family archives, Mason City Library, Mason City, Iowa.

Willson, Meredith. "A Special Tribute to Pennsylvania Band," *Mason City Globe-Gazette* 23 August 1962: n.p.

Willson, Meredith. *A Suite for Flute*. New York: Frank Music Corporation and Rinimer Corporation, 1974.

Willson, Meredith. *And There I Stood With My Piccolo*. New York: Doubleday and Company, 1949.

Willson, Meredith. Audio cassette. "'1491' OC Live." Los Angeles: 1969.

Willson, Meredith. *But He Doesn't Know the Territory*. New York: G.P. Putnam's Sons, 1959.

Willson, Meredith. *Eggs I Have Laid*. New York: Henry Holt and Company, 1955.

Willson, Meredith. *1491*. Los Angeles: Richard Morris draft, 22 March 1969.

Willson, Meredith, guest conductor. The University Symphony Orchestra, Tilson Music Hall, Indiana State University, Terre Haute, Indiana, 13 May 1970. Open reel audio recording and program.

Willson, Meredith. "Here's Love," *Playbill*. Sam S. Shubert Theatre 30 September 1963.

Willson, Meredith. "Hometown (Mason City) Revisited." *Mason City Globe-Gazette* 25 November 1950: 12.

Willson, Meredith. *Mass of the Bells*. Boston: Frank Music Corporation and Rinimer Corporation, 1970.

Willson, Meredith. "Meredith 'Music Man' Willson Views Music, Lyrics and Poetry," *New York Herald Tribune* 1961 n.p.

Willson, Meredith. "Meredith Willson Tells of Proud Moments in his Life," *New York Herald Tribune* wire service dispatch dated 19 August 1958 and reprinted in the *Mason City Globe-Gazette* 25 August 1958.

Willson, Meredith. *Music Man, The*. New York: G.P. Putnam's Sons, 1958.

Willson, Meredith. "The Music Man," *Playbill*. The Majestic Theatre 16 December 1957.

Willson, Meredith. "New Shows, New Woes: The 'Biz' Is Mysterious," *New York Herald Tribune* 30 October 1960: 4:1.

Willson, Meredith. "Nocturne for Piano." New York: Frank Music Corporation and Rinimer Corporation, 1977.

Willson, Meredith. *O.O. McIntyre Suite*. New York: Robbins Music Corporation, 1934.

Willson, Meredith. "Playing in a Band Instead of a Gang," *New York Herald Tribune* 1 February 1959: n.p.

Willson, Meredith. Radio scrapbook. Mason City Public Library.

Willson, Meredith. "Show Us the Way, Blue Eagle." San Francisco: Sherman, Clay, & Co., 1932.

Willson, Meredith. *Symphonies Nos. 1 & 2*. Dir. William T Stromberg. NAXOS, 8.559006, 1998.

Willson, Meredith. "TV Is Just Not Show Business," *Oakland Tribune* 21 June 1959: B-3+.

Willson, Meredith. *What Every Young Musician Should Know*. New York: Robbins Music Corporation, 1938.

Willson, Meredith and John Nesbitt. "House of Melody." San Francisco: Sherman, Clay & Co., 1937.

"Willson Play for Broadway," *Mason City Globe-Gazette* 5 October 1964: n.p.

Willson, Rosalie. Family scrapbook collection at the Kinney Pioneer Museum, Mason City, Iowa.

"Willson Writes Lyrics for Newman School Song," *Mason City Globe-Gazette* 11 September 1961: n.p.

Wilson, John S. "Meredith Willson, Composer of 'Music Man' Dead at 82," *The New York Times* 17 June 1984: n.p.

Witbeck, Charles. "Music Man Meredith Willson Planning Summer TV Specials." Mason City Public Library clipping, 1964: n.p.

Wright, Carl. "Mason City Had Its First Movie Premiere for 'Music Man,'" *Mason City Globe-Gazette* 21 June 1962: 33.

Wright, Carl. "Mason City To Raise $35,000 for Big Festival," *Mason City Globe-Gazette* February 1962: n.p.

Wright, Carl. "There Stood Willson With His Piccolo in River City," *Mason City Globe-Gazette*, 1958: n.p.

Wright, Carl. "U.S. Newspapers Laud 'Music Man' Festival," Mason City Globe-Gazette 22 June 1962: n.p.

Wright, Carl. "Willson Show Hails Young America," *Mason City Globe-Gazette* 24 July 1964: n.p.

"Wyler, William." *Cinemania '95*. CD-ROM. Redmond, WA: 1995.

Wyler, William. *The Little Foxes*. With Bette Davis, Herbert Marshall, and Teresa Wright. RKO/Radio, 1941.

Zell, Marty, producer-director. "Iowa Impressions," *The Iowa Heritage*. Iowa Public Broadcasting, 1979.

Zimmer, Norma. Letter to author. 23 July 1995.

Zimmer, Norma. *Norma*. Wheaton, IL: Tyndale House, Publishers, 1976.

Index

A

ABC (American Broadcasting Company) 92, 104, 134, 142, 147
Academy Awards, The 71, 72
Ace, Goodman 94, 106, 110
Affair of the Follies, An 25
AFRS (Armed Forces Radio Service) 33, 61, 75, 76, 77, 78, 79, 80, 81, 82, 83, 85, 125, 165, 179
Ainsworth, Ed 170
Alexander, Joan 92
Allen, Betty 86
Allen, Ethan 4
Allen, Fred 77, 93, 94, 100, 101, 107
All Star Revue (Four Star Revue) 105, 106
"Always and Always" 64
Amans, John 37
"American Anthem" 152
American Bandmasters Association 177
American Broadcasting System (Seattle) 41
American Home 88, 167
American Legion, The 170, 175
American Philharmonic Orchestra 42
America Calling 66, 182, 194, 195
America Sings 51
Amsterdam, Morey 105
And Then I Wrote the Music 125
And There I Stood with My Piccolo 11, 18, 32, 45, 46, 71, 89, 102, 107
Annual Award of Masquers 164
"Answer the Call" 99
"Anthem of the Atomic Age" 98
"Are You Sure?" 150
Arlen, Steven 172
Armour Institute 5, 13, 127
Arnett, Judd 158
ASCAP (American Society of Composers, Authors and Publishers) 45, 64
"Ask Not" 162

B

Baird, Bertha 113
Baird, Bil and Cora 122
"Band, The" 139
Bankhead, Tallulah 50, 72, 93, 94, 96, 105, 110
"Banners and Bonnets" 98, 99, 184
Barmak, Ira 170
Barrere, Georges 27
Barrett, Lydia Margaret 113
Barry, Bud 106
Barrymore, Ethel 105, 106
Bay, Howard 124, 132
BBC (British Broadcasting Company) 58, 100
Beatles, The 138, 161
"Being in Love" 141
Bell, Jack 35
"Belly Up to the Bar, Boys" 150

Berle, Milton 120, 133
"Big Bopper" (J.P. Richardson) 139
Big Brothers, The 132, 164, 165, 175
Big Show, The 8, 50, 83, 93, 94, 95, 96, 97, 99, 100, 101, 102, 104, 105, 106, 110, 112, 184, 197, 205
Big Ten, The 51, 194
Blaine, Vivian 94, 110
Blakesley, Doris viii, 116, 163
Blevins, Winifred 172
Bloomgarten, Kermit 119, 120, 123, 124, 128
Blue Monday Jamboree 48, 49, 50, 193
BMI (Broadcast Music, Inc.) 64
Bolton, Whitney 149
Boswell, Connie 66
Branstad, Governor Terry 178, 179
Brighton, Illinois 5, 6, 127
Broderick, Matthew 134
Brown, Johnnie and Maggie 2, 139, 140, 147, 148, 149, 150, 151, 155, 156, 157, 158, 163, 170, 171, 175, 178, 188, 189, 200
Buchwald, Art 101
Buffalo Bills 121, 125, 135, 140, 144, 145
Bunce, Charles 49
Burns, George and Gracie Allen 2, 46, 62, 85, 86, 87, 89, 91, 102, 110, 116, 133, 196, 197
Burrows, Abe 92
Bushgens, Mr. 117

But He Doesn't Know the Territory xii, 117, 120, 124, 139
Bye, Bye Birdie 141, 148

C

California Story, The 99, 118, 152, 184
Camelot 141, 148, 149, 150, 172
Canada Dry 85, 98, 183, 187
Capitol Records 99, 125, 150
Captain Dobbsies Ship of Joy 46, 194
Carefree Carnival 48, 51, 56, 194
Carney, Art 112
Carr, Vicki 163
Carter, Paulina 87
CBS (Columbia Broadcasting System) 41, 46, 56, 58, 66, 76, 77, 78, 82, 85, 93, 104, 118, 131, 132, 139, 147, 162, 163, 164, 189, 193, 194, 195, 196, 197, 198
Cedar Lake, Iowa 139
Cedar Rapids, Iowa 96, 177
"Centennial March" 97, 111
Cerro Gordo County, Iowa 2, 3, 4, 20, 24, 103, 110, 117
Charles City, Iowa 5, 14, 42
Chicago, Illinois 3, 5, 13, 18, 23, 24, 30, 46, 48, 55, 73, 98, 103, 127, 146, 152, 160, 174
"Chick-a-Pen" 156, 188
"Chicken Fat" 163, 164
Chiffon Jazz 51
Willson, Robert Meredith 15
Christmas Seals 86, 165, 168, 196
Cliburn, Van 133
Coe College 177

220

Colman, Ronald 66, 81
Colt, Alvin 161
Columbus, Christopher 167, 169, 170, 171
Conforti, Gino 172
Conn Musical Instrument Company 123, 136, 137, 138
Cook, Barbara 121, 122
Cooke, Richard 149
Cougat, Xavier 46
Crosby, Bing 50, 56, 65, 76, 77, 78, 81, 140, 178, 200
Cullen, Bill 92
Cullum, John 172, 173
Curran Theatre 173

D

Dailard, Wayne 152
Dailey, Dan 120, 122
Damrosch, Walter 37, 38, 39, 144, 193
Damrosch Institute 26
Darrin, Bobby 133
Davis, Valentine 158
Day, Doris 107
"Defiance" 44, 181
DeForest, Dr. Lee 35
Des Moines, Iowa 2, 21, 32, 146, 168
Diamond, Selma 94
Dickirson, James 2
Diljas, Tommy 115
Disney, Walt viii, 72, 78, 134, 158, 164, 174, 175
Disneyland 174, 175
Dobbs, Hugh 46, 194
"Dolce Far Niente" 148
Dorsey, Tommy 65

Doyle, David 160
Dubuque, Iowa 5
Durante, Jimmy 80, 93, 95, 96, 105, 106, 184

E

Edwards, Frank 42
Eggs I Have Laid 106, 176
Elkhart, Indiana viii, 136, 137, 167
Elmwood Cemetery 89, 178
Encore 104, 105, 197
Englebach, Dee 106
Estherville, Iowa 5, 6, 22
Every Day 98, 105, 114, 183, 197, 198

F

Falstaff Show, The 87, 184
Fenn, Jean 172
Feurer, Cy 113, 114, 119
Fibber McGee and Molly (Jim and Marian Jordan) 48, 66, 82, 102, 194, 195
First Congregational Church 7, 153, 178
Fischer, Edna 48, 182
Fletcher, Ron 105
Florida Tech University 176
"Fluff of Gold" 23
Ford, Paul 141
Ford, President Gerald 174
Ford Sunday Evening Hour, The (also Ford Summer Hour, The) 169, 183, 194, 195
Foster, George 94
Foster, Phil 102
1491 167, 169, 170, 171, 172,

173, 189
Fowler, Gene 66, 83, 100
Franchi, Sergio 163
Franklin, Aretha 150
Frank Music Company 150
Fulton, James M. 31

G

Gage, Ben 87
"Gary, Indiana" 127, 187
General Foods 61, 85, 86, 87, 91, 97, 169
George Burns and Gracie Allen Show, The 46, 82, 85, 86, 87, 91, 110, 196, 197
Gershwin, George 37, 110
Gibson, Harry and Betty 49
Gingold, Hermione 141
Gleason, Jackie 120, 146
"Gloryland" 173, 189
Godfrey, Arthur 107, 121, 144
"God Gave Me Twenty Cents" 24
Goetchus, Dr. Herman 27
Golden Gate Bridge 51, 52
Golden Globe, The 141
Golden State Eggs 50
Goldovsky, Boris 139
Goldwyn, Samuel 72
"Gone To Chicago" 98
Goodman, Benny 65
Goodman, Bill 92
"Goodnight, My Someone" 125
Goodwin, Bill 46, 87
Grammy (National Academy of Recording Arts and Sciences) 133, 167, 198
Grant, Cary 140
Grauer, Ben 105

Great Dictator, The 68, 69, 70, 71, 72, 182
Greek War Relief 65, 66, 195
Green, Mort 94
Greene, Herb 119
Green Springs, Ohio 5
Griffith, Andy 120, 141
Griffith, Jim 116
Grimes, Tammy 148, 149, 158
Grofé, Ferd 49
Guys and Dolls 110, 113, 129
Gwynne 160
Gypsy 140

H

Hackett, Buddy 141
Hadley, Henry 27
"Hail, Alma Mater" 139
Hall, Cliff 160
Hall, Earl 116, 145, 176
"Hallelujah, It's Tallulahvision at Last" 105
Hallmark Playhouse, The 90, 197
Hamlin, John 86
Hammerstein, Oscar, II 110, 111, 140, 146, 148, 150
Hancher, Virgil M. 177
"Handful of Stars, A" ("Pockets Full of Stars") 83, 95
Hanover College 139, 176, 189
Harris, Phil 46, 87, 122
Hart, Moss 120
Haverdegrain, Charlie 115
Hazelton, Squiz 18, 123
Heckler Surprise Party 51, 193
Heindorf, Ray 74, 142
Hellman, Lillian 72
Henry Aldrich Show, The 91

Herald-Examiner 172
Here's Love 115, 131, 152, 158, 159, 160, 162, 184, 188, 199
"Here Comes the Springtime" 96
"Here Y'Are Brother" 25
Hewitt, Joseph 2
Hickox, Harry 141
Hitler, Adolph 68, 71
"Hit the Leather" 75, 177
Hoare, Frank 123
Hodges, Eddie 124
Hogue, Pastor S. Mark 98
Holliway, Harrison 48, 49
Holly, Buddy 139
Hollywood Museum 165
Honey Bear 15, 26
Hope, Bob 78, 79, 81, 94, 107
Hopper, Hedda 145
House of Melody xi, 47, 48, 182
Howard, Ronnie 141, 143, 145
"How I Love the Music of a Band" 96
How To Listen to Long Hair Music 114
How To Succeed in Business Without Really Trying 161
How To Write a Script 195
Hubbell, Frank Allen 152
"Hullabaloo" 96

I

"I'll Never Say Never Again" 148
"If I Knew" 148, 188
Illinois Association of Broadcasters 164
Indiana Institute of Technology 177
Indiana State University ix, 175, 176
International Institute of Arts and Letters 164
"Iowa" 97, 178, 179, 200
"Iowa – A Place To Grow" 173
Iowa Award 177
"Iowa Fight Song, The" 96, 184
"Iowa Stubborn" xii, 113, 187
Irma La Douce 148, 149, 150
"It's Beginning to Look A Lot Like Christmas" 160, 178, 184
"It's Easter Time" 96
"It's You" 125, 187
"I Ain't Down Yet" 148, 178, 188
"I See the Moon" 98, 114

J

"Jamboree March, The" 50, 181
Jeffers, James W. 16, 124
JELL-O 86, 91, 97
Jenkins, Gordon 66
"Jervis Bay, The" 65, 66, 83, 100, 183
Johnson, Ernie 32
Johnson, President Lyndon 165
Johnson, Van 133
Jones, Jack 163
Jones, Shirley 140, 142, 143, 145
Juilliard School of Music 27

K

Kansas Story, The 152, 173
Kaufman, Dave 146
Kaye, Danny 98, 120, 122, 200
Kaye, Sylvia Fine 122
Keeler, Harry 31
Kelly, Gene 120, 122
Kelly, Patsy 106

Kelton, Pert 121, 140
Kennedy, Jimmy 47
Kennedy, President John Fitzgerald 162, 164, 165
Kew, Mayor Kenneth 178
KFRC 45, 46, 48, 49, 51, 193
KGLO 64, 111, 128, 155
KGO 51, 193
KHJ 45, 46, 51
Kidd, Michael 121, 161
Kiley, Richard 162
Kirk, Lisa 162
KJR 42, 193
Kohl, Jack 116
KPO 51, 193, 194

L

Lacey, Frank 118, 119
Lahr, Bert 60, 106
Laine, Frankie 93, 106
Lampert, Benjamin 23
"Last Days of Pompeii, The" 34
Lauck, Chester 84
Lee, Don 41, 45, 51
Lerner, Alan Jay 110, 150
Lester, Jerry 92
"Let's All Do the Festival Waltz" (The Margaret Waltz") 101
Lewis, Robert Q. 92
"Lida Rose" 6, 125, 127, 136, 178
Lime Creek 2, 13
Linden, Adolph 42
Little Foxes, The 64, 72, 73, 83, 93
"Local Boy Makes Good" 50, 182
Lock, Tom 116
Loesser, Frank 109, 110, 119, 126, 150, 161, 162, 168

Loewe, Frederick 150
Lost Zeppelin 43, 44, 213
Los Angeles, California 35, 38, 45, 46, 51, 53, 55, 56, 62, 63, 76, 77, 84, 89, 94, 98, 132, 133, 162, 164, 165, 166, 168, 169, 170, 172, 173, 174, 175
Los Angeles City Council 164
Los Angeles Civic Light Opera Company 162, 169
Los Angeles Times 170, 173
Lovelace, Governor Herschel C. 135
Luckey, Susan 141
Lucky Strike Hit Parade 51

M

MacLaine, Shirley 151
MacNider, Charles 143
MacNider, Hanford 33, 146
Macy's Department Store 161
Majestic Theatre xi, 120, 128, 150
Mamoulian, Robert 118
Martin, Ernie 110, 112, 115, 117, 118, 119
Marx, Groucho 93, 94, 105
Marysville, California 3
"Mason City, Go, Go, Go" 97
Mason City, Iowa (also Masonville, Mason Grove) vii, viii, xi, xii, 2, 3, 4, 5, 6, 7, 9, 10, 11, 12, 13, 14, 15, 16, 17, 18, 19, 20, 21, 22, 23, 24, 25, 26, 27, 28, 29, 30, 31, 32, 34, 35, 41, 53, 60, 68, 80, 88, 89, 92, 97, 103, 106, 109, 110, 111, 112, 113, 115, 116, 117, 122, 123, 124, 127, 128, 135, 139, 142, 143, 144, 145, 146,

150, 153, 163, 167, 178, 179, 180
Mason City Globe-Gazette 26, 31, 42, 152
Mason City High School 5, 15, 17, 21, 22, 26, 27, 97, 112, 116, 144
Mass of the Bells 173, 189
Matthews, Merle 45
Maynard, Bassoon Master 26
"May the Good Lord Bless and Keep You" 7, 96, 106, 114, 150, 151, 176, 178, 200
McIntyre, O. O. (Oscar Odd) 29, 50, 182, 183
Melendy, Dr. Earle R. ix, 175
Mendon, Mayor George E. 145, 146
Mengleburg, Willem 36
Meredith Willsons Marching Band 99
Meredith Willsons Musical Revue 66, 82, 195
Meredith Willson Show, The 58, 91, 197
Merrill, Robert 104
"Metropolis" 49
Meyer, Abe 43, 51, 168
MGM (Metro Goldwyn Mayer) 57, 58, 59, 60, 61, 67, 72, 119, 145, 151, 157
Milligan, Lester 144
Miracle on 34th Street, The 158
Missions of California 53, 63, 68, 81, 173, 183
Modern American Music 99, 200
Monroe, Marilyn 149
Moore, Gary 139, 170, 198
Moray, Joseph and Miranda 87

Morris, Richard 147, 148, 170, 171
Murray, Mae 43
Music Award of Texas 164
Music Man, The xii, 1, 2, 6, 7, 8, 9, 10, 11, 12, 15, 16, 17, 19, 20, 22, 29, 33, 35, 45, 51, 52, 74, 83, 89, 97, 99, 103, 104, 105, 106, 107, 109, 111, 112, 113, 114, 115, 116, 117, 118, 119, 120, 121, 122, 123, 124, 125, 126, 127, 128, 129, 131, 132, 133, 134, 135, 136, 137, 138, 139, 140, 141, 142, 143, 144, 145, 146, 147, 148, 149, 150, 151, 155, 156, 157, 158, 160, 167, 169, 170, 173, 175, 178, 179, 180, 184, 187, 188, 198, 199, 200, 203, 204, 215, 216
Music Room 85, 87, 105, 114, 197, 198
Mussolini, Benito 68
"My Cavalier" 45, 181
My Fair Lady 129, 134, 141, 150
"My Kansas, My Home" 152, 164
"My White Knight" 127, 141, 167

N

Naismith, Lawrence 160, 161, 162
Name's the Same, The 92, 197
National Conference of Christians and Jews, The 165
National Foundation on the Arts and Humanities 165
National Library Week 164
NBC (National Broadcasting Company) 1, 39, 41, 45, 46, 47, 50, 51, 52, 55, 56, 57, 58,

225

62, 77, 78, 80, 82, 84, 85, 91, 93, 94, 95, 96, 97, 100, 101, 104, 105, 106, 110, 144, 146, 147, 168, 169, 174, 179, 193, 194, 195, 196, 197, 198
Nesbitt, John 48, 83, 182
"Never Feel Too Weary To Pray" 64, 73, 83
New York City, New York xii, 15, 18, 22, 24, 25, 27, 28, 30, 36, 37, 38, 39, 41, 42, 43, 50, 53, 86, 89, 93, 102, 103, 106, 110, 111, 112, 115, 120, 122, 123, 126, 128, 132, 140, 141, 149, 158, 159, 160, 177
New York Critics Circle 133
New York Herald Tribune 156
New York Institute of Music 27, 35, 36
New York Philharmonic Orchestra 38, 43
New York Times, The 123
1947 Christmas Seals Show 86, 196
Nixon, Vice President Richard 164, 174
Noble, Ray 84
"Nocturne for Piano" 174
Norman, Lucille 152
North Iowa Band Festival 129, 135, 136, 139, 143, 144, 145, 146, 180
Notre Dame University 5

O

O. O. McIntyre Suite 50, 182, 183
O'Leary, Florence 113
O'Neill, Eugene 146
Oakie, Jack 68, 71

Oklahoma! 111, 122, 134, 140
One Man's Family 46
Oregon Story, The 152
Ostrow, Stuart 125, 157, 158
Owens Township, Iowa 3

P

Pacific Pioneer Broadcasters 177
Paige, Janis 159
"Parade Fantastique" 35, 44, 50
Parents Magazine Award 164
Paris, Illinois 3
Parks 120, 133
Parsons, Louella 149
Parsons College 177
Passing Parade, The 48, 83
Patchen, Ed 17, 115
Payne, John 162
Peacock Alley 43
Pearce, Al 49
Pene du Bois, Raoul 124, 132
"Peony Bush, The" 98, 200
"Phenomena" 44
Philadelphia, Pennsylvania xi, 13, 26, 54, 89, 116, 119, 123, 124, 125, 126, 127, 128, 131, 148, 149, 155, 157, 158, 160, 161, 178, 179
Piazza, Margaret 104
"Pine Cones and Holly Berries" 160
Pinza, Ezio 95, 106
Powers, Fr. William 139
Presidential Medal of Freedom 177
Presnell, Harve 149, 151
Preston, Robert 122, 123, 127, 128, 132, 134, 140, 141, 142,

143, 145, 148, 149, 157, 158, 162, 164, 172, 199

R

Radio France 101
Radio Suite 75, 88, 183
Rarig, John 86
Rau, Charlie 8
Reagan, President Ronald 177
Red Cross, The 75, 99, 184, 187
"Red Sails in the Sunset" 47
Reed, Paul 160
Reid, Toby 88
Reiniger, Gustavus 5
Reiniger, Lida Mecham 5, 6
Reynolds, Bernard 3
Reynolds, Debbie 151, 163
Rialto Theatre 35
Richards Music Corporation 144
Riesenfeld, Hugo 35, 181
Righter, Charles 97
Rinimer Corporation 150
Rivera, Chita 172
Robards, Jason 120
Rodgers, Richard 110, 111, 140
Roosevelt, President Franklin Delano 66, 80, 160, 194, 195
Rosling, Vladimer 152
Ross, Vicki 145
Rusty Hinge, The 135

S

"Sadder But Wiser" 119
Sailor on Horseback 176
Salvation Army 99, 168, 184, 198
Sams, Lynn 123
Sanders, George 100, 101
"San Diego Waltz, The" 99

San Francisco, California viii, 29, 38, 45, 46, 47, 48, 51, 52, 53, 55, 56, 57, 63, 89, 99, 169, 172, 173, 183, 193, 194
San Francisco Chronicle 52
San Francisco Examiner 45
San Francisco Symphony 38, 52, 53, 57, 63, 194
"San Juan Bautista Suite" 63, 81, 175, 196
Saroyan, William xi
Schary, Dore 147
Schlatter, George 164
Scott, General Winfield 2
Seattle, Washington 2, 42, 45, 193
Seattle Times 42
"Seventy-Six Trombones" 34, 109, 115, 119, 125, 126, 136, 160, 164, 174, 176, 177, 178, 187
Shapiro, Ted 83, 95
"Show Us the Way, Blue Eagle" 47
Shubert, John 120
Shubert Theatre 126, 148, 158, 161
"Siege, The" 44, 189
Silk Stockings 113, 115
Simon, Frank 31, 34, 123
Sims, Jay 32
Sinatra, Frank 79, 80, 106, 134, 140, 200
"Sincere" 127, 187
"Skyline" 45
Songwriters Hall of Fame 177
Sound of Music, The 112, 148
Sousa Band Fraternal Society 35
Sparkle Time 85, 107, 196

SPEBSBQSA (Society for the Preservation and Encouragement of Barbershop Singing in America) 168
Sprague, Elizabeth 4
Squires, Clell 106, 112, 116, 163
"Stars and Stripes Forever, The" 21, 30, 32, 34, 43, 54, 60
Star Parade, The 147, 198
Stevens, Bob 86
Stevens, Craig 159, 162
Stewart, Carleton 144
Stone, Irving 176
Stone, Pastor Robert 178
Storer, W. A. 123
Suite for Flute, A 174, 189
Sundell, Cora 116
Surf Ballroom 139
Symphony Number One in F Minor (A Symphony of San Francisco) 51, 53, 63, 183
Symphony Number Two in Minor (Missions of California) 53, 63, 68, 81, 173, 183

T

Talking People 85, 86, 87, 91, 97, 98, 99, 107, 118
Tank, Alvin 113, 115
"Tew" 159
"That Man Over There" 158
"Thingamabobs" 50
"This Is It" 96
"Thoughts While Strolling" 50, 155, 200
"Three Chimes of Silver" 100
Tiffany-Stahl 43, 44, 45
"Till There Was You" 125, 138

Titanic 147, 148
Tobin, Margaret 147, 148
Todman, Mark 92
Toffelmeyer, Ethel 116
"Tornado" 44
Toscanini, Arturo 36, 37, 105, 109, 179
"Trouble" 12, 119, 122, 139, 162, 187
Truman, Margaret 95
Truman, President Harry S. 81, 101, 107
Tucker, Forrest 132
"Two in Love" 65, 98, 182

U

Understudy, The 157, 158
United Artists 44, 70, 72
University of California at Los Angeles, The 166, 169
University of Iowa, The 96, 97, 136, 139, 176
University of Washington, The 42
Unsinkable Molly Brown, The 89, 139, 140, 147, 148, 149, 150, 151, 155, 157, 158, 163, 170, 175, 188

V

Valens, Richie 139
Valenti, Caterina 163
Van Dyke, Dick 133
Van Hoogstraten, Willem 36, 62
Van Horne, Harriet 91
Variety 51, 58, 128, 141, 159, 160, 172, 179
Vermont, Monique 141

Von Bomel, Elizabeth (Peggy) Wilson 21
Von Bomel, Leroy 89

W

"W.I.N." 174
Wall Street Journal, The 149, 160
Waltz Time 51, 193
Walt Disney World 175
Warner, Jack 140, 142
Warner Brothers Pictures, Inc. 57, 59, 67, 78, 116, 122, 135, 140, 144, 145, 151, 200
Warran, Richard 4
Wartburg College 177
Washburn, Marcellus 115, 121, 134, 141
Waverly, Iowa 177
Weekday 105, 198
"Wells Fargo Wagon, The" 120, 187
West Side Story 128, 129, 133, 134, 141
We Take the Town 157, 172
White, Oona 121, 132
Who Did What to Fedalia? 24, 102, 103, 104, 184
"Why Not?" 173, 189
Williams, Hugh 47
Willow Grove 33, 174
Willson, Alonzo 2, 3, 4, 179
Willson, Benjamin 4
Willson, Catharine Reynolds 3
Willson, Elebel 4
Willson, Elizabeth (Peggy) Wilson (see Von Bomel) 4, 21, 27, 28, 29, 42, 45, 50, 53, 58, 65, 80, 88, 89, 168
Willson, Elizabeth Sprague 4
Willson, John David 5, 6, 8, 9, 12, 14, 23, 53, 54
Willson, Lucille "Dixie" 23
Willson, Ralina "Rini" Zarova xi, 89, 102, 105, 106, 107, 110, 114, 115, 118, 119, 120, 122, 124, 126, 128, 131, 133, 137, 138, 139, 140, 147, 150, 162, 163, 165, 166, 167, 168, 169, 170, 175, 179
Willson, Robert Meredith
 birth of 6
 childhood of 6, 7, 8, 9, 10, 11, 12, 13, 14, 16, 17, 18, 19, 20, 21, 22
 death of 177, 178
 honorary degrees and awards of 176, 177
 motion picture scores of 43, 44, 45, 67, 68, 69, 70, 71, 72, 73, 74
 musicals of
  (*1491*) 167, 170, 171, 172, 173
  (*Here's Love*) 158, 159, 160, 161, 162
  (*The Music Man*) 107, 109, 111, 112, 113, 114, 115, 116, 117, 118, 119, 120, 121, 122, 123, 124, 125, 126, 127, 128, 129, 131, 132, 133, 134
  (*The Unsinkable Molly Brown*) 147, 151
 New York Philharmonic years of 36, 37, 38
 radio career of 38, 39, 41, 42, 43, 55, 56, 57, 58, 59, 60, 61, 62, 63, 64, 65, 66
 Sousa years of 31, 32, 33, 34, 35
Willson, Rosalie Reiniger xii, 6, 7,

8, 12, 13, 14, 23, 29, 53, 115, 116, 125, 127, 150, 151, 178
Willson, Rosemary Sullivan viii, 169, 170, 174, 175, 177, 178, 179
Willson Symposium on Expansive Cement 27
"Will I Ever Tell You?" 125
Wilson, Frank 94
Winchell, Walter 132
Winter Garden Theatre 27, 150
Wolfington, Iggy 121, 134
Wooley, Monty 92, 121
Words and Music by Meredith Willson 99
Wright, Frank Lloyd 11

Y

Yoder, Paul 139, 188
Young Americans, The 163
Your Hit Parade 51, 65
"You and I" 55, 64, 98, 199, 200
"You Can't Have a Show Without Durante" 96
"You Got Trouble" 119

Z

Zacheis, Les 96
Ziegfeld Follies 24, 112
Zimmer, Norma viii, 86, 87, 91, 118
Zinneman, Fred 118

Made in the USA
Lexington, KY
03 April 2011